Routledge Revivals

The House of Lords and Contemporary Politics

Originally published in 1958, the essential purpose of this book was to present a picture of the unreformed House of Lords at work as part of the effective system of government in Britain at the time, going back to the passing of the Parliament Act of 1911. When the Parliament Act of 1911 was passed, both its advocates and its opponents expected that it would soon be replaced by a comprehensive reform both of the powers and of the composition of the House of Lords. The previous forty years had in fact seen innumerable proposals, modest and ambitious, in Parliament and Party Conferences, but all had been abortive. The powers of the House had been left unchanged until 1958, except by the new Parliament Act of 1949, which merely modified the provisions of the old by reducing from three sessions to two the Lords' power to delay bills passed by the Commons. The Life Peerages Act, discussed in this book, which authorised the creation of life baronies with no numerical limits, was passed in 1958.

The House of Lords and Contemporary Politics
1911–1957

P. A. Bromhead

First published in 1958
by Routledge & Kegan Paul Ltd

This edition first published in 2025 by Routledge
4 Park Square, Milton Park, Abingdon, Oxon, OX14 4RN

and by Routledge
605 Third Avenue, New York, NY 10017

Routledge is an imprint of the Taylor & Francis Group, an informa business

© 1958 P. A. Bromhead

All rights reserved. No part of this book may be reprinted or reproduced or utilised in any form or by any electronic, mechanical, or other means, now known or hereafter invented, including photocopying and recording, or in any information storage or retrieval system, without permission in writing from the publishers.

Publisher's Note
The publisher has gone to great lengths to ensure the quality of this reprint but points out that some imperfections in the original copies may be apparent.

Disclaimer
The publisher has made every effort to trace copyright holders and welcomes correspondence from those they have been unable to contact.

A Library of Congress record exists under LCCN: 58001920

ISBN: 978-1-032-89904-6 (hbk)
ISBN: 978-1-003-54527-9 (ebk)
ISBN: 978-1-032-89922-0 (pbk)

Book DOI 10.4324/9781003545279

THE HOUSE OF LORDS AND CONTEMPORARY POLITICS
1911-1957

by
P. A. BROMHEAD
M.A., D.Phil.
Senior Lecturer in Politics, University of Durham

ROUTLEDGE & KEGAN PAUL
London

*First published 1958
by Routledge & Kegan Paul Ltd.
Broadway House, Carter Lane, E.C.4
Printed in Great Britain
by Butler & Tanner Ltd.
Frome and London*
© *copyright 1958 by P. A. Bromhead*

TO
MY WIFE

PREFACE

WHEN the Parliament Act of 1911 was passed, both its advocates and its opponents expected that it would soon be replaced by a comprehensive reform both of the powers and of the composition of the House of Lords. The past forty years have in fact seen innumerable proposals, modest and ambitious, in Parliament and in Party Conferences, but all have been abortive. The powers of the House have been left unchanged until now, except by the new Parliament Act of 1949, which merely modified the provisions of the old by reducing from three sessions to two the Lords' power to delay bills passed by the Commons. At last, in November 1957, a Conservative Government brought forward a proposal to reform the composition of the House with a serious intention that it should go through; but the modest provisions of the Life Peerages Bill came as something of an anti-climax. Both socialists and conservatives would have liked a more far-reaching reform, but they are still far from agreeing on the objectives at which larger reforms should aim. The differences between the Parties have become narrower as time has gone by, but the restricted and essentially uncontroversial scope of the Life Peerages Bill recognizes the need for caution.

Thirty years ago the Conservatives apparently wanted to restore the formal power of the House of Lords to obstruct socialistic legislation; now, however, they have abandoned this aim as unrealistic. Their present purpose seems to be more limited; they hope to improve the effectiveness and increase the prestige of the upper House, and would be prepared to accept a reduction of their own excessive numerical superiority in it in order to achieve that objective. The Labour Party has lost its former attitude of active hostility to the House of Lords, but still has little enthusiasm for any change which might enhance the prestige of the House, without guaranteeing a Labour majority there in periods of Labour majority in the Commons. People of the Left find it hard to forget the Lords' record of resistance to the popular will under Left governments during the past hundred years, and particularly between 1892 and 1914. While recognizing the usefulness of the House of Lords within a restricted sphere, socialists in general prefer that it should either remain politically weak or be entirely transformed. Knowing that the transformation that they would like would be unacceptable to the Conservatives, and believing that the power of the Lords to obstruct is now adequately limited, they are not very interested in reform.

The Bryce Conference of 1918 tried to define the functions which the House of Lords could usefully perform in the context of modern British Government, but the most important of the recommendations —that the House should have power to impose so much delay on legislation as might enable public opinion to express itself—has a meaning which is very obscure. Because of this obscurity it seems that this principle cannot now be accepted without reservations.

The other functions which the 1918 Report considered to be appropriate may be fairly generally accepted. The amending of bills sent up from the Commons, the prior discussion of uncontroversial bills in order that the legislative burden of the Commons may be lightened, the discussion of topics of current political interest— these are fields in which a second Chamber has surely useful work to perform.

But it is not only, or even mainly, with the actual powers and functions of the Lords that most recent discussion has been concerned, but rather with the composition of the House. It is hoped that this book will make some contribution to the discussions on this subject, by presenting an analysis of the total membership, which is very large, and of the active membership, which is very small, by examining the strength of the various parties, by assessing the distinctive contributions of peers of first creation and of peers who have succeeded to their titles, and by enquiring into the character of the relationships between government and opposition in the light of the theory of governmental responsibility. Attention will be paid to the rôle of groups of peers such as bishops and doctors, in order to illustrate the contribution but may be made by members who possess special knowledge and qualifications.

It will be necessary, for the sake of completing the picture of the House itself, to examine briefly some of the proposals that have been made for the reconstruction of its membership. It is hoped also that the broader description of the actual composition of the unreformed House, and of its work, will serve as a background against which any current proposals may be discussed.

The essential purpose of this book is, however, to present a picture of the unreformed House of Lords at work as a part of the effective system of government in Britain in recent times, going back to the passing of the Parliament Act of 1911. If little is said about the earlier history of the House, the reason is that the subject has already been

PREFACE

thoroughly treated elsewhere; a reappraisal of the earlier history, to be of much use, would need a volume to itself. Similarly, there is no detailed description of the procedure for issuing writs of summons or for introducing new peers into the House, or about the ceremonies connected with the Royal Assent to bills. All these things are important; they are indeed inseparable from the very nature of the House, the continuity of whose existence is embodied in them. While it is not necessary to describe here in detail that which has often been described elsewhere, the importance of the symbols of continuity with the past must not be forgotten.

Again, as this book is concerned with the House of Lords in relation to national politics, it passes over in silence two important aspects of the work of the House—its judicial functions and its functions with regard to private bills. The judicial functions, which it performs as the highest court of law in the land, have become by now clearly distinct from its functions as a deliberative parliamentary assembly, and they are performed by peers who possess special qualifications. The functions with regard to private bills are not so clearly distinct, but they are distinct enough to be omitted in the present context. Nearly all the work on private bills is performed by small select committees, which consist of ordinary peers who are prepared to give time to this work, but which proceed rather like judicial bodies. When a local council or some other such body wants Parliament to give it a new power or a new status, it must present its case, and the opponents may also present their case, before a select committee, sometimes of one House of Parliament only and sometimes of each House; the select committee decides whether to grant or to refuse the request after hearing all sides. In this matter the House of Lords is in no way inferior to the House of Commons. Many private bills are first introduced in the Lords, and many are in effect settled there. The peers who sit in the select committees perform very important and responsible functions, to which due regard must be paid in assessing the value of the House as a whole. If the House of Lords were abolished some new kind of machinery would have to be devised, perhaps with difficulty, to take over this work.

The sources mainly used for this study have been official publications, particularly *Hansard* and the Lords Journals, supplemented by yearbooks and *Vacher's Parliamentary Companion*. Reference has also been made to Erskine May, and to numerous biographies and memoirs. There is a considerable literature devoted to the House of Lords; the most recent additions to it have been the Hansard Society's book, *The Future of the House of Lords* (1954) and the Fabian Society's pamphlets *Reform of the Lords* (1954) and *The Privy Council as a Second Chamber* (1957). I have tried to avoid covering

PREFACE

the same ground as is covered in these works; nevertheless, I must acknowledge a debt to the authors of them for a number of facts and ideas, and for findings which I have set beside my own. To the Rt. Hon. Lord Chorley, who was one of the three co-authors of the 1954 Fabian pamphlet, I must express my warmest gratitude for the great amount of help that he has given me, by answering questions and explaining points of difficulty, and by reading through an early draft and proofs; he removed many errors and made many invaluable suggestions for improvements. The Most Hon. the Marquess of Salisbury, K.G., has most kindly read the proofs and pointed out errors of fact or emphasis; I am greatly in his debt for the advice and encouragement that he has given. Mr. H. M. Burrows, C.B.E., Clerk of Public Bills at the House of Lords, Professor F. C. Hood and Professor Wilfrid Harrison have read through all or part of the work in typescript, pointed out mistakes and omissions, and shown the way to many improvements. Sir James Fergusson of Kilkerran, Bt., Keeper of the Records of Scotland, has given the immense benefit of his knowledge on the subject of the Scottish Representative Peers, without which it would have been difficult indeed for me to deal with this subject. Commander Christopher Powell has given expert advice regarding private members' bills, and Canon H. E. W. Turner regarding the position of the bishops in the House of Lords. To those whom I have named, as well as to others who like them have so generously put their knowledge at my disposal in discussion and in correspondence, I must express my thanks for making possible so many improvements.

I should like also to thank my father for reading the work and making many suggestions, my wife for her patient collaboration and for the many ideas which I owe her, and Mr. Michael Topping for much valuable assistance in gathering material.

For all errors of fact or judgment I alone am responsible.

CONTENTS

Preface   vii

PART I: BACKGROUND AND STRUCTURE

Chapter I. The House of Lords and Constitutional Development   3

Chapter II. The Composition of the House of Lords   17
1. FORMAL CLASSIFICATION OF PEERS   17
2. HOW ARISTOCRATIC IS THE HOUSE OF LORDS?   20
3. THE PRINCIPLES GOVERNING THE CREATION OF NEW PEERS   22
4. NEW PEERAGES CREATED, 1916–56: AN ANALYSIS   26

Chapter III. Active and Inactive Peers   31
1. THE ACTIVE ELEMENT IN THE HOUSE   31
2. PEERS WHO ATTEND OCCASIONALLY   46
3. THE CONTRIBUTION OF PEERS OF FIRST CREATION   49

Chapter IV. Special Classes of Peers   52
1. INTRODUCTION   52
2. ARCHBISHOPS AND BISHOPS   53
3. THE LAW LORDS AND OTHER LEGAL PEERS   67
4. MILITARY COMMANDERS   72
5. CIVILIAN PUBLIC SERVANTS, DOCTORS, ETC.   75

PART II: THE ORGANIZATION OF THE HOUSE

Chapter V. Procedure and Organization of Business   81
1. GENERAL PRINCIPLES   81
2. TIMES OF SITTING   83
3. TYPES OF BUSINESS AND ARRANGEMENT OF TIME   89

CONTENTS

4. THE PHYSICAL ARRANGEMENTS OF THE HOUSE OF LORDS	93
5. OFFICERS OF THE HOUSE	95

Chapter VI. The Representation of the Government in the House of Lords — 99

Chapter VII. Party Organization and Discipline in the House of Lords — 110

PART III: THE LORDS AT WORK

Chapter VIII. Legislative Procedure in the Lords — 127

Chapter IX. The Parliament Act of 1911 and Its Effects — 134
1. THE ACT AND ITS BACKGROUND — 134
2. THE IMMEDIATE SEQUEL — 136
3. THE LORDS AND LEGISLATION TODAY — 140

Chapter X. Conservative and National Government Bills, 1922–39 — 147

Chapter XI. Labour Government Bills in 1924 and 1929–31 — 151

Chapter XII. Labour Government Bills in 1945–51 — 157
1. THE NATURE OF THE LORDS' CONTRIBUTION — 157
2. THE GREAT SOCIALIST REFORMS — 159
3. ORDINARY LEGISLATION — 170
4. CONCLUSION — 176

Chapter XIII. Conservative Government Bills of 1951–6 — 177

Chapter XIV. Bills First Introduced in the Lords — 186

Chapter XV. The Lords and Private Members' Bills — 196
1. BILLS FIRST INTRODUCED IN THE LORDS — 196
2. BILLS BROUGHT UP FROM THE COMMONS — 210

Chapter XVI. The Death Penalty Question — 216

CONTENTS

Chapter XVII. The House of Lords and General Debates
1. PARLIAMENTARY QUESTIONS IN THE LORDS
2. GENERAL DEBATES IN THE HOUSE OF LORDS

PART IV: THE MOVEMENT FOR REFORM

Chapter XVIII. The Question of Reform of Powers

Chapter XIX. Proposals for Minor Modifications of Composition
1. INTRODUCTORY SURVEY
2. LIFE PEERAGES
3. EXCLUSION FOR NON-ATTENDANCE
4. SHOULD PEERS BE ALLOWED TO SIT IN THE HOUSE OI COMMONS?
5. THE ADMISSION OF WOMEN
6. ABOLITION OF THE RIGHT OF TRIAL BY PEERS
7. PAYMENT OF PEERS

Chapter XX. Proposals for Wholesale Reconstruction of the House

Chapter XXI. Conclusion

Appendix: The Election of the Scottish Representative Peers
Bibliographical Note
Index

PART I

BACKGROUND AND STRUCTURE

Chapter I

THE HOUSE OF LORDS AND CONSTITUTIONAL DEVELOPMENT

IN most of the states which comprised earlier Western civilization some part in the management of affairs was played by non-elected senates or councils of persons distinguished by birth or wealth or both. In most countries such councils were prior in time to the more popular assemblies to which they were eventually required to transfer most of their powers. Modern democratic theories tend to be hostile to the notion that any part of real political power should be in the hands of hereditary notables; nearly everywhere the old 'upper' houses, based on hereditary right or nomination, have been transformed into assemblies based on election, direct or indirect.

Even now, it is still fairly generally accepted that popular assemblies need to be supplemented by others not based on direct, equal and universal suffrage. In every large modern state of the West there is some kind of 'second chamber', though Britain alone keeps to heredity as a basis of membership. The members of the Canadian Senate are appointed for life; vacancies are filled (often very tardily) as they arise, on the advice of the Government of the day. In most other modern states members of upper Houses are elected, though the basis of representation always differs from that of the lower House, and senators are generally elected for relatively long terms. Many upper Houses are never completely dissolved. In this respect the United States Senate, with one-third of its members retiring or seeking re-election every two years, is typical. Continuity of membership, for half or two-thirds of the members, over election times, necessarily implies that individuals must be elected for relatively long periods. It is supposed that this device makes upper Chambers less easily the prey of rapidly-changing public sentiments.

THE HOUSE OF LORDS AND CONSTITUTIONAL DEVELOPMENT

In federal states senates generally have the special function of representing the constituent parts; each of the States of the American Union, from Nevada with 150,000 inhabitants to New York with a hundred times as many, has two senators. Such 'unfair' representation is acceptable in federal countries, in which the constituent units are equal with one another in status; in unitary states, however, public opinion tends to rebel against over-representation of the country-side and small towns. In federal countries, because of the peculiar strength of local allegiance, upper Chambers tend, like the United States Senate, to have relatively great prestige. In unitary states on the other hand, even when they represent local communities, they are widely considered to be superfluous obstacles to the will of the popular assemblies.

Most modern second chambers are artificially-created bodies, with their powers and composition closely defined in constitutional documents, and with their existence corresponding to some theoretical and practical purpose in the minds of the constitution-makers. The British House of Lords on the other hand grew slowly and remains essentially unchanged from the days when its position as an assembly of notables was unchallenged. It is only the character of its contribution to the nation's affairs that has been transformed, and this transformation has proceeded entirely without plan, through a succession of individual actions related to particular circumstances and shaped usually by the attitudes of individual personalities.

Its background of evolution, rather than deliberate creation or reconstruction, is an essential part of the character of the House of Lords even today. Its organic quality is palpable and impressive. Most would-be reformers have recognized this and have wanted to leave undisturbed as far as possible such ancient devices as the writ of summons. It would be easy enough, if it were thought desirable, to alter the form and the meaning of a writ of summons, but the House has shown its respect for its own foundations by the exhaustive enquiries which it has conducted into the meaning of the existing unwritten, customary rules. It would have been easy, at any time in the past half-century, to provide for the admission of women and of life peers, and to provide for the exclusion of some peers, either at their own request or otherwise. But Parliament has been loath to solve these problems by methods such as an engineer might use in converting a ship from coal-burning to oil-burning; it has preferred to begin, at least, by enquiring whether it would be possible to place a new interpretation on ancient rules.

A good illustration of this tendency is provided by the setting-up and the proceedings of the 1955 Select Committee on the Powers of the House in relation to the Attendance of its Members. A suggestion had been put forward that peers might be excluded for non-attendance. It was considered that such exclusion might be possible without legislation. So the Select Committee, composed of fifteen of the most prominent members of the House, was set up. Several experts went to immense trouble to produce memoranda for the Committee's guidance, and appeared before it to give evidence during four afternoons of hearings. After five further meetings the Committee produced its Report, which, though largely negative in its results, sums up the findings of much scholarly research.[1]

It is not possible to say just when or how the House of Lords originated. Before 1066 the Saxon kings took counsel of the Witan, an assembly of great and wise men, of whose composition we know little, though it appears not to have been fixed. Under the Normans the King's Court was composed of magnates, who held their land directly from the King in return for the feudal services, essentially military, which they owed him. The word 'baron' originally meant a man, or vassal, who owed homage to a great lord; a special use of the word expressed in particular (though for a long time not exclusively) the relation of a tenant in chief to his lord, the King. It did not, in Norman times, connote any definite political status or right to be summoned to the King's Court, and not all the King's barons were magnates, for many of them held little land and were men of little account.

Three times a year the Norman kings were accustomed to summon assemblies of magnates, of 'all the great men of England, archbishops, bishops, abbots, earls, thegns and knights', as the Anglo-Saxon Chronicle called them, to discuss with them the important questions of the moment, including pleas. Many of the functions performed by these enlarged meetings of the King's Court, which came in time to be called great councils, were judicial in character, though much of the judicial work soon came to be performed in the first instance by more permanent courts which were offshoots of the main body. The day-to-day work of government was performed by royal servants, chosen by the King. They were drawn at first from the baronage, but later on some were chosen from among men who were not barons. By the time of the minority of Henry III it was possible to speak of the advisers collectively as 'the council'. In an age in which relationships were largely prescribed by custom, there was no legislation as we understand it, so the early assemblies could not properly be called 'legislative' in character; the boundaries between legislative, executive and judicial functions were not fixed or even apprehended. The magnates did, however, have a sense of a responsibility, not only to themselves and to the community, but to the King, for ensuring

[1] It made certain positive proposals. Cf. below, p. 251.

that the King did right. Their loyalty to the King did not prevent them from obliging King John to promise, in Magna Carta, to observe the law; their exaction of his promise did not conflict with that loyalty, but fulfilled it. Twenty years later they resented Henry III's attempts to govern without consulting them; they were particularly angry when, on being summoned to a great council in 1237, they were only asked to grant an aid, without engaging in any discussion of general affairs. The King's action was an injury, not to them alone, but to the whole community.

During the thirteenth century we may observe a certain confusion of two ideas about the rôle of the magnates. On the one hand there was the idea that their proper function consisted in giving advice to the King and in furthering his ends, which ideally were supposed to be identical with their own and with those of the community; on the other hand there was the idea that the barons in some sense represented the whole community as an entity distinct from the King. It was perhaps this second idea which was expressed by the incipient use of the word *parliamentum* (which seems to have been clearly established by 1258) to describe the meetings which the magnates attended.[1]

Although the word 'parliament' was becoming current, the assemblies so designated still fell far short, at the end of the thirteenth century, of having acquired the form of our modern parliament. The King could choose more or less arbitrarily those to whom he would send personal writs of summons; the notion that a man who had once received a writ had a right to be summoned in future, and that his heirs inherited his right, grew at first out of custom and little else.

At the same time a distinction had already been recognized between greater and lesser barons. It had been the practice to send a personal summons to attend the council only to the greater barons; Magna Carta stipulated that the lesser were to be summoned through the sheriffs. In practice there seems to have been little regularity, even after 1215, about the summoning of the lesser barons. From their occasional presence there appears to have sprung, however, the germ of what was later to become the House of Commons, which we see in the practice of summoning representatives of the shires to the parliamentary assemblies, on occasions when it seemed to the King advisable to obtain the agreement of the people from whom he hoped to collect money. But there was no regularity about the summoning of these representatives, and no notion that any special capacity to make laws resided in an assembly in which they were present, or was

[1] Cf. J. E. A. Jolliffe, *The Constitutional History of Medieval England* (A. & C. Black, 2nd. ed., 1948), p. 286.

lacking in an assembly from which they were absent. In 1290 the statute *Quia Emptores* was passed a week before the day for which the knights of the shire had been summoned.

During the fourteenth century the representatives of the shires and boroughs, who were coming to be called 'the Commons', developed a practice of meeting separately from the magnates, in order to discuss the current problems which were the cause of their having been summoned. But the full parliament, meeting together, returned answer to the King. In the judicial sessions the magnates sat together with the King, and the commons appeared in the rôle of petitioners.[1]

Meanwhile, the right of individuals to receive personal writs of summons as great barons was gradually becoming established. It was never laid down (not, at any rate, until much later) that the King ought not to omit a man who had once been summoned, or his heirs after him, and such omissions were still not infrequent. Nevertheless, it was undoubtedly the usual practice to repeat the summons to an individual once summoned, and to summon his heir after him. The attitude of the barons to the business of attending at parliaments probably had something to do with the growth and establishment of a firm tradition there was a hereditary right to the writ. In the earliest times, the writ was seen merely as a command, which of course it has always continued to be (in form), but as presence at the meetings of parliament became, for various reasons, more and more desirable, so the reception of a writ of summons came to be highly prized and therefore claimed when there seemed good grounds for claiming it. As the claim was made, so it became more and more usual for the King to behave as though the claim had a firm foundation. That which had been merely usual came to be expected, and it became rarer for the King to withold a summons from a man once summoned or his heir, and finally so rare that a denial of a writ appeared to be 'illegal', or a denial of a right.

The permanent and hereditary nature of the right to receive the writ of summons, and therefore membership of the Lords' House of Parliament, is generally held to have been confirmed and finally settled only in 1625. In that year the King refused to issue a writ of summons to the Earl of Bristol, who was out of favour, and the Earl presented a petition to the House of Lords. His petition was referred to a committee, which reported that 'no precedent could be found for withholding a writ from a peer capable of sitting in Parliament'.[2] It was left to the House of Lords itself to build up, on a basis of

---

[1] Cf. Jolliffe, op. cit., p. 374.
[2] Cf. Memorandum by Sir Reginald Manningham-Buller and Mr. D. G. Squibb to the Select Committee of the House in Relation to the Attendance of its Members, in the Committee's Report (1956), at p. 3.

precedents derived from individual cases, rules regarding the exclusion of individuals considered unsuitable for membership, usually because of misdeeds. An order for the exclusion of minors was made in 1685.

The introduction of ranks among the magnates may have had, indirectly, some bearing on the development of the idea of a right to be summoned to parliament. As we have seen, the term 'baron' at first merely described a given feudal relationship, and was not equivalent to 'recipient of a writ of summons', though it did come to be used in that particular sense. In Anglo-Saxon times the term 'earl' (meaning noble man or chieftain) was associated with the possession of special hereditary authority in a shire or in several shires. After the Norman conquest the functions of the earl in the shire moot disappeared, but the title survived, and new men, great noblemen, were granted the dignity of 'earl'. Thus the temporal lords included earls and barons. The title of earl was still always associated with the name of a county or county town, but there was no exact title to correspond with the status of baron; a magnate might be called 'Lord A', but the same dignity was given also to men of lower status.

The title of 'duke' first made its appearance in England in 1337, when it was conferred on the King's eldest son. Later other members of the royal house were created dukes, and before the end of the fourteenth century other magnates too. The titles of 'marquis' and 'viscount' were also introduced, the latter only in the fifteenth century. The new ranks had little importance except for the sake of precedence and distinction, but the manner of their establishment had repercussions of some interest for the developing structure of the peerage. The new titles were granted by letters patent under the great seal, which conferred the specific rank on the recipients and their heirs. Here was a new and more definite foundation of a right to receive a writ of summons, though that right was only assumed to follow from the possession of a given rank. The use of letters patent was soon extended to the older ranks of magnates. In 1387 Richard II created John de Beauchamp a baron, 'unum parium et baronum regni nostri', by patent,[1] and although it was nearly fifty years before the next creation, from 1446 all new peers were created in this way.

This then is the story of the development of our practice with regard to the members of the body which has come down to our time as the House of Lords. The procedure for the grant of membership went through a gradual evolution, as Parliament itself evolved, until

---

[1] The patent conferred no right on the new baron, and gave him no seat in Parliament, but there was a reference to the duties that he was to perform 'in future in our councils and Parliaments'. He received a writ of summons for the first Parliament to be held after his creation, but was beheaded three months later.

five hundred years ago the practice became established which it has not, until now, been found necessary to alter.

The use of the term 'peer' became current during the fourteenth century, and was connected with the idea that accused noblemen ought to be tried by their equals or 'peers'. The term was also useful because it was a convenient designation of members of what was coming to be the upper House of Parliament, though the designation 'House of Lords' was not used until the time of Henry VIII. At the same time the lower House was also acquiring a clear identity and procedure of its own, and was developing a close concern with the nation's finances.

From the old petitions of the Commons there slowly grew a system of parliamentary legislative activity, in which both Houses played their part. Before the middle of the century some statutes were passed 'by the advice and assent of lords and commons', but the older formula, 'by the advice of the lords and request of the commons' was still sometimes used. The assent of the commons as well as the lords was coming to be necessary.

In 1454 the number of lay peers was 56; it was almost equal to that of the spiritual lords, and continued to be so (and sometimes inferior) until the dissolution of the monasteries removed the abbots from membership of the Lords' House of Parliament. The number of the temporal lords fell to only 28 in 1485, and rose gradually to 60 by the end of the sixteenth century. Throughout the Tudor period the House of Commons gained strength and importance in relation to the upper House, though not necessarily at its expense. If few new peerages were created, it was because the Lords generally acquiesced in the royal wishes, for the attainment of which Henry VIII preferred to make use mainly of the House of Commons, over which he was able to exercise a considerable influence. The importance and vitality of the Commons made further progress under Elizabeth.

During the reigns of the first two Stuart Kings the House of Lords remained generally loyal to the Crown. There was indeed an element which was inclined to reflect the radical attitude of the Commons, but this element remained in a minority. The Lords were not always ranged against the Commons, and sometimes supported them, as for example over the Commons' claims to freedom from arrest in 1626 and 1642. In general, however, the majority in the Lords were inclined to try to preserve the established order, and to oppose the claims of the Commons to restrict the power of the Crown. Furthermore, James I and Charles I created new peerages with great liberality. The older nobility disliked the influx of new men, but the new peers were not, on the whole, inclined to oppose the Stuarts. Thus it was that on 5th February 1649 the Commons declared: 'the House of Lords is useless and dangerous and ought to be abolished'; for the next eleven years the House did not meet.

A few Presbyterian peers sat in the Convention during the time in which the House of Lords was abolished, but in 1660 the separate sittings of the upper House were resumed, and the House took its place alongside the revived House of Commons. The only legislation that was necessary in order to restore the former composition of the House was the Act of 1661 by which the Bishops' Exclusion Act of 1642 was repealed.

The most important developments in the years following the Restoration were in the field of the relationship between the two Houses in financial matters. An attempt by the Lords in 1661 to substantiate a claim to a right to originate, amend or reject financial bills led to the passing by the Commons in 1671 of a resolution declaring that 'in all aids given the King by the Commons the rate of tax ought not to be altered by the Lords'. The Lords were not ready to hand over all financial control, but when they made an attempt to amend a financial bill seven years later the Commons passed a stronger and more comprehensive resolution in which they asserted their sole right to grant aids and supplies and to determine the purposes for which they were to be used; financial bills were not to be altered or changed by the Lords. The Lords had to give way; something like a constitutional rule had been written down to express a disability of the House of Lords that had already been inherent in the origins of the bicameral Parliament. Even now, there was not universal agreement about the scope of the rule. In 1726, when a request for an increase in the number of seamen for the navy was addressed to the Commons only, some peers objected and argued that demands for Supply ought to be sent to the Lords. It was even claimed that, notwithstanding the Commons Resolution of 1678, the Lords had an undoubted right to amend money bills. When a motion hostile to the Government was put to the vote, however, it was defeated. A similar incident occurred in 1740; the majority of the peers were not inclined to dispute the claim of the Commons to control finance.

As a corollary to their acceptance in principle of the claims of the Commons, the Lords were careful to insist that the Commons should not improperly use their financial privileges in order to extend their power in other spheres. In 1700 they protested against 'the tacking of so many and different matters to a money bill', and in 1702 they resolved 'that the annexing any Clause or Clauses to a Bill of Aid or Supply, the Matter of which is foreign to, and different from, the Matter of the said Bill of Aid or Supply, is Unparliamentary, and tends to the Destruction of the Constitution of this Government'.

Thus the declarations of the first fifty years following the Restoration, for all that they were contained only in orders of the two Houses, defined the relations between the Houses in this matter in terms such as might have been found in a written constitution, if such a constitution had ever been found necessary. Nevertheless, the declarations remained as orders and no more, and an attempt by the Lords to introduce, by statute this time, an element of constitutional definition of the composition of their House, was unsuccessful.

The prerogative of the Crown to 'create' new peers had not previously been seriously questioned, though, as we have seen, there were some objections to the lavish creations of the first two Stuart kings. In the conditions of parliamentary supremacy which arose from the abdication of James II, however, it was to be expected that the Administration, if in danger of seeing its policies frustrated in the House of Lords, might be tempted to give itself a majority there by the use of the expedient of granting peerages to its friends. The temptation arose in 1712, and the Government created twelve new Tory peers, with the help of whose votes it was just able to obtain a majority.

It was clear that a precedent had been established which might, if followed frequently, threaten the very existence of the House, and in 1719 the Lords approved the Peerage Bill, whose main provision was 'that the number of English peers should not be enlarged beyond six above the present number, which upon failure of male issue, might be supplied by new creations'. Had the Bill been passed into law, it would have destroyed a safety-valve whose usefulness was to be seen in 1832 and 1911. In the Commons, however, after the Bill had been vigorously attacked by Walpole, it was decisively rejected. The way was now clear for any future government to coerce the Lords; the precedent of 1712 had been upheld.

As responsible government developed in the eighteenth century the House of Lords left to the Commons the power of exercising control over the executive. It was to the Commons and not to the Lords that ministers were held to be responsible. Nevertheless the Lords did not simply acquiesce in the constitutional superiority of the Commons; on the contrary, members of their House not only held most of the great offices of State,[1] but also established something like an ascendancy over the Commons by holding effective control over the process of election of members to fill many of the seats in the lower House. The Duke of Newcastle and his friends operated the system and kept themselves in power until 1760; then, however, King George III

[1] It is, however, significant that, while Harley chose to go to the House of Lords in 1711, when his power was at its zenith, Walpole a little later remained in the Commons until his pre-eminence was at an end.

himself took charge of the machine. After 1810, when King George went mad, the old system of corrupt elections worked less effectively, until its foundations were swept away in 1832. The Lords' resistance to the Reform Bill was overcome by a threat to create new peers as in 1712.

During the first decades after the passing of the Reform Act of 1832 the House of Lords generally acted with moderation, and no acute conflict between the Houses developed. During the later years of the nineteenth century, however, and indeed right up till 1914, the rôle of the House of Lords in the British constitution could hardly be described except in terms of a permanent conflict between its majority and the Liberals in the House of Commons. With the passage of time, as the number of peers increased, and as the Liberals' policies became more and more objectionable to the established interests represented by the Conservative element in the Lords, the conflict became sharper until it came to a head in the crisis of 1909-11.

The solution which was imposed in 1911, against bitter opposition in the House itself, was intended, even by its authors, to be only temporary and provisional, but it has endured with slight modification until now. Nevertheless the House of Lords of 1957, though superficially unchanged, is really a very different body from that against which Asquith and Lloyd George battled in 1909-11. With its powers formally limited by law, the House of Lords has used even its remaining powers with so much restraint and moderation that its proceedings of 1945-51 hardly seem to belong to the same body as that which resisted the Liberal Government of 1906-14.

The process of adaptation over the past half-century, though in one sense without precedent, in another sense can be seen as a continuation of the process of development and adaptation which has been going on for the past nine hundred years. The process has not gone smoothly or deliberately or steadily; rather there has been a series of conflicts, in which, at various stages, crown, ministers and Commons have been involved, and which have usually been resolved by inconclusive settlements. But each settlement, whether it dealt with the power of Parliament to restrict the King's prerogative, or with the privilege of the Commons to control finance, or with the right of the administration to create new peers, has produced consequential adaptations of practice which in their turn have become part of the character of the House, whose permanence and flexibility are complementary to one another.

There are perhaps two important weaknesses in the position of the House of Lords in the modern British constitution. In the first place its claims to exercise any power at all would probably be rejected by a big section of the population—by that part which thinks that the popular will ought to prevail. It may be true that at any given time it is not the will of the people which prevails, but the will of the government which the people have placed in office. Nevertheless the people's will is still supposed to be translated into action by the government which they place in power at a general election. Thus if the House of Lords frustrates the intentions of ministers who are supported by a majority in the Commons, its action is widely regarded as an unjustifiable interference with the expression of the will of the people. Egalitarians may tolerate the House of Lords so long as it does not attempt to exercise real power; they can hardly be expected to do more.

In the second place, the exercise of real power by the upper House would be inconsistent with the theory of governmental responsibility in the extreme form in which it is generally accepted today. As long ago as 1719 it was being argued that if the House of Lords were to be protected by the proposed Peerage Bill against massive creations of new peers, it would be 'an end of responsibility of Ministers to the House of Commons'.[1] In modern conditions this argument is unanswerable. Practically all important legislation is necessarily introduced by the government of the day, which makes itself responsible for it. We do not expect a government to remain in office, taking responsibility for its stewardship in running the affairs of the country, unless it can obtain the consent of Parliament to the measures which it regards as a necessary condition for continuing to accept that responsibility. If the Government is responsible in this way it seems illogical to expect it to continue to accept responsibility for public affairs if the House of Lords refuses to allow it to put its policy into effect. This doctrine is really the foundation, if not of the historical origin, at least of the persistence in modern times, of the long-established rule that the House of Lords should not interfere with the control of the Commons over finance. In recent times the Government's responsibility for its legislative proposals is felt to be little less complete than its responsibility for the raising and spending of money.

It is true that in some federal states this difficulty about the responsibility of the Government is left unsolved. In the United States it does not arise, because the President has no parallel responsibility to Congress. The system of checks and balances in the United States makes it possible for the two houses of Congress to exercise power co-equally without upsetting the theoretical balance of the constitution, although the practical effect of the duality may sometimes be

[1] *Further Reasons against the Peerage Bill*, a tract of 1719, quoted by Turberville, *The House of Lords in the XVIIIth Century*, p. 179.

exceedingly inconvenient, if not disastrous. In Australia, where the Government is supposed to be responsible in the same way as the British government, great difficulties have arisen both through the intervention of the Senate, and (more still) through the intervention of the referendum. The makers of the Australian constitution prevented the Senate from producing a deadlock by providing for a simultaneous dissolution of both Houses in case of need. They provided, however, for a referendum in relation to constitutional amendments. On a number of occasions the people have shown themselves unwilling to allow a particular government to put into effect a particular item in its policy, yet they have at the same time shown a preference for that government as compared with any other.

It is by now accepted that the House of Lords, however constituted, should not be able to thwart permanently the intentions of a government which enjoys popular support. It is still argued, however, that the Lords should have power to delay legislation passed by the Commons 'until public opinion shall have had an opportunity of expressing itself'. But this notion involves difficulties. There is no means whereby the state of public opinion on any particular issue may be conclusively ascertained. Some people sometimes speak as though a general election showed the state of public opinion on all the political questions of the day. If this were really so, it must be supposed that public opinion was in favour of the nationalization of steel and possibly of sugar and cement in 1950, but not in favour of those nationalizations in 1951. In reality, a general election usually produces many distinct and more or less unconnected issues. When the people vote in favour of a particular party at a general election they do not show themselves in favour of every single item in that party's programme; they show simply that they prefer to be governed by that party rather than any other party during the ensuing five years. The electors do indeed make their choice to some extent on the basis of their study of the party's record in the past and of its programme for the future. It seems, therefore, legitimate to argue that a government has no mandate for a wholly new policy which is manifestly at variance with the record and the programme. But if the Lords are to have power to protect the people against such wholesale innovations, it must be a power to force a dissolution of the House of Commons.[1]

The proposition of the Bryce Conference, about delay until public opinion has time to express itself, could very well be interpreted as meaning a power to delay a bill, not for one year or two years, but merely for perhaps one or two months until the bill has had a chance

[1] For further discussion of this question, cf. C. S. Emden, *The People and the Constitution* (Oxford U.P., 2nd edition, 1956), p. 226.

of going through the Commons again. This is indeed just the rôle which the constitution of the Fourth Republic in France assigns to the Council of the Republic. It is also the rôle which Mr. Anthony Wedgwood Benn, in his 1957 Fabian tract, suggests as appropriate to a second chamber.[1] Fortunately, with two important exceptions (apart from the Parliament Bill itself), the House of Lords has in fact not since 1945 claimed any more power or authority than this. It seriously interfered with some of the legislative measures of governments between the wars, but in these cases its interference could hardly be said to have been based upon the principle of giving public opinion time to express itself.

But to discuss the contemporary House of Lords in terms of conflict and delay is really to present a very misleading picture of its rôle in the modern state. Far from having been destroyed by the Parliament Act of 1911, the House was in the long run given an opportunity to develop a new sense of its purpose, infinitely better adapted to the needs of the modern world than the old. In recent years the House of Lords has not been moribund; it has discussed more topics, and it has proposed—and passed—far more amendments to bills in each year than it did before the passing of the Parliament Act. It is true that it has at no point seriously thwarted the policy of the Government of the day—not even on the death penalty in 1948 or 1956—but then the modern doctrine of governmental responsibility appears to make it impossible that any government whose will had been seriously thwarted could remain in office at all. The will of governments is now thwarted neither in the House of Commons nor in the House of Lords. But just because of this, governments tend to be particularly ready to temporize, and to give way (within the limits of the main lines of their policies) to any sort of claim that may appear to them to be legitimate. Parliament is above all a place where the work of the Government is criticized and discussed; in this field the House of Lords is fulfilling its rôle alongside the House of Commons. The most that a member of the House of Commons can expect to do by speech is to persuade the Government to modify a policy which it is pursuing. A peer has as much chance of doing this through a speech in the House of Lords as has a member of the House of Commons in the lower House.

We are thus confronted with a paradoxical situation. On the one hand the House of Lords is in two essential ways an unacceptable piece of machinery in the modern state. It cannot properly be allowed to exercise power however it is constituted, and its composition makes it inherently objectionable to half of the British public. Yet on the

[1] A. Wedgwood Benn, *The Privy Council as a Second Chamber*, Fabian Tract no. 305, January 1957, p. 21.

other hand, as there is a useful function for a second chamber to perform in this country, the unreformed House of Lords performs that function supremely well. Minor reforms, such as the introduction of devices to increase the strength of the Left, and perhaps to increase the numbers of politically unattached 'experts', might make the House a still more effective instrument, but it is doubtful whether any fundamental reconstruction would produce a more useful second chamber.

The conclusion would seem to be that so long as the House of Lords continues by the exercise of voluntary restraint to perform a restricted function in the exercise of political power, there is in a sense little reason for altering either its powers or its composition. At the same time, as the character of its composition gives such great offence to such large elements of the population, and as some sort of reform could clearly be achieved on the right lines without seriously affecting the character of the House, there seems much to be said for the acceptance of some reform designed to lessen the power of the 'backwoodsmen' and strengthen the Left. Mr. Macmillan's Government, in the Bill which it introduced in November 1957, proposed to aim at only the second of these two objectives. In a preliminary debate on 30th and 31st October the Government's plans were received with little hostility but also with little enthusiasm. They were criticized from Left and Right for their failure to attempt to deal with the first objective also; but the critics were so far from agreeing with one another that it soon became clear how difficult it would be to achieve agreement over any more ambitious reform. At the same time, most of the criticism was put forward rather in a vacuum, and there would be little point in discussing here the Government's plans or the criticism levelled against them. Such discussion will be deferred until after the factual examination of the rôle of the unreformed House in recent years, which will be undertaken in the ensuing chapters.

Chapter II

THE COMPOSITION OF THE
HOUSE OF LORDS

WITH some 860 members the House of Lords has the distinction of being the largest legislative assembly in the world. Yet the number of members who take an active part in its proceedings is very small. The combination of these two facts makes the description of the membership of the House a peculiarly complicated task.

It is necessary to begin with a formal statement of the classes of persons who together comprise the membership, but such a statement tells us little about the House as a working part of the machinery of government, as almost half of its members never attend and many others attend very rarely. If we wish to give a satisfactory picture of the House as a working institution we must make a special study of the active element within the total membership (cf. Ch. III).[1]

1. FORMAL CLASSIFICATION OF PEERS

In classifying the members of the House of Lords we may begin by distinguishing between hereditary peers—that is, peers who hold hereditary titles, including the first holders of such titles—and other members.

The non-hereditary element, which is very small in relation to the total membership of the House, is composed of two groups, bishops and judges. There are now—and have been for the past three hundred years—26 episcopal members of the House. Spiritual Lords were summoned to the court of the Norman Kings, and have been among the members of the House ever since Parliament began to take shape. For a time they were more numerous than the temporal peers, and often also more influential in state affairs. It was not until the

[1] These two chapters deal with the House up to 1957, without the addition of life peers.

suppression of the monasteries that the spiritual Lords were permanently outnumbered by the temporal.

From 1550 to 1847 the two archbishops and all the 24 diocesan bishops had seats in the House of Lords. During the past 110 years, however, fifteen new sees have been created by the sub-division of old dioceses which had grown too populous for convenient administration. The bishops of the new dioceses have equal status with those of the old, but the number of spiritual Lords in the upper House has not been correspondingly increased. The two Archbishops and the Bishops of London, Winchester and Durham are automatically members of the House of Lords; the other seats are held by the 21 bishops who have the longest seniority. Archbishops and bishops keep their seats in the House of Lords only during their tenure of office. In a few cases peerages have been granted to retiring Archbishops in order that they might continue to be members of the House.

The second class of non-hereditary peers is of modern origin, going back to the passing of the Appellate Jurisdiction Act of 1876. Under that Act the Crown was empowered to grant life peerages to four 'Lords of Appeal in Ordinary', in order to improve the capacity of the House to carry out its tasks as the highest court of appeal in the land. The number of Lords of Appeal has been increased by subsequent legislation, until it is now nine. As these peerages are granted for life and not only during tenure of office, the number of the members of the House holding life peerages at any given time may be somewhat in excess of nine.

Next there are two groups of members who owe their seats to a combination of inheritance and election; the 16 Scottish representative peers and the few remaining Irish representative peers have inherited their peerages but not their seats in the House of Lords.

Under the Treaty of Union between England and Scotland (1707), not all the peers of Scotland, but only 16 representatives elected by them at each General Election, may sit in the Lords.[1] The creation of Scottish and English peerages ceased after 1707; new peers since then, whether Englishmen or Scotsmen, have received peerages of Great Britain (or, sometimes, of Ireland) or, since 1801, of the United Kingdom. But there are still today 86 holders of peerages of Scotland created before the Treaty of Union, who are not entitled as such to sit in the House of Lords, but only to elect their representatives. Many of them may in fact, however, sit in the Lords in their own right because they also hold, as well as their Scottish peerages, peerages of England, or of Great Britain (created since 1707) or of

[1] For a description of the process of election of the Scottish Representative peers, and for an analysis of the voting in 1955, when an election took place, cf. Appendix, below, p. 276.

FORMAL CLASSIFICATION OF PEERS

the United Kingdom (created since 1801). Under the terms of a resolution passed by the House of Lords in 1793, peers of Scotland who also hold English, British or United Kingdom peerages are entitled to vote in the election of the Scottish Representative Peers.[1] On the other hand, neither minors nor peeresses in their own right may vote or stand for election. As eight of the 86 peerages mentioned above are at present held by women, and one by a minor, the total number of electors is reduced to 77. No peer of Scotland may either vote or be elected in an election for the House of Commons; peeresses on the other hand, under the Representation of the People Act, 1918, do not suffer from this disability.

Similarly, Irish representative peers were, until 1922, elected to the House of Lords by the holders of Irish peerages, under the provisions of the Act of Union of 1800. The Act fixed their number at 28, but with the creation of the Irish Free State in 1922, and the abolition of the office of Lord Chancellor for Ireland, the machinery for their election ceased to operate, and they are now almost an extinct species; only four of them remain.[2]

The rules regarding Irish representative peers differ in two important ways from those regarding the Scottish peers; the representatives are elected for life, instead of for a single Parliament, and Irish peers who have not been elected as representative peers may, unlike their Scottish equivalents, vote in elections for the House of Commons and themselves be elected to that House. Lord Palmerston, for example, was an Irish peer, but sat in the Commons as M.P. for Tiverton. More recently Earl Winterton sat in the Commons from 1918 to 1955, and was then given a United Kingdom peerage.[3]

Finally we come to the main part of the membership of the House —some 800 hereditary peers of England, Great Britain or the United Kingdom, each owing his seat to the fact that he has a hereditary right to a write of summons at the beginning of each Parliament. On the death of the first holder of a peerage, it passes to his eldest

---

[1] Thus the holder of the Scottish Dukedom of Buccleugh, which was created in 1663, also holds the English Earldom of Doncaster. He may sit in the House of Lords by virtue of the latter, and vote in the election of the Scottish Representative Peers by virtue of the former.

[2] Cf. Wade and Phillips, *Constitutional Law* (Longmans, 1946 ed.), p. 70, and Commons Debs., 2nd May 1927, vol. 205, col. 1296. One of the last remaining Irish Representative Peers, the Earl of Drogheda, was given a United Kingdom peerage in 1954.

[3] The grant of new Irish peerages continued after 1800, and the recipients were sometimes men having nothing to do with Ireland. It was sometimes useful for a man to be given noble rank without being excluded from the possibility of being elected to the House of Commons. Lord Curzon was given an Irish peerage in 1899, when he became Viceroy of India, but had cause to regret it later. (Cf. Lord Ronaldshay, *Life of Lord Curzon*, Benn, 1928, vol. iii, p. 39.)

surviving son, and then to *his* eldest son, if he has one, or by primogeniture to the next male descendant of the first holder. Among the hereditary peers (apart from the peers of the blood royal who do not speak or vote in the House) are five ranks; in July 1956 there were 21 dukes, 27 marquesses, 135 earls, 106 viscounts, and 537 barons. These five ranks have little importance for the purposes of our present discussion; a more important distinction for our purpose is that between those who have themselves been ennobled and those who have inherited their peerages.

Peers who are the first of their creation are presumably men of the kind we would expect to see in a nominated House of Lords. All have rendered distinguished service in some field or other, and it will be necessary to attempt to classify them according to their several backgrounds. Among those who have inherited peerages it is worth distinguishing between the peers of the second or third generation and those who hold ancient titles. Most peers who are the second holders of their titles have been born as the sons of commoners; on the other hand, being the sons (or in a few cases the grandsons) of men themselves raised to the peerage, they have nearly all been brought up in the midst of power and success, political or commercial. Peers who hold older titles, on the other hand, have generally been brought up in households whose prestige is already well established. This is not always so, however. If the holder of an ancient peerage has no male heir, the title passes to the next available descendant of the original holder, who may conceivably be a remote cousin whose personal background is far removed from the ruling class.

2. HOW ARISTOCRATIC IS THE HOUSE OF LORDS?

As the House of Lords is supposed to be an aristocratic assembly (and the House of Commons a popular assembly), we must concern ourselves particularly with the attempt to answer the question just how far the House of Lords can be regarded as being pre-eminently aristocratic in its composition. The answer to this question, whether we concern ourselves with the total membership of the House or whether we limit our enquiry to the relatively small number of active peers, is exceedingly intricate. Half of the total membership of the House in 1957 consists of men holding peerages originally created during the present century. More than a fifth of the peers of today were themselves ennobled, and almost a fifth are the sons of the first holders of their titles. Even before 1945 many of the newly-ennobled peers, particularly among the industrialists, were men who had made their way by their own efforts. If an aristocrat is a person of ancient noble lineage it seems then legitimate to deny that the composition of the House as a whole is essentially aristocratic. This denial must however be made subject to a number of important modifications. In the first place it is doubtful whether a person needs to be of ancient lineage to be considered aristocratic in Britain. The British aristocracy, with its background of centuries of fluidity, assimilates new members very rapidly, so that in outlook and manner of life a person brought up in ease and affluence based on a recently acquired fortune differs little from one whose fortune has a more ancient origin. The educational system plays a most important part in achieving this end. A self-made tycoon can send his son to Eton, where he will mix on equal terms with children of the older aristocracy, and the same mixing continues, though very much less exclusively, in the six most favoured colleges of Oxford and Cambridge. As was recently pointed out in an article in the *Economist*, 'rather more than half of those who are ennobled send their heirs to Eton and Harrow and another 20% to 30% to other public schools. Thus are the old and new nobility welded together, learning *noblesse oblige* . . . at academies especially fitted to inculcate it.'[1]

[1] *The Economist*, 21st July, 1956, p. 201. In the study which follows, frequent references will be made to the educational background of peers. Most entries in *Who's Who* tell us where the subjects were at school and university, and the information we may thus easily obtain and apply to groups of persons tells us much about their solid composition. There is a fairly high degree of correlation between 'being an old Etonian' and 'belonging to the aristocratic class'. A citation of two sets of figures can be used to test the reliability of this statement. According to the *Economist's* survey, just cited, of all peers who are the 'seventh holders of a title and above', 59% went to school at Eton, 18% at other public schools, and a further 15% do not say, in the reference books, where they were at school. As a check on this information it can also be mentioned that of all the 176 peers of the first three ranks (excluding first creations) in 1954, the 126 who give information about their schooling were distributed in almost the same way—83 at Eton, 8 at Harrow, 8 at Winchester, 23 at 22 other first-class public schools (five of them at Catholic schools), 3 at other public schools (two Catholic), and only one at any other sort of school. 'Most aristocrats go to school at Eton' does not imply 'most of those who go to Eton are aristocrats', but when we remember that old Etonians cannot be more than 0·5% of all men who have received full secondary education, we can readily see the implications of these figures.

The 22 'first-class' schools are those cited by Mr. R. K. Kelsall for the purposes of his book *Higher Civil Servants in Britain* (Routledge, 1955, p. 120), namely Charterhouse, Cheltenham, Clifton, Fettes, Haileybury, Loretto, Malvern, Marlborough, Oundle, Radley, Repton, Rossall, Rugby, Sedbergh, Sherborne, Shrewsbury, Uppingham and Westminster, with the addition of four 'special' schools which he omits, namely Ampleforth and Downside (Catholic), Wellington, with its military connection, and the Royal Naval College. The same list, without the four special schools but with the addition of two London day schools, is also used by Hester Jenkins and D. Caradog Jones for their study 'Social Class and Cambridge University' in *British Journal of Sociology*, vol. i, 1950, p. 96.

With further education, we can make use of parallel illustrations. Of the 65 peers of the rank of Earl and above who give any information in *Who's Who*

Secondly, although the House of Commons is popularly elected, it is doubtful whether, in comparing it with the House of Lords, we really ought to describe it as a popular assembly without qualification. Even now a rather large proportion of Conservative Members of Parliament are men of upper-class background, and about a quarter of all Conservative Members of Parliament have been educated at Eton. (This proportion has altered little during the past fifty years.) Among Conservative ministers the proportion of men with aristocratic connections tends to be even larger. As Conservative members of the House of Commons, and particularly Conservative ministers, have provided the largest single element in the recruitment of peers in the past fifty years, a fairly large proportion of the newly ennobled peers have been men who already have aristocratic connections. The social composition of the House of Lords, or at any rate of its Conservative element, is thus really more aristocratic than would seem from a consideration of the large number of newly-created peers, but not very much more aristocratic than the Conservative element in the House of Commons. The atmosphere of the modern House of Lords is remarkable for its friendliness and lack of aristocratic exclusiveness. It has been completely transformed since the time (1891) when Archbishop Benson lamented of his brother archbishop, Frederick Temple: 'his accent a little provincial . . . his figure square and his hair a little rough, he is not listened to at all by these cold, kindly, wordly wise, gallant landowning powers.'[1]

3. THE PRINCIPLES GOVERNING THE CREATION OF NEW PEERS

All new peerages are granted by the Crown on the advice of the Prime Minister of the day. The number of new creations varies from year to year and over longer periods. It rose in 1916–22, then fell. In 1945 there were 32 new peers, in 1949 only six. The average from 1941 to 1955 was twelve a year. Peerages are granted as rewards for particularly distinguished service in politics or in other fields of the national life, or because the Government of the day wishes to have

about having been to a University, 83% were at one or another of the six colleges of Oxford (Christ Church, Magdalen, New College and Balliol) or Cambridge (Trinity and King's). Yet former students of these colleges are under 5% of all university graduates.

The references to educational background which follow are based, then, on the assumption that if a large proportion of a given group of men consists of old Etonians, etc., it is legitimate to suggest that the group as a whole has a large element of upper-class members. The same assumption can be made, though with much less confidence, with regard to the 'six colleges'; for many years past they have drawn their students from very varied social backgrounds, and not only from the upper class.

[1] Quoted in A. C. Benson, *Life of Edward Benson*, vol. ii, p. 394.

the recipients in the House of Lords where it has work for them to do. Until thirty-five years ago it was often possible for a man to buy a peerage by making a large contribution to the funds of the political party in power, but the blatant use of this practice during Mr. Lloyd George's tenure of office as Prime Minister caused such a scandal that the sale of honours was brought to an end.[1]

The main basis of distinction among men who have peerages conferred upon them is that between former members of the House of Commons and others. Over half the new peers of the past few generations have been men from the House of Commons. These in their turn may be divided into a number of loosely defined groups. First come the ministers on whom peerages are conferred as rewards for their services when they retire from office. Certain conventions govern the granting of peerages to distinguished politicians. Any outgoing Prime Minister has by convention a right to have an earldom conferred upon him either immediately on resigning or later. Of recent Prime Ministers only Baldwin took a peerage immediately on retiring. Most others have preferred to remain in the House of Commons for some time and some have died without having gone to the House of Lords at all. Clement Attlee took his earldom in the autumn of 1955, after four years as Leader of the Opposition in the House of Commons. Sir Anthony Eden declined a peerage in 1957, although he also resigned his seat in the Commons.

Apart from former Prime Ministers, politicians these days normally receive peerages only at the hands of their own parties, though this is by no means a hard and fast rule. A minister who goes out of office with his party as a result of defeat at a general election does not normally stand a chance of receiving a peerage while his party is in opposition. If a minister wishes to retire, however, at the moment of a general election, he may be given a peerage in the dissolution honours. These days a senior minister who retires with a peerage is usually made a viscount rather than a baron.

It would be an over-simplification to suggest that peerages conferred upon ministers are always conferred at the end of glorious careers crowned by voluntary retirement. Two variations on this theme must be noticed. In the first place the conferment of a peerage often accompanies dismissal, when a Prime Minister wishes to rid himself of a minister whom he no longer wants—either because he is old but fails to realize that his powers are declining, or because, though comparatively young, he has been a failure in office, or because the Prime Minister simply wants him out of the way in order that he may reconstruct his government. The Prime Minister is able

[1] Cf. Gerald Macmillan, *Honours for Sale* (Richards Press, 1954). This question was debated in the Lords in 1918 and 1922, and in the Commons in 1919.

to achieve a dual purpose by the grant of a peerage in such a case. He may soothe and gratify the individual concerned, or at any rate his family, and he may remove him from the House of Commons where his continuing presence might otherwise have been embarrassing to the Government. Secondly, peerages are sometimes conferred upon ministers while in office, because the Prime Minister wishes to have them in the upper House for some special reason. A minister who accepts a peerage knows that by so doing he is making himself ineligible for the premiership and some of the other highest offices.

Peerages are often granted also to members of the House of Commons who have held no ministerial office. Back-bench members who are ennobled have usually many years of faithful party service to their credit. On occasion an M.P. may find himself prematurely ennobled as a result of the operation of what Sir Stephen King-Hall has called 'the co-incidental operation of the honours list'. If a prominent member of the Government party has been defeated at the polls, the Prime Minister may wish to find a seat in the House of Commons for him quickly. The most convenient way of doing this is usually by giving a peerage to a back-bencher who holds a safe government seat. The offer of a peerage can usually be relied upon to induce a suitable man to sacrifice his seat for the sake of the party's interests. The co-incidental operation of the honours list may have been a fairly prolific source of recruitment to the peerage in the past, particularly when incoming ministers, on first taking office, were obliged to submit themselves immediately for re-election in their own constituencies, but nowadays, with the great power of party organizations, the party leaders in the House of Commons are very often provided with safe seats there in any case.

The new peers from outside the House of Commons are generally men who have distinguished themselves in particular branches of the national life. The largest group consists of men whose distinction lies in the field covered by the wide terms 'commerce and industry'. They may be divided roughly into heads of large manufacturing or commercial concerns on the one hand and financiers or bankers on the other. As the peerage has always tended to assimilate the most important self-made magnates in the land, this group may be said to provide a continuity of a sort with the past, running right back to the Middle Ages. Even during the industrial age it has undergone a certain change. In the nineteenth and early twentieth centuries the founders of many of the great businesses whose names are now household words were given peerages. In some cases it was not only for their pioneering work in industry that they were rewarded, but also for their public benefactions. In more recent times, however, the biscuit kings and the baking powder kings of an earlier generation have tended to be superseded, among the ranks of the newly-ennobled, by 'managers' who have risen in the service of already established companies.

Many of the business men who receive peerages have also sat in the House of Commons. In some cases it is difficult to say whether it is really because of his parliamentary services or because of his commercial distinction that a particular man has received his peerage. Account must be taken of this difficulty in regard to the classification which follows later in this chapter.

Apart from the business men the largest individual groups of new peers until very recent years have been members of the armed forces and other public servants. Peerages are given to military commanders more readily after a war than in peace-time. With civilian public servants it is mainly those who have served overseas, as ambassadors or proconsuls, who are ennobled. When we consider that retired home civil servants, with their experience of administration, would apparently be peculiarly well able to make useful contributions to the work of the House, we may be surprised that so few of them have been given peerages. Not only they, but distinguished men in all fields of activity other than those already mentioned, are very thinly represented among the newly-created peers. There are generally two or three of the most distinguished members of the medical profession in the House of Lords, and a few scientists and dons, but taken together the numbers in all these groups have been very small indeed. During 1945–51 the Labour Government did something to redress the balance, but several of the non-parliamentarians ennobled during this period were ennobled mainly in order that they might speak for the Party, in some cases from the front bench. Though they had not sat in the House of Commons, these new peers were quickly assimilated with the 'politicians'.

The past fifty years have produced a gradual change in the popular feeling about the proper financial and social status of members of the House of Lords. Eighty years ago it was fairly generally accepted that one of the main arguments against giving ordinary peerages to judges was that they were generally of insufficient financial substance to be able to leave their heirs with the means of living on a scale appropriate to men of noble rank. Yet the salary of a judge at that time was the equivalent, at present values, of more than £20,000 a year after tax. In 1919 Field-Marshal Haig informed the Prime Minister that 'unless an adequate grant was made to enable a suitable position to be maintained', he must decline any offer of a peerage. He eventually accepted an earldom, together with a gratuity of £100,000.[1]

[1] Haig's note to the Prime Minister is quoted in Robert Blake (ed.), *The Private Papers of Douglas Haig* (Eyre & Spottiswoode, 1952), p. 357.

THE COMPOSITION OF THE HOUSE OF LORDS

Even in 1930 Mr. Ramsay MacDonald, when distributing peerages to political supporters as a Socialist Prime Minister, showed a certain preference for men whose social background would make them inconspicuous in an aristocratic assembly. During the past generation, however, as the public respect for wealth has declined, so the opinion that a peer ought to be a man of substantial independent means has become rare. Anxiety has, however, been expressed in some quarters, even very recently, about the future situation of the heirs of working-class peers.[1]

4. NEW PEERAGES CREATED, 1916–56: AN ANALYSIS[2]

The actual operation of the principles regarding the creation of new peers is illustrated in Table I. It cannot be claimed that this table is entirely accurate, because there are so many individuals whom it is very hard to classify, but it can be claimed that the general picture

TABLE I

PROFESSIONAL BACKGROUND OF NEW PEERS CREATED, 1916–56

	M.P.s	Lab. Party workers.	Commerce and industry.	Military, etc.	Other public servants.	Lawyers (exc. Law Lords).	Others.
1916–19	32	—	14	9	2	—	3
1920–29	46	—	26	1	5	6	3
1929–31	9	2	—	1	1	2	4
1932–39	37	2	23	3	8	—	7
1940–44	18	2	3	4	3	5	2
1945–51	24	10	—	16	—	—	10
1951–56	27	—	4	—	2	2	2

probably corresponds fairly well with the reality. The compiler of a table of this sort cannot escape from the need to make rather arbitrary decisions from time to time in individual cases. The chief source of possible misleading impressions is probably with relation to the former Members of Parliament. We have already seen that many ennobled M.P.s have also been prominent in business. Others have been prominent men in other fields too. In many cases a man's extra-parliamentary activities have contributed largely to the decision to award a peerage to him. A man such as Lord Percy of Newcastle,

[1] L. G. Pine, *The Story of the Peerage* (Blackwood, 1956), p. 260. Mr. Pine expresses concern at the danger of the future appearance of a race of *hidalgos de la gutiera*.

[2] For an analysis covering the period 1832–1928, cf., H. R. G. Greaves, 'Personal Origins and Interrelations of the Houses of Parliament', in *Economica*, vol. ix (1929), pp. 173–84.

who received a peerage in 1953, is hard to classify. He was a member of the House of Commons from 1921 to 1937; he was Minister of Education in Mr. Baldwin's second cabinet, from 1924 to 1929, and Minister without Portfolio in 1935-6. In 1937, however, he withdrew from politics and for the next fifteen years was Rector of King's College in the University of Durham. He could presumably have had a viscounty in 1937 had he wished, so although the peerage he eventually received could well be deemed a recognition of his later work, he is classed for our purposes among the former Members of Parliament. Lord Beveridge, on the other hand, who was in the House of Commons for only a few months, has been included under the heading 'others', because it seems obvious that it was mainly because of his distinguished career outside the House of Commons that he was made a peer.

Sixteen Members of the House of Commons whose eminence in industry and commerce alone might well have entitled them to receive peerages, but who had sat for long periods (ten years or more) in the Commons, have been classed among the former M.P.s. A few others whose House of Commons careers were short, are placed, like Lord Beveridge, in other classes. Table I may tend to overemphasize the element 'politicians' (ex-M.P.s) at the expense of the other classes, but the distortion to the whole picture cannot be very serious.

Of the 280 new peerages granted between 1916 and the accession of the Labour Government in 1945, just over half were given to Members of Parliament, of whom only a quarter had been ministers. Thirteen of the M.P.s (seven of them ennobled in 1929-31) had been Labour members. Another 66 new peers, or a quarter of the whole, were rewarded for their prominence in business, and to these we might add 16 Members of Parliament who were also very prominent business men. Of the total of 82 more than a quarter had deployed their talents in shipping, newspaper-owning or the brewing or distilling of strong drink. Eighteen others were military commanders, of whom half received their peerages during 1916-19. There were ten civilian public servants, including colonial governors, ambassadors and officials of the Royal Household and of Parliament. None of these were ordinary members of the Administrative Class of the Home Civil Service. There were seven men who had served the nation chiefly as advisers to the Government, as members of Royal Commissions or as arbitrators or makers of reports. There were nine who could be most conveniently classified as magnates—men of great eminence in local life and generally possessed of inherited wealth and land, by means of which, together with their own activities, they had already acquired a social status of such a kind that they seemed to merit recognition by the grant of peerages. There were also six men whose chief claim was the work they had been doing for the Labour Party outside Parliament; they were brought in partly to strengthen the Labour Party in the House of Lords.

The smallest element consisted of men of great distinction in less easily classifiable fields of the national life. Lord Baden-Powell, the Chief Scout, was given a peerage in 1930, as was Archbishop Davidson when he retired from the see of Canterbury. The world of learning was represented by Lord Rutherford. The list was completed by two members of the medical profession and seven judges in addition to those who were made Lords of Appeal in Ordinary.

After the second world war, with the Labour Government in power for six years consecutively, the new peers came from new and more varied backgrounds. Forty-four supporters of the Labour Party were ennobled between 1945 and 1951. Twenty-four of these were Members of Parliament, two were trade union officials, and eight had been prominent in other work for the Labour movement. Ten others were made peers not so much because of their political activity up to that point, but rather because, being experts or men of standing in various fields of life, it was felt that they would have something of value to contribute to the proceedings of the House of Lords from the Socialist point of view.[1]

Labour leaders and ardent supporters of the Socialist movement are generally supposed not to want to be peers, so it is perhaps scarcely correct to say that the peerages have been conferred upon such persons wholly as rewards for their services. They should perhaps rather be said to have accepted peerages as a duty and as a token of acceptance of a task of furthering the interests of the Party through work in the House of Lords. A number of prominent Socialists accepted peerages at the hands of the National Government before 1939, and again under the wartime Coalition Government.[2] Since 1951, however, the only Labour Party supporter to have accepted

[1] In addition, Air Chief Marshal Lord Douglas of Kirtleside and Admiral Lord Mountevans, who received peerages as rewards for their wartime services, were classed by *Vacher* as supporters of the Labour Party.

[2] The difficulties of the Socialist conscience with regard to Labour representation in the Lords are well illustrated by the events of 1935-6. The Labour Party Conference in 1935 instructed the Executive to draw up a report on Honours. The report, which was produced a year later, emphasized the need for competent representation of the Labour case in the upper House so long as the House existed. But the next Party Conference decided, by 185 votes to 174, to refer the report back, and no agreed statement of policy emerged. (Cf. G. D. H. Cole, *History of the Labour Party from 1914*, Routledge, 1948, p. 344.) In 1945-51 the Party did not allow the demands of practical politics to be sacrificed for the sake of any pedantic adherence to egalitarian principles. From Lord Attlee's sensible policy over peerage-creations both the Labour Party and the House of Lords have profited.

NEW PEERAGES CREATED: AN ANALYSIS

a peerage at the hands of the Conservative Government is Lord Attlee, who received his earldom as his due under the convention regarding former Prime Ministers. Even his acceptance of a peerage was rather sharply criticized by some 'diehard' Socialists.

The Labour Government did not give peerages only to its own supporters, but also rewarded men who had no political connections; no less than sixteen wartime military leaders, for example, were ennobled between 1945 and 1951.[1]

Since 1951 former members of the House of Commons, and in particular former ministers, have received a larger proportion of the new peerages than under earlier Conservative administrations. Two-thirds of the new peers of 1951-6 were ennobled from the House of Commons. Sixteen of the twenty-eight M.P.s thus ennobled (including Earl Attlee) had served as ministers; two of them were granted peerages in order that they might perform special functions as ministers in the House of Lords, one took office on being made a peer, and the remainder were for the most part ennobled on retirement from office.[2] The greatest change as compared with the earlier period dominated by the Conservative Party is to be found in the great decline of the granting of peerages to men of commerce and industry. Only four big industrialists were given peerages in 1951-6, though it would perhaps be advisable to add four other men prominent in the City or in industry who have earned their peerages principally by their long service in the House of Commons.

Taken as a whole, the new peers of the past forty years do not include an unduly large proportion of men who were born in the highest social class. According to the 1954 Fabian Society pamphlet, just half of the 116 men created peers in 1945-54 could be regarded as 'upper class'; 35 of them are classified as 'middle class' and the remaining 23 as 'working class'.[3] According to the *Economist's* survey, only 18% of all living peers of first creation were at school at Eton. When we look more closely at this figure, however, we see that nearly all of the old Etonians were also former Conservative members of the House of Commons. As soon as we look at the other groups of newly-created peers we find a much wider spread of social origins. Most ennobled judges[4] and military commanders were educated at

---

[1] This figure includes Lord Mountbatten, who had a special claim on appointment as Viceroy of India, and Lord Freyberg, who received his peerage only after he had served as Governor of New Zealand.

[2] Earl Winterton is included in these calculations. As an Irish Peer he had sat for thirty years in the Commons.

[3] Lord Chorley, Bernard Crick and Donald Chapman, *Reform of the Lords* (Fabian Research Series, no. 169), 1954, p. 10.

[4] For an analysis of the social and educational background of the whole of the judiciary, cf. *The Economist*, 15th December 1956, p. 946.

public schools suggesting a relatively affluent middle-class origin, but most of the industrialists, particularly before 1940, appear to have been self-made men. Of the 36 ennobled between 1920 and 1929, for example, only one (according to Cokayne's *Complete Peerage*) was at school at Eton and one at one of the 'first-class' schools. Some of the others appear not even to have had full secondary education at all, though detailed analysis is impossible because so many give no specific information about their educational background.

The present discussion of the personnel of the House of Lords would not be complete without some reference to the position of the peerage in the contemporary social structure. We need not here examine the intrinsic merits or demerits of an aristocratic principle in society, or the nature of mere snobbery, to which the peerage gives a focus and from which it derives some sustenance. We must observe, however, that, for all the progress of radical and egalitarian doctrines, some of Mr. Russell Kirk's 'canons of conservatism', such as 'belief in the necessity of orders and classes' and 'love of the proliferating variety and mystery of traditional life',[1] have a real force in our national and local affairs. Many peers, particularly those who hold long-established titles, are great men in their own parts of the country. They embody the community's sense of its own continuity; they are tokens of its stability. Their fellow-citizens elect them to local councils, appoint them to public boards and to the governing bodies of institutions, entreat them to be presidents and officers of innumerable societies for doing good, invite them to be directors of banks and insurance companies and other commercial and manufacturing firms.[2] The peerage as a whole, old as well as new, is in fact constantly and closely in touch with the manifold concerns and interests of the community, and can draw on a wide experience whose value we ought not to fail to take into account when we assess the House of Lords as a working institution of government.

[1] Russell Kirk, *The Conservative Mind* (Faber, 1954), p. 17.
[2] *The Economist*, 28th July 1956, p. 297, gives some statistics on this.

Chapter III

ACTIVE AND INACTIVE PEERS

1. THE ACTIVE ELEMENT IN THE HOUSE

WE may now turn from the consideration of the whole membership of the House of Lords to a special study of the active element. There are today some sixty peers who may be regarded as a nucleus of regular attenders and contributors to debate. These peers treat the House of Lords much as the elected members of Parliament treat the House of Commons. They come down to the House on most sitting days and may be regarded as 'politicians'. A quarter of them hold office in the Government and receive salaries. Of the whole sixty nearly two-thirds are Conservatives, a third are Labour peers, and a few others support neither of the main parties. The balance of parties in the day-to-day House is thus by now not so overwhelmingly in favour of the Conservatives as may be commonly believed.

There are in addition about 500 peers who come to the House from time to time, some very rarely and some fairly often. Many of these are elderly, or have quite time-consuming avocations outside the House; most of them attend, as a rule, only for debates of particular interest to themselves. Sir Ivor Jennings in 1939 referred also to the drawing power of 'entertainment'. Most peers come to the House at some time, though not all of these participate in debate and not all of them take part in any division. During the session of 1956, according to Mr. Wedgwood Benn's 1957 Fabian tract, 310 peers attended ten times or more and 280 attended less than ten times; the average daily attendance throughout the session was 104.[1] It may be assumed that rather more than half of the peers present on a 'typical' day would be regular attenders, another quarter fairly frequent attenders,

---

[1] *The Privy Council as a Second Chamber*, op. cit., p. 5.

and the remainder members who are aptly classified in the 1954 Fabian Society pamphlet as 'casuals'.[1]

For the whole period since 1919 the average number voting in divisions has been around eighty; there has been no significant change during the period. A debate of special interest produces an exceptionally large attendance; such occasions are, however, not usually concerned with ordinary political questions. In the past thirty years only two purely political questions have produced divisions with over 200 peers voting—a series of divisions on the Commons' rejection of Lords amendments to the Coal Mines Bill in 1930, and the plans for Indian constitutional reform in 1934 and 1935.[2] On the other hand a bill to allow peeresses to sit in the House brought out 206 peers to vote in 1926, and over 200 voted on each of two other proposals for the reform of the House, in 1927 and 1933; 216 peers voted on a liquor control bill in 1924, and 289 on the Prayer Book question in 1927. Coming down to more recent times, we find 258 and 238 peers voting on the two second readings of the Parliament Bill in 1948, 244 on a motion condemning independent television in 1954, 209 on the death penalty in 1948 and 333 on the same subject on 1956. For the rest, no division in the past thirty years has brought out over 200 peers to vote; the number voting on really important political questions has usually been around 150. 112 peers voted on the Anglo-French ultimatum to Egypt on 1st November 1956 (with many abstentions), and 188 in the divisions on the same question at the end of the three-day debate six weeks later—though there were abstentions on this occasion also.

The fluctuating attendance is well illustrated by the votes on the Labour Government's Parliament Bill, which came up to the Lords for second reading three times during 1948 and 1949. According to the authors of the Fabian Society pamphlet, 91 peers voted in all three divisions, 108 in two, and 154 in one only. They suggest that, in divisions attracting say 250 votes, about half of the peers voting may be 'casuals' who are 'attracted by the occasion to make their infrequent visits on those days'.

Although the average daily attendance at the House is so small, the Chamber is not usually as empty during a sitting as one might expect. The number present may tend to dwindle after about 5.30 p.m., but until that hour there are generally at least thirty peers

---

[1] Lord Chorley, Bernard Crick and Donald Chapman, *Reform of the Lords*, op. cit., p. 9.

[2] Conditions were very different in 1906–14. The controversial debates of that period regularly drew very large attendances. On the Education Bill of 1906, during the sixteen-day committee proceedings, there were many days on which the numbers voting in divisions greatly exceeded 200.

present. In the House of Commons (or, for that matter, the French National Assembly) the attendance of members actually listening to a debate is often little more than this, at any rate when back-benchers are speaking.

Some detailed studies of the active element of the House have already been published. In the *Spectator* for 20th November 1953, pp. 561 f., Mr. Sydney Bailey analysed the participation of peers in all the divisions in the first two sessions of the Parliament of 1951. He found that in the thirty-one divisions which took place the average number of peers participating in each division was 78; in four of these divisions (three of them on the National Health Service Bill) more than one hundred peers took part. Altogether 296 peers voted at least once during this two-year period. Of these 296, 51 were Labour peers, 14 Liberals, 8 Independents, and 218 peers who 'could be regarded as Conservatives'.[1] The figure of 51 Labour peers includes almost all of the peers belonging to the Labour Party, whose total number at that time was 55.

Mr. Bailey classified as regular attenders all those peers who took part in at least 15 of the 31 divisions during the two years under review. Of these he found that there were 65; 43 Conservative and 22 Labour. All but two of the 22 Labour peers were first in the line of creation. Of the Conservatives on the other hand, 33 had inherited their titles, though of these 33, eight were the sons of appointed peers. Only ten were the first of their creation.

The results of another survey were published in the *Manchester Guardian* on 17th May 1950. This survey did not distinguish between peers according to party allegiance, but concentrated on ascertaining the relative amounts of participation in the work of the House by peers of first creation on the one hand and peers who had inherited their titles on the other hand. It was found that, in the 65 divisions which took place between 15th August 1945 and 17th May 1949, 461 peers voted at least once each. Of these just two-thirds had inherited their titles. During three short sample periods of 1949, peers who had inherited their titles made 54% of the 311 speeches and asked 37% of the 141 questions. According to another source, the researches of Lord Moran, 147 of the 318 peers who spoke in the four sessions 1947–51 (or 46%) were peers of first creation.[2] These figures, taken together, suggest a greater intensity of participation by peers of first creation.

[1] Mr. Bailey's figure of 218 includes many peers who do not formally adhere to the Conservative Party or accept its Whip. In the discussion which will occupy most of the rest of this chapter these peers will be counted separately from the avowed Conservatives.

[2] Lord Moran cited these figures to the House during a debate on a Life Peers Bill (Lords Debs., 3rd February 1953, vol. 180, col. 163).

We may now proceed a little beyond the results produced by these surveys, and attempt to supplement them by some further statistics of the same sort, based on different criteria. The chief method used for this study is a classification of peers into a number of groups according to the frequency of their interventions in two chosen three-year periods, one in the immediate past and the other, for the sake of comparison, immediately after the passing of the Parliament Act in 1911. Each peer has been credited with the number of interventions shown against his name in the *Hansard* index, and then classified as 'active' (group I), 'moderately active' (group II), or an 'occasional contributor' (group III) according to the number of his interventions. The qualification for inclusion in the first group is to have spoken on 25 or more occasions in three years. The second group consists of peers who contributed from 10 to 24 times, and the third, that of the 'occasional' speakers, those who spoke at least once each, but less than ten times.[1]

The first period examined is that of 1911–13. These years are not typical of the pre-1914 period, because the activity of the House was exceptionally intense in 1911, when the debates on the Parliament Bill, and on the Lords' own proposals for reform, were not only controversial but long drawn-out. Even so, the total time spent in session in 1911 and 1912 was less than in most recent years, and the session of 1913 (which began late and was short) produced very little discussion in the Lords at all. Most of the time in 1911 and 1912 was taken up with debates about the House of Lords or Irish home rule; the Scottish Small Landholders' Bill of 1911 took up a good deal of time, and brought into action some Scottish peers who might otherwise have had less to say.[2] There was also a fair amount of discussion of defence and of merchant shipping.

[1] This method of classification fails to take into account the (not very numerous) peers who attend often but never speak. It seems better, for the purposes of this study, to concern ourselves with contributions to debate rather than with attendance. The classification is inevitably subject to error, particularly on the borderlines between the groups, but the same could be said about any other basis of classification which might be employed. It has been difficult, for example, to decide how best to deal with speeches in committee. How are we to classify a peer who has made, say, 30 speeches in committee on a bill in which he is particularly interested, and only four interventions on other matters during the whole three-year period? It would clearly be wrong to classify him as a member of the nucleus of 'active' peers who speak regularly or very frequently. In order that distortions produced by this factor may be minimized, all speeches made by a peer in committee on a particular bill on any one day have been counted, for the purpose of the classification, as one speech. Some other similar arbitrary decisions have had to be made, but it seems fair to claim an adequate degree of accuracy for the classification as a whole.

[2] It might be suggested that the inclusion of the year 1911 would distort the result. In fact, however, the peers who spoke often in 1911 spoke often also in

THE ACTIVE ELEMENT IN THE HOUSE

In 1911–13, 38 peers spoke often enough to be placed in the first, or 'active' group. All, with perhaps one exception, could be described as 'politicians'. All those who had themselves been ennobled had served in the House of Commons. The others, with one exception, had either served in the House of Commons or inherited peerages early in life, and followed their political bent in the upper House. The exception was the fifth Lord Ellenborough, an eminent sailor who inherited a peerage late in life. More than two-thirds had inherited their peerages, and were thus in the House of Lords as a result of the accident of birth.

The most striking feature of the whole 'active' group is the complete absence from it of men ennobled because of their eminence in fields of activity other than politics. Lord Halsbury, who was a most eminent lawyer and judge, might have had a claim to be counted as a non-politician, but as he outdid all his colleagues in purely 'political' activity in 1911, and was a most impassioned partisan, he can hardly be counted as a non-politician for our purposes. Lord Ellenborough comes nearest among this group to our conception of a non-political senator. His interventions were almost entirely restricted to questions concerning the Navy, on which public attention was focused more than usual at that time.

Even among the peers whom, for the purposes of this study, we call 'class II' (each of whom spoke on between 10 and 25 occasions in the three years) none had earned distinction outside Parliament before entering the upper House. More than half of all the peers in the two groups had served in the House of Commons; almost half of these had inherited their peerages, but had been elected to the House of Commons before succeeding. Many of them had been elected to the lower House while still in their early twenties.[1] Among this group the holders of great and ancient titles, such as the Duke of Devonshire and the Earl of Derby, form a large proportion. Even the enlarged electorate had still often been eager, in the late nineteenth century, to give old family seats to men of under 25.[2] Of the peers of group II who had never sat in the Commons, seven-eighths had inherited their peerages while under the age of 35. There were only four (as compared with one in the first group) who had reached the House of Lords in middle age without having sat in the Commons first.

1912. Only one of those included in this list concentrated his speeches in 1911. This was Lord Courtney of Penwith, who spoke little in 1912 or 1913.

[1] Sir Lewis Namier has shown that in 1761, of the 23 M.P.s who were the eldest sons of peers, 21 had entered the House of Commons at the first available opportunity after reaching the age of 21. (*The Structure of Politics at the Accession of George III*, vol. i, p. 55).

[2] Cf. W. L. Guttsman, 'Aristocracy and the Middle Class in the British Political Elite, 1886–1916,' in *British Journal of Sociology*, vol. v (1954), p. 13.

In each group more than three-quarters of the active Conservatives had inherited their titles, though sons of first creations were fairly numerous. The proportion of peers of high rank was nearly twice as high among active Conservative peers as among the membership of the House as a whole. Two reasons for this suggest themselves. On the one hand several of the peers of high rank were continuing a tradition of political leadership built up by their families; on the other hand there was still at that time a fairly strong tendency for public opinion to look upon heads of the great families as the natural leaders of the nation—a tendency which is weaker today, though still in evidence.

Of the 26 Conservatives in the first group only two admitted, for the purpose of the reference books, to having been to schools other than Eton. One of these went to Harrow and the other to Charterhouse. On the other hand, against the 16 old Etonians we have to set the relatively large number (eight) who gave no information about their schooling. The Conservatives of the second group have a very similar educational background. When we look at University education we find the same story. Of all the Conservatives in the two groups, 34 admit to having been to a university, all of them to Oxford or Cambridge and over three-quarters of them to one or other of the six most favoured colleges[1] of those two universities.

The Liberal peers who were active included a larger proportion of men promoted from the House of Commons, and a leavening of men of middle-class rather than aristocratic origins. Half of them had been promoted from the Commons.

Active Peers in recent times

For the attempt to present a picture of the active element in the House of Lords in recent times two periods have been studied, the first three sessions following the general election of 1951 and the two last sessions before that of 1950. The figures given here will be based on the period 1951–4; the period 1947–9 has been used mainly as a check for the purpose of ascertaining how far peers tend to speak more when their own Party is in Opposition.

The first change to be noticed when we compare the recent period with 1911–13 is the greatly increased number of peers who participate in the debates. As will be seen later, the quantity of work done by the House, measured in hours of sitting per year, is far greater nowadays than forty or even twenty years ago. The House discusses a wider variety of subjects. When we look at the debates in terms of participation by individuals, we find a corresponding increase at all levels.

[1] Cf. above, p. 21 note. Most of the others were at University College, Oxford.

TABLE II

	Number of peers who qualified for inclusion in 1911–13 and 1951–54.			
	Class I.	Class II.	Class III.	Total.
1911–13	38	33	128	199
1951–54	68	58	192	318
Excess of 1951–54 over 1911–13 (%)	79	76	50	60
Proportion of total membership of the House: 1911–13 (%)	7	7	23	37
1951–54 (%)	8	6	23	37

The total number of peers who made some contribution in three years was 60% greater in the recent period than in the earlier; the rate of increase was greater among regular participants than occasional participants. These figures must be set against the increase in the total membership of the House from about 600 to about 850, itself an increase of nearly 50%. We cannot, however, be satisfied that the increase in participation was caused entirely by the increase in total membership; the change in the character of the work of the House (which itself reflects the increase in numbers) is also an important contributory factor.

Among the frequent participants the balance between Conservatives and others is about the same in the recent period as in the earlier—though it was different during much of the intervening period.

The tally of peers in the first class according to the criterion of participation corresponds almost exactly with Mr. Bailey's classification according to frequency of voting, both in general and when broken down according to party allegiance.[1] The only difference is with the Liberals and non-party peers; the tiny handful of Liberals who spoke frequently did not vote often enough to qualify for inclusion in Mr. Bailey's list of frequent voters.

	Conservative.	Labour.	Liberal.	Other.	Total.
Frequent speakers, 1951–54	40	23	4	1	68
Frequent voters, 1951–53	43	22	—	—	65

When we set these figures against the total membership of the House

---

[1] It also corresponds with the results of the researches embodied in the 1954 Fabian Society pamphlet, where it is shown that of the 166 peers who voted on the Parliament Bill on 29th November 1949, 60 had attended at the House at half or more of the sittings during the three sessions in which the Bill had been before Parliament (op. cit., p. 10).

we find that the proportion of Conservatives among 'active' peers (60%) is about the same as their proportion to the total membership (494 out of 850, or 58%). On the other hand, as might be expected, the proportion of Labour peers is much higher among the active membership (34%) than among the total membership (7%). To put it in another way, less than one-tenth of all Conservative peers are regular contributors to debate, as against two-fifths of all Labour peers. Of the total of over 230 non-party peers only one, Lord Vansittart, spoke often enough to be included in this list.

Of the 68 who may, according to this criterion, be said to form the regular nucleus of the active House as it performs its business from day to day, half (33) had been in the House of Commons before entering the Lords by way of succession or ennoblement (Table III). Another 12 (11 of them Conservatives) had succeeded to peerages when they were under 35 years old, and therefore too young, in the normal course of events, to enter the House of Commons.[1] Fourteen (six of them Labour) had themselves been given peerages as rewards for their distinction in fields of public affairs outside the House of Commons. The remaining nine had inherited peerages when aged more than 35, but had never been in the House of Commons.

This total of 23 peers who had neither succeeded when young nor served in the House of Commons stands in striking contrast to the corresponding figure for 1911–13, when there was not one 'active' peer of first creation who had not been in the Commons, and only one who had succeeded when over the age of 35. This important change in the balance of the composition of the active element in the Lords should surely be a healthy one. It is not by any means entirely due to the intrusion of Labour creations into the House; the 23 were from both main Parties and included many peers on the cross benches (see Table III). We have here a development which probably has a relation both of cause and of effect to the modern tendency for the Lords to devote infinitely more time to the discussion of questions of a non-political character.

Among the second group, consisting of peers who spoke fairly often, we would perhaps expect to find a larger proportion of peers of first creation, and particularly of men ennobled as a result of their great distinction outside politics. The contrary is in fact the case, among the Conservatives at any rate. Of the total of 33 Conservatives in the group, only six were first creation peers. The proportion of first creation peers among the Conservatives is thus only half as great in the second group as in the first.

[1] This assumption can only be made with appropriate reservations. Heirs to peerages do indeed still sometimes enter the House of Commons when well under 35, but it happens less frequently now than in the nineteenth century.

THE ACTIVE ELEMENT IN THE HOUSE

TABLE III

PARLIAMENTARY BACKGROUND OF ACTIVE PEERS, 1911–13 AND 1951–54

	Former M.P.s.		Never in Commons.		
	First holders.	Inherited titles.	Inherited at age under 35 yrs.	Others inherited.	First holders.
1911–13.					
Class I: Cons.	6	8	11	1	0
Liberal	6	0	6	0	0
Class II: Cons.	2	8	10	3	0
Liberal	4	0	1	1	0
Total	18	16	28	5	0
1951–54.					
Class I: Cons.	10	6	11	8	5
Labour	14	1	1	1	6
Others	3	1	0	0	2
Class II: Cons.	4	6	14	7	2
Labour	4	0	2	1	5
Others	2	0	1	3	8

It is proposed now to analyse the active peers in some detail, treating each Party separately, but taking the second group (class II) together with the first.

Among the Conservatives the proportion of peers who had inherited their titles (five-eighths of the whole) was slightly less than forty years earlier. It was particularly high (over four-fifths) among the peers of class II, and lowest (56%) among the back-benchers of class I. Only a third of the peers who held office during the period were peers of first creation.

When we compare the office-holders[1] (including Lords in Waiting)

[1] All peers of classes I and II who held office at any time during the period under review are here classed as 'office-holders'. The office-holders counted here include Lords Leathers and Alexander of Tunis, because they spoke often enough during the period under review to warrant their inclusion here. It is really wrong, however, to include them as part of the nucleus of Conservative peers regularly attending. Neither has spoken much when out of office, and Earl Alexander does not even acknowledge himself as a Conservative. Lords Ismay and Cherwell have been omitted from the list, because they spoke rarely even when they were in office. (Lord Cherwell had, however, spoken more frequently during the previous few years.)

with the others we are struck in particular by the very high proportion of holders of old titles; almost half of the office-holders were at least the fifth in line of succession to their titles. Similarly, we notice an unduly large proportion of peers of high rank. Over half of the office-holders were dukes, marquesses or earls; yet of the active Conservative peers who did not hold office less than a fifth held titles of the three higher ranks.[1]

The relatively high proportion of peers with inherited titles among the office-holders can be easily explained. It is now impossible for any substantial number of important ministers to be in the House of Lords; most of the ministerial posts held by peers must in modern conditions be posts carrying little power or prestige. Such posts are rarely likely to be acceptable to Conservative peers of first creation, whether they have been ennobled from the House of Commons or because of their distinction outside politics. We find that the six office-holders of first creation all held senior ministerial posts with seats in the cabinet.[2] Of the 13 peers who had inherited their titles

TABLE IV

ACTIVE CONSERVATIVE PEERS CLASSIFIED ACCORDING TO AGE OF TITLE

	1st.	2nd.	3rd or 4th.	5th or Older.	Total
1911–13.					
Class I:	6	6	2	12	26
Class II:	4	3	4	12	23
Total	10	9	6	24	49
1951–54.					
Class I: Ministers	6	4	0	9	19
Others	9	3	2	7	21
Class II:	6	10	7	10	33
Total	21	17	9	26	73
Percent of total 1911–13 Classes I and II combined.	20·4	18·4	12·2	49	
1951–54	28·7	23·3	12·3	35·7	

[1] If Earl Alexander of Tunis and Lord Leathers were omitted, the proportion of old titles would be even greater (9 out of 17); the proportion of peers of higher rank would not be affected.

[2] To them we might add Lord Cherwell and Lord Ismay. Cf. above, p. 39.

only one (the Marquess of Salisbury) had a seat in the Cabinet,[1] and nine were men of under 50 holding relatively unimportant posts for which it might have been hard to find occupants among ennobled Conservatives.

The predominance of holders of old titles, and of titles of high degree, among these minor office-holders, may be partly coincidental, but does not appear to be wholly so. The same phenomenon can be observed in earlier Conservative governments. In 1905, 14 out of 17 office-holding peers were of the rank of earl or above; in 1925, seven out of twelve; and in 1938 eleven out of sixteen. We must apparently return to the twofold explanation offered for the parallel phenomenon with regard to the active Conservative peers of 1911–14, when the Party was in opposition. A theory of continuous political service by the heads of ancient families, carried on from generation to generation, could find some support from the evidence, but not very much.[2]

When we look at the active Conservative peers (groups I and II) according to their educational background we find a pattern similar to that of 1911–14. Almost nine-tenths of them, including all the peers of first creation, were not merely at public schools, but at public schools belonging to the first class. Forty-one (more than half of the total) were at Eton, ten at Harrow or Winchester, and fourteen at other leading public schools. Five give no information about their schooling, or say that they were educated 'privately'.[3] For the rest, the whole mass of middle-grade and minor public schools, and of secondary and grammar schools, privately or publicly maintained, is represented by only three peers, all of them men of singular personal ability and distinction, and even these three were all at independent day schools of high standing and belonging to the Headmasters' Conference.

With the background of further education it is the same story.

[1] In 1956, however, after the end of the period now under review, the Earls of Home and Selkirk were both given posts with seats in the Cabinet. The balance among office-holders had shifted in favour of the aristocratic element. Only two out of the 17 office-holders were peers of first creation and three were the second holders of their titles. Holders of old titles and of peerages of the higher ranks were still in a majority. Three of the four peers in the reconstructed Cabinet held old earldoms.

[2] Cf. W. L. Guttsman, 'Social Structure of the Political Elite', in *British Journal of Sociology*, 1951, pp. 132 f.

[3] One of these was Lord Leathers, who could perhaps be called a self-made man, and who was brought into the wartime Government and into the Lords in 1941 to be Minister of War Transport. In 1951 Sir Winston Churchill brought him into the Cabinet as Minister for Co-ordination of Transport, Fuel and Power. But he only figures in our list because the period covered by this survey includes the time while he was in office, and therefore called upon from time to time to speak for the Government. At other times he had taken little part in debate.

Half of the active Conservative peers (36) were at one or other of the six leading colleges of Oxford and Cambridge, 11 at the rest of Oxford and Cambridge and only two at other universities. Thus of those who admitted having been to universities three-quarters passed through the most aristocratic part of the university system, representing about one-thirtieth of the total of university students even at the time when most of the men concerned were students. A further 12 were at military or naval establishments.

Although it could be argued that much useful and constructive work had been done in the Lords by men with inherited peerages, this brief study of the active members on the Conservative side of the House could be made to provide support for the opinion that the hereditary element is unheathily large. The reason is evident; there are plenty of Conservative peers of first creation in the House, but many of them are either retired from active politics or very busy with other activities.

We are confronted with the inescapable fact that among the Conservative peers, who dominate the House, the great majority of the active members owe their seats to the accident of birth, and also belong to a very restricted social group. Some people might well be inclined to condemn the House of Lords on this ground, and to say that so long as it is not completely reconstructed it must be an unhealthy institution in a modern state.

In reply to such an argument it might well be pointed out that the Conservative Party remains in a high degree aristocratic even when it is required to submit to the test of the polls. Conservative Party selection committees, particularly when they have safe seats in the House of Commons to bestow, are inclined to look with favour on aspirants with aristocratic connections. Recent Conservative Prime Ministers have, perhaps not deliberately, given a very large proportion of ministerial offices to aristocratic M.P.s; ten of the fourteen members of the Cabinet in November 1956 who sat in the Commons are closely related, either themselves or by marriage, to holders of British hereditary titles, and two of the four others figure in Burke's *Landed Gentry*. It could be plausibly stated that the Cabinet did not include a single middle-class Englishman, except perhaps Mr. Butler. The slight tendency away from aristocratic domination of the higher ranks of the Conservative Party during the 1920s and 1930s has been reversed.

In view of these considerations it seems fair to assume that the few dozen active Conservative peers who hold old titles would in general find no difficulty in obtaining seats in the House of Commons; many of them have in fact previously sat in the Commons. Egalitarians who resent the presence of these unelected, unappointed aristocrats in the upper House of the Legislature would do well to turn their resentment against the whole process of selection of men for political leadership in the Conservative Party, both in the constituencies and in the House of Commons. Lord Woolton's reforms have, as yet, been slow to bear fruit.

Active Labour Peers

While the active Conservative peers constitute only a small part of the total Conservative membership of the House, the contrary is, as we would expect, the case with the Labour peers. Two-thirds of their total number spoke often enough to be included in one or the other of the first two groups, and only one-sixth of them failed to speak at all during the three years under review. It is true that, as the Labour peers created before 1951 become older, and receive no reinforcements in the form of new creations, the attendance on the Labour benches tends gradually to decrease; nevertheless, the figures do reflect the supposed attitude of ennobled Socialists to their membership of the House. If a man has accepted a peerage, not as a reward but in order that he may support his Party in the House of Lords, he can be expected to attend the debates.

The Labour peers, active and inactive, have, as a group, many characteristics which distinguish them sharply both from the Conservatives and from the Liberals who were their predecessors on the Left. The group resembles the Conservatives chiefly in including many former members of the House of Commons; indeed, with two-thirds of their number former M.P.s the Labour peers of group I resemble the active Conservatives of forty years ago more closely in this respect than do the active Conservatives of today.

As soon as we leave this matter of former membership of the House of Commons, we find the Labour peers so different in some respects from the Conservatives that we can scarcely use the same headings for classification. When we look, for example, among the Labour peers of group I, for the proportion of peers who are the second or third holders of their titles, we find that there are none at all. Not many heirs of ennobled Socialists are yet to be found among the membership of the House, and such as there are are not necessarily themselves Labour supporters. Only a handful of holders of old titles are Labour supporters.[1]

The active Labour peers who were never members of the House of Commons are men of most varied backgrounds—so varied indeed

---

[1] It is sometimes suggested, not altogether without justification, that heirs to Labour peers tend to desert the Party of their fathers. Some of the original Labour peers of first creation have by now died and been succeeded by their sons. At least five of these successors now in the House of Lords are described in *Vacher* as non-party or Liberals, and two as Conservatives. But the numbers are as yet too small to serve as a basis for valid generalization.

that it is scarcely worth attempting to classify them. Most have been to some extent active in work for the Labour movement in some form, but the proportion of trade union officials is less than is commonly supposed.

When we look at the educational background we find it worth while to make a distinction which was irrelevant with the Conservatives (as it is also with active non-party and Liberal peers)—between those who have been to 'grammar schools' and those who only received elementary education. A fair proportion of Labour peers are not merely men of working-class origin, but men who have made their careers within the working class; about a third of all those in the two active groups received no secondary education.[1] Interestingly enough, the same number went to first class public schools, and among these the old Etonians outnumber the former pupils of all other public schools put together.[2] About half of all the active Labour peers received university education; seven of the sixteen are shared between the 'six colleges' of Oxford and Cambridge, and another seven among the provincial universities.

On the whole, the active peers who are members of the Labour Party tend to form a rather self-consciously coherent group—more so at any rate than their Conservative opposite numbers. In view of the circumstances of their appointment to the House of Lords this is hardly surprising, and the fact that they are in a permanent minority accentuates the same tendency. Furthermore, a relatively large proportion of the active Labour peers sit on the Front Bench.

Active Liberal and non-party Peers

The Liberal and non-party peers of the first two groups are not numerous enough for classification in separate tables.[3] With both

[1] We noticed above that many men ennobled by Conservative governments, particularly before 1930, had received no secondary education. But the self-made business men of a generation ago have not, for the most part, taken a very active part in the proceedings of the House.

[2] With both of the main parties we are struck by the thin representation of the public schools generally patronized by the middle classes, the prosperous business and professional people who are often said to form the backbone of the community. Of all the 99 active peers of groups I and II, belonging to one of the two main political parties, we find only 15% from the 22 leading public schools, other than Eton, Harrow and Winchester, and only one single individual from the mass of about 50 middle and minor public schools (whose former pupils are more numerous than those of all the 25 'first class' schools), to set beside the 60% who went to Eton, Harrow or Winchester.

[3] The Second Marquess of Reading has been omitted from the list of Liberals, because as he held office in the Conservative Government throughout our period it seemed that he should be included among the Conservative office-holders. He was, however, active among the Liberal peers before he accepted office.

Liberal and non-party peers, particularly the latter, the 'moderately active' peers (group II) were more numerous than those who qualified for inclusion in group I (cf. Table V). Taken together, however, the 18 peers who, while outside the two main parties, spoke fairly frequently, add up to nearly a sixth of the total relatively active membership, and thus provide the House of Lords with an element without parallel in the Commons.

The four Liberals of group I included the first Viscount Samuel, an elder statesman and former M.P. and minister. The five group II Liberals included Lord Beveridge, who, though he was in the House of Commons for a few months in 1945, had until then adhered to no political party, and had earned his claim to a peerage by his activities outside the field of politics. Of the nine Liberals included in our groups I and II, Lord Elibank was the only other to have sat in the House of Commons, and he sat only from 1918 to 1922. Five of the Liberals were the second holders of their titles; only Lords Samuel, Layton and Beveridge had themselves been ennobled.

Nine non-party peers spoke often enough to be placed in our second group, in addition to Lord Vansittart, who was in the first group. All of these ten peers had themselves been raised to the peerage. They included two who could be classified as public servants, one Air Force commander, one industrialist–M.P.–Indian Governor, one scientist (Lord Boyd-Orr), one don (Lord Elton), Lord Waverley, the Archbishop of Canterbury and Dr. Bell, Bishop of Chichester. Two had spent periods in the House of Commons as Conservatives or the equivalent. One of these two (Lord Waverley), had held high office in Conservative and Coalition Governments. He had spent twelve years as a University Member of the House of Commons, where he never adhered to the Conservative Party. Before entering Parliament he had been for ten years Permanent Under-Secretary of State at the Home Office. Of the others Lord Hankey had been a minister during his first years in the House of Lords, after a distinguished career as secretary to the Cabinet.

As a group, these non-party peers (except for Lord Boyd-Orr) must be considered to be closer in their sympathies to the Conservative than to the Labour Party. In divisions on party lines, when they voted at all, they mostly voted with the Conservatives. This fact lends a little weight to the suspicion of the Left that a reformed House of Lords composed of eminent men could safely be expected to give the Conservatives an unfailing majority.

Although Conservatives and Conservative sympathizers form such a large majority of the active membership of the House, the Conservatives themselves can never be made so much subject to party discipline as the Conservatives in the House of Commons. There are some non-party peers who can generally be better relied upon not to vote against the Conservative leadership than some of the Conservative peers themselves. The subject of party discipline is, however, not a simple one, and will have to be treated separately in another chapter.

2. PEERS WHO ATTEND OCCASIONALLY

So far we have concerned ourselves only with the relatively active element among the peers. We must now go on to examine the rest of the membership, and consider both the peers who attend occasionally and those who never attend. Over a third of the peers can be counted as permanent absentees, but this still leaves us with some 400 to account for, who come to the House occasionally but too rarely to be included among the active element. However small and responsible the group of peers who constitute the active House, any adult holder of a peerage, provided that he has gone through the necessary formalities, and is not subject to certain obvious disqualifications, may attend at any time, speak and cast his vote. The less well-known of the peers, particularly those who never speak, but come down to listen and vote on explosive occasions, are commonly called 'backwoodsmen'. The backwoodsmen are generally—and it may be rightly —regarded as a limitless reservoir of Conservative votes upon which the party leaders can rely in case of need. Certain special occasions do, in fact, bring out great numbers of backwoodsmen. The Finance bill of 1909 brought out 425 peers to vote, or nearly three-quarters of the total membership of the House, and even as recently as 1956 no fewer than 333 peers voted (without any prompting from Party leaders) on the bill which proposed to abolish the death penalty.

During the period 1951–4, 192 peers spoke at least once but less than ten times each. For the purposes of the present study we may call these 'group III'—the occasional contributors to debate. Thirteen of these were Labour supporters: the rest were mainly Conservatives or Conservative sympathizers. One third were peers of first creation, though the proportion of these was rather low among the Conservatives. A few of the 192 could probably be regarded as 'backwoodsmen', but most could certainly not. Some, not all of them peers of first creation, are acknowledged authorities in their own fields, men who have time-consuming commitments of their own, and could not possibly attend at the House of Lords very frequently. Such men do, nevertheless, come to the House from time to time to give it the benefit of their special knowledge. A few of the peers included in group III took a very prominent part in debates on particular bills; if we had counted every single intervention, instead of each occasion of intervention, some of them would have qualified for inclusion among the active peers. Lord Ridley, for example, took a large part in the committee stages of the Transport and Town and Country Planning Bills, Lords Radnor and Falmouth on the Transport Bill, and the Earl of Crawford on the National Gallery and Tate Gallery Bill. On the other hand, 30 of the 192 peers in the group spoke only once each during the whole of the three years under review.

In the group as a whole, Conservatives are relatively more numerous (and Socialists less numerous) than they are among the first two groups, but this is only to be expected. Former members of the House of Commons are relatively less numerous. We do not find any striking difference, as compared with the other groups, in the proportions either of peers of first creation or of non-party peers.

However much it may be argued that the active House of Lords, as a working and effective part of the British system of government, is composed of just those very people who ought to be in an upper House, it is still true that the vast number of inactive peers can at any time come down and swamp the House with their votes. For nearly a hundred years men of the Left have insisted that the existence of this large body of potential voters, most of them with inherited peerages, owing no responsibility to anybody but themselves, but possessing wealth and privileges which they are chiefly concerned to protect, makes the House of Lords a body not deserving to have any effective power placed in its hands. Now that Conservative opinion has shown itself ready to favour the establishment of machinery to remedy this situation, the Left's lack of enthusiasm for reform seems to some people to suggest a preference for a discredited House of Lords, shorn of all real power, rather than a House enjoying greater popular prestige.

The term 'backwoodsmen' has not a very complimentary sound; it is applied in general to those peers who are not regularly in touch with public affairs, but emerge from obscurity on occasion in order to vote in the House of Lords. The term is used above all in connection with those rare divisions in which exceptionally large numbers of peers vote. As so much has been said about the 'backwoodsmen's vote', it seems worth while to attempt to discover what meaning that concept has, and to enquire whether it has any real influence on the course of events. Such an enquiry cannot be carried very far, as it is impossible to say exactly who is a backwoodsman; furthermore, the incursion of peers who might be regarded as backwoodsmen, in any substantial numbers, is very rare. A study of the division on the death penalty in 1956, when the vote was said to be 'swelled by noblemen whose more natural medium of public service would be a rural district council', and Lord Salisbury was said to be followed by 'a rabble similar to that with which the late Sir John Falstaff refused to march through Coventry',[1] may serve our purpose most effectively.

On 10th July 1956 the House of Lords, by 238 votes to 95, rejected the Death Penalty Abolition Bill. The number of peers voting was thus 333, or 250 more than in the average division of recent times. It is fair to assume, as has been generally assumed, that many of those who voted on this occasion were 'backwoodsmen', and although their irruption in such large numbers into the division lobbies may have been an isolated performance, it is important as a demonstration of the potentialities of the unreformed House.

This division is made particularly interesting by the fact that the voting, though it was for the most part on party lines, was entirely free. Twenty-five Conservatives (or one in seven) voted on the opposite side to the main body of their Party. The proportion of Labour dissentients (4 against the Bill to 27 for it) was almost exactly the same.

In order to discover the part played by 'backwoodsmen' we may enquire how many of those who voted had failed to speak in any debate in the period we have been considering (1951–4). If we leave out of the calculation the 17 peers created since the end of 1953, who could not be included in our earlier classification, the number of 'backwoodsmen', thus crudely defined,[2] taking part in the division was 124 out of 316. Twenty-two of them voted for the Bill, 102 against it. The corresponding figures for peers of our class I are 17 for, 37 against, divided mainly on party lines. Thus the ratio of retentionists to abolitionists was more than twice as high among the 'backwoodsmen' as among the nucleus of regular attenders (three-quarters of whom voted in this division).

Two-thirds (84) of the 'backwoodsmen' were avowed Conservatives, 73 of them holders of inherited peerages. The latter voted 67 to 6 against the Bill, a ratio which differs strikingly from that among all the peers of first creation (including bishops), who voted 66 to 50 against it. Thus the total vote in favour of retention was swollen to a significant extent by the participation of Conservative 'backwoodsmen' with inherited titles.

It does seem, then, that a study of the figures in this particular case lends some force to the popular conception about the power of non-responsible elements to come down and distort the vote of the House

[1] Lord Altrincham, 'The People's Bobbety', in *The Spectator*, 20th July 1956, p. 89.

[2] This definition of 'backwoodsmen' is clearly not exact. Some peers are included who had voted in several other divisions, and some of the peers who had spoken once or twice each in 1951–4 would probably deserve to be called 'backwoodsmen' more than some of those whom we are including in that category. But this definition is probably as satisfactory as any other would be.

CONTRIBUTION OF PEERS OF FIRST CREATION

on particular occasions. It is only fair to mention, however, that although the majority was swollen by the 'backwoodsmen', the result would have been the same if they had not participated. The distortion which they produced was not absolute, but only relative.

To some observers it may indeed seem rather deplorable that a vote on a matter such as this should bring out to vote a number of peers so enormously greater than the average. It is hard to see how this affair can have failed to damage the reputation of the House of Lords in the public estimation.

3. THE CONTRIBUTION OF PEERS OF FIRST CREATION

If radical opinion looks askance at those who belong to the House by the accident of birth, it is on the whole well disposed towards peers of first creation, the senators who have earned their honours by their own merits. It seems worth while, therefore, to see how much statistical enquiry can tell us about the specific contributions to debate of the peers of first creation. With this end in view, a study has been made of the amount of participation in 1951-4 by all the 190 men who had themselves received peerages and were still alive at the end of 1953.

Sixty-nine, or more than a third of the peers who had themselves been ennobled, did not speak at all. Half of these were over 70 years old in 1952. Some of them (and perhaps some of the younger men too) were probably not robust enough physically to be able to take part in the debates, but poor health can only be the explanation in a few cases.

Some of these silent peers held exceedingly powerful positions in industrial and commercial life; others were men of the highest renown in various other spheres of the nation's activities. It can only be assumed that many of them regarded their titles as marks of honour or distinction like knighthoods or other orders, rather than as valuable for the opportunity of contributing to debate in the House.

It thus appears that many of the men who have themselves received peerages for their distinction in fields of activity outside Parliament are rather slow to give the House the benefit of their expert knowledge. Perhaps this will not always be so; there is room yet for the House to increase the scope of its activities as a substitute for an Economic Chamber.

The number of first creation peers who did speak during the three years (121) was slightly less than the corresponding number (147) noted by Lord Moran for the four-year period 1947-51.[1] Of the 121,

[1] Cf. above, p. 33, and Lords Debs., 3rd February 1953, vol. 180, col. 163.

40 spoke often enough to be included in our 'class I', and indeed formed a majority of this most active group. Thirteen of them had never sat in the House of Commons, and therefore brought to the Lords the benefit of their experience in fields outside politics. (Cf. Table III, above.) Only half of them were Labour supporters.

As a group, the 25 first creation peers who were moderately active (class II) differed greatly from those of class I. There were fewer of them, and they formed a much smaller proportion of the whole of the peers in the class. Less than a quarter of them—only six—were Conservatives. It is here that the men of distinction outside politics become an important element. There were eight non-party peers who had never been in the House of Commons, as compared with four Conservatives and four Labour peers who had been M.P.s.

It appears, then, that, on the whole, ennobled party politicians from the House of Commons tend either to be very active in debate in the Lords or to take hardly any part at all; men of distinction from outside politics, on the other hand, tend to be moderately active rather than to place themselves among the nucleus of peers who sustain the main burden of day-to-day business. This finding agrees closely with what might be expected, but the number of peers even in the moderately active class who have been ennobled from outside political life may appear to be disappointingly small.

It is often claimed—and with much justification—that whatever may be the subject of discussion the House can expect to hear contributions from peers who are among the greatest experts in the land on that particular subject. The peers who have received their peerages solely because of their useful work and expert knowledge in special fields are not numerous, and some of them attend rarely, but it happens that many of the former M.P.s and of the peers who do acknowledge some party allegiance, have expert or special knowledge or experience in particular fields in addition to the wider political experience which they also possess. The 'experts' who speak in the House of Lords tend not to be specialists in the narrow sense of the word.

When we examine the list of peers of first creation according to party allegiance, we are at once struck by the way in which the centre of gravity differs from that of the whole House, including peers who have succeeded to their titles. Apart from the men ennobled from the House of Commons, and from the non-parliamentary Labour peers, most of the new peers created since 1939 acknowledge allegiance to no party. Only a third of all the peers of first creation now surviving are avowed Conservatives; if we count the bishops the proportion is under a third. The Conservatives only just outnumber the Labour and Liberal peers together. Among the peers of first creation who

CONTRIBUTION OF PEERS OF FIRST CREATION

actually take part in the proceedings of the House, whether we count them all (classes I, II, and III) or only the more active ones, the Conservatives are actually outnumbered by the Labour peers, and the peers who are committed to no party, if we include the Law Lords and bishops, just outnumber the Labour peers. It must of course again be pointed out that most of the 'non-party' peers of first creation are Conservative sympathizers, and in general as likely to produce pro-Conservative votes as the Conservative Party peers themselves. All the same, the fact that avowed Conservatives are only a quarter of the first creation peers who actually spoke in the House in 1951-4 is noteworthy, and deserves to be emphasized.

It would not be right to conclude this chapter without a reminder that its statistics are based on a rather arbitrary classification, which obviously cannot take into account the special and varied qualities of individuals. The House of Lords includes among its membership most of the elder statesmen of the day. Some of them, and of the distinguished men from outside politics, speak often, and others speak rarely, but the cumulative effect of the wisdom and experience which they can offer is something which defies statistical analysis.

As far as can be seen at present, the addition of some life peers, including at last some women, as proposed by the Bill of 1957, will not fundamentally change the nature of the composition of the House, and will only slightly alter the balance of the Parties. Its main effect will be to make possible the addition of worthy new members, in slightly larger numbers than hitherto, without further increasing the numbers of potential backwoodsmen in future generations. The House has already absorbed Lord Attlee's massive creations of 1945-6, which enriched it by bringing in members of more varied backgrounds, and widened she scope of its debates. The new Bill will encourage further development in the same direction.

Chapter IV

SPECIAL CLASSES OF PEERS

1. INTRODUCTION

IT has often been suggested that a reformed House of Lords might include some members nominated, by the Government or by some other agency, as representatives of particular groups within the community. The advocates of reform along these lines do not normally envisage an upper House consisting of spokesmen of rival groups; they hope rather that some of the most distinguished men in each of the main fields of the nation's activities would be sent to the House of Lords, where they could give the benefit of their special knowledge and experience in the counsels of the nation. One of the strongest arguments against such a change is that it would merely formalize, and perhaps devitalize, a practice which already exists in fact, and which works very well without the need of formal definition. The present system, whereby some five to twenty new peerages are granted each year to distinguished men, already produces an upper House which includes, at any given time, two or three, or in some cases more, of the most distinguished men from each of the main professions and classes of activity. The many ennobled industrialists and men of commerce represent between them most of the main industries, and besides these there are usually a few doctors, educationalists, Labour leaders, former ambassadors, colonial governors, generals, admirals and air marshals.

The Law is represented by the nine Law Lords, the retired Law Lords and the ex-Lord Chancellors, together with a few judges who have received ordinary peerages, and the Church by the two Archbishops and 24 bishops. In a formal sense the Law Lords and bishops hold positions very different from those held by the men who have received hereditary peerages, and some real differences flow from the formal ones. Spiritual lords and Law Lords appear nowadays to be debarred from belonging—publicly at any rate—to political parties, and a loosely-defined convention discourages them from making partisan speeches.[1] Distinguished men who have received hereditary peerages are not subject to such limitations, though many of them feel it appropriate to abstain from open partisanship.

As so much has been said of the potential advantages of a system of appointment of a given number of peers from certain walks of life, it should be rewarding to make a special study of the contributions made to debate, and to the general life and activities of the House, of peers belonging to some of these distinguishable classes.

2. ARCHBISHOPS AND BISHOPS

We may usefully begin with the archbishops and bishops. Their part in the work of the House has greatly changed during the past hundred years. In the Middle Ages the spiritual lords took their part in the functions of the great offices of state. After the Reformation their share in the executive offices declined,[2] but the bishops continued to form an integral part of the membership of the upper House.

Although their constitutional position in the upper House is different from that of the ordinary peers, the two archbishops and 24 bishops who sit in the contemporary House of Lords may now be regarded essentially as a group of specialist members of the House, having the function of stating, where appropriate, Christian opinions on the problems of the day.

The formal procedure for the appointment of bishops, which is prescribed by an Act of Henry VIII, re-enacted by the Act of Supremacy, 1599, is well known. On being notified of a vacancy the Crown sends to the dean and chapter a *congé d'élire*, together with a letter missive containing the name of the person to be elected. The appointment is thus effectively made by the Prime Minister. Great changes in the actual working of the system have taken place in the past 200 years, but the real process of choice is still discreetly concealed.

[1] A very distinguished parliamentarian, the first Lord Wedgwood, is on record as having felt, in 1942, that bishops and Law Lords had become over-cautious. He wanted them 'to do their duty by their country as leaders and not as servants'. (Cf. C. V. Wedgwood, *The Last of the Radicals*, Cape, 1951, p. 238.)

[2] Juxon, Lord Treasurer, 1636-41 (while Bishop of London), was the last to hold office save Robinson the diplomat, who was made Privy Seal in 1711 when Bishop of Bristol. The Archbishop of Canterbury continued, by virtue of his ecclesiastical office, however, to be at least a nominal member of the Cabinet during the formative years of that body in the eighteenth century. Archbishop Secker attended what was probably a meeting of the Cabinet council as late as 1763. (Cf. E. R. Turner, *The Cabinet Council* (John Hopkins U.P., 1930), vol. ii, p. 80.

SPECIAL CLASSES OF PEERS

In the eighteenth century, before the wholesale creation of peers by the younger Pitt, the bishops still formed a numerically important part of the House. The effective power of appointing and promoting bishops was a useful part of the administration's apparatus of patronage. In the words of Turberville, 'appointments to sees were as important, politically, as elevations to peerages. Episcopal vacancies afforded a government with most useful opportunity for increasing its strength in the upper House.'[1]

It was, in general, only when ecclesiastical matters came before the House that bishops were inclined to show independence. On ordinary questions a bishop would generally consider himself beholden to the Government at whose hands he had received his diocese, and indeed in difficult questions the Government of the day might regard the votes of its appointees on the ecclesiastical bench as useful supports and bulwarks against the possibility of defeat.[2] During the nineteenth century this attitude became less and less common, both among the bishops and among the politicians, as the old system of patronage disappeared. Queen Victoria took a close personal interest in the appointment of bishops. She often disagreed with her Prime Ministers, but the disagreements generally had nothing to do with party-political affiliations.[3] Well before 1900 bishoprics had ceased to be part of the system of political patronage by means of which governments sought to maintain their parliamentary strength. Lord Salisbury, for all his interest in Church matters, found the task of making ecclesiastical appointments very burdensome,[4] and Asquith considered the system 'in these times not only anomalous but, on paper, almost indefensible'. Asquith writes that he relied to some extent on the advice of the Archbishop of Canterbury, but that he nevertheless 'took the utmost trouble to find the best man, and, so far as was compatible with the needs and traditions of particular dioceses, to hold the balance even between the different parties in the Church'.[5]

There is, however, some evidence for a supposition that around the turn of the century and for some years afterwards, suspected political leanings might affect, favourably or adversely, a particular clergyman's prospects of promotion. It may not be entirely due to coincidence that some of the more radically-inclined prelates of recent times have been appointed under Liberal or Labour Prime Ministers.

---

[1] A. S. Turberville, *The House of Lords in the Eighteenth Century*, p. 422.

[2] Cf. Cyril Garbett in *The Future of the House of Lords* (Hansard Society, 1954), p. 96 f. Dr. Garbett cites two occasions in 1733 when Walpole was saved from defeat by bishops' votes.

[3] For a full treatment of this subject, cf. G. K. A. Bell, *Randall Davidson* (Oxford U.P., 1938), specially at pp. 163 ff.

[4] Cf. Gwendolen Cecil, *Life of Lord Salisbury*, vol. iii, p. 194.

[5] Earl of Oxford and Asquith, *Fifty Years of Parliament*, vol. ii, p. 217.

Lord Rosebery, in pressing Dr. Percival (then Headmaster of Rugby) to become Bishop of Hereford in 1895, wrote to him: 'I have some reason to hope that your views and my own are, to a considerable extent, in agreement. . . . It is extremely desirable that a bishop of your opinions should be placed on the marches of Wales.'[1] In the same year Dr. Talbot, who was also to show Liberal sympathies in the House of Lords, was appointed to Rochester; he was translated to Winchester in 1911. Charles Gore was appointed to Oxford in 1911, Dr. Barnes to Birmingham in 1924 and Dr. Temple to York in 1929.[2]

The citation of these few cases, all of them before 1931, does not invalidate a general assertion that political considerations were coming to count for less and less in relation to appointments to the bishops' Bench. Recent Prime Ministers appear to have relied greatly on the advice of their patronage secretaries, who are civil servants and who can be assumed to pay great attention to the wishes of the Church in general and of the individual dioceses concerned in particular.[3] They no doubt consult the Archbishop of Canterbury before advising the Prime Minister.

Bishops have long since ceased to feel any sort of obligation to come down to the House of Lords to support with their votes the Party under which they have been appointed, and they no longer regard a record of faithful voting as a means of obtaining translation. Nevertheless, in the nineteenth and early twentieth centuries bishops often spoke in a highly partisan way, and thought that there was nothing strange in their doing so. Most of them tended to support and vote with the Conservatives. Dr. Benson, Archbishop of Canterbury from 1883 to 1896, disliked the House of Lords but thought it his duty to attend, and encouraged the other bishops to do so too.[4]

During the present century, the rôle of the bishops seems to have undergone some further change. As long ago as 1909 Archbishop Davidson, recognizing the tendency for bishops to abstain more and more from political controversy, preferred not to take part in the struggle over the Finance Bill, though he wrote that he would be 'sorry to seem to urge silence on any of our body if they . . . think it really expedient to say their say.'[5] Now, in the middle of the century,

---

[1] Quoted in William Temple, *Life of Bishop Percival* (Macmillan, 1921), p. 130
[2] Cf. Sir W. Ivor Jennings, *Cabinet Government* (Cambridge U.P., 1936), p. 392. Bishop Gore had, however, received his first episcopal appointment, as Bishop of Worcester, under a Conservative Government in 1901, at a time when he had just been embarrassing the Government with his activities in relation to the South African war. (Cf. G. L. Prestige, *Life of Bishop Gore*, Heinemann, 1935, pp. 227 f.)
[3] Cf. *The Economist*, 20th October 1956, p. 214.
[4] Cf. A. C. Benson, *Life of Edward Benson*, vol. ii, p. 66.
[5] Cf. his letter to the Bishop of Wakefield, quoted in Bell, *Randall Davidson*, op. cit., p. 595. The Archbishop seems to have been more positively discouraging

there is less general participation by bishops in debate than there was fifty years ago. Archbishop Davidson's interpretation of the changing rôle of bishops has been proved correct, and the trend which he observed and encouraged has continued. With a few exceptions, bishops appear to consider that they should intervene only on appropriate occasions, usually on questions concerning moral or social welfare or education, and there seems also to be a tendency for them not, for the most part, to speak in so personal and individual a way as their predecessors of fifty years ago.[1] It is rare for more than one bishop to intervene in a debate, and a bishop's speech is sometimes regarded, rightly or wrongly, as an expression of the general opinion of the Church of England (and perhaps, in a way, of the whole of English Protestant Christianity) on a particular subject. This is particularly the case with the Archbishop of Canterbury, though there is evidence of a feeling of uneasiness lest the Archbishop should regularly be regarded as the accredited mouthpiece of the Church.[2] In divisions bishops rarely vote, and they hardly ever do so when party-political questions are involved.

Although the bishops have in general withdrawn from party politics, a feeling seems to have grown up that they ought to show interest in debates on moral, educational or social questions. But even for a debate of this type, an attendance of four or five bishops might now be expected for a subject which would have brought twenty to the House fifty years ago. Most of the bishops attended all through the debates on the Education Bill in 1906. In 1912, when the Lords debated a bill dealing with prostitution and the punishment of procurors, the debate had to be postponed at the last minute, owing to the needs of the business of the House. When the debate eventually took place, Dr. Davidson felt it necessary to give an explanation for the small attendance of bishops. 'Many bishops had arranged to be here for the 27th,' he said, 'but cannot change their plans so as to be here now. They have too many long-standing

to some other bishops' ideas of intervening in the controversy. Mr. J. G. Lockhart, in *Cosmo Gordon Lang* (Hodder & Stoughton, 1949), p. 236, suggests that Dr. Davidson 'advised the bishops to take no part in the debate', and was doubtful of the wisdom of the intervention (against rejection) of his brother Archbishop, Dr. Lang.

[1] Cf. H. Hensley Henson, *Retrospect of an Unimportant Life* (Oxford U.P.), vol. ii (1943), p. 86.

[2] Thus at the Bristol Diocesan Conference in May 1956 the Bishop (Dr. Cockin) was asked if there was a conspiracy on the part of bishops to refrain from speaking out on things of national and international importance, if they discussed them in private and left the Archbishop of Canterbury to make public statements. The Bishop answered the question with a qualified negative. (*Manchester Guardian*, 24th May 1956.) The *Guardian's* sub-editor headed this report 'No cabinet of bishops'.

engagements at home.'[1] No doubt the Archbishop intended to imply some displeasure at the change which had been made, but his words suggest a feeling that a debate of this character ought normally to produce a fairly large attendance of bishops. The Archbishop also said that if there had been a prospect of opposition on second reading the number of bishops present would have been larger, in spite of the change of day, in order to assist the passage of the Bill by their votes. Such an attitude to the functions of bishops in the votes of the House would hardly be expected today, even on a matter such as the Bill in question.

A more recent instance of an episcopal apology for a sparsely-filled bishops' bench was in 1951, when the House was debating a motion that children of divorced persons should be better protected by the law. Only one bishop was present, and in supporting the motion he expressed regret that his colleagues were 'collectively occupied elsewhere'.[2] In 1955, when there were no bishops present at a debate on prisons, Lord Moynihan was 'very critical that no one from this bench was there or seemed to take any interest'; in 1956, in another debate on the same subject, two bishops spoke.[3]

When we look back at the period before 1914 we find that there was a good deal of participation by bishops in the debates on the great issues of that time, which involved probably more violent controversy than has been seen in Parliament since then. Bishops took a leading part in the impassioned debates on the Education Bill of 1906. In 1909 five bishops spoke on the Finance Bill; in 1911 six spoke on the Parliament Bill or in the other debates connected with the status and composition of the House. In 1913 the two Archbishops and 15 bishops voted with the Opposition to contribute to the defeat of the Irish Home Rule Bill. Bishops Gore of Oxford and Percival of Hereford, both Liberal appointments, voted with the Government. Archbishop Lang of York, in a speech in which he said that the Bill ought not to become law without a mandate from the people, did indeed refer to 'the hesitation with which one of the spiritual Lords enters upon a discussion of a question on which Party divisions are so deeply marked'.[4] When the Bill came up again under the procedure of the Parliament Act six months later the two Archbishops and six bishops voted against it.

Welsh Church disestablishment was a topic of a special kind;

[1] Lords Debs., 28th November 1912, vol. 12, col. 1191. At the Committee stage there were two divisions, in each of which the majority in favour of the extension of corporal punishment included five members of the ecclesiastical bench.
[2] Lords Debs., 14th February 1951, vol. 190, col. 346.
[3] Ibid., 31st July 1956, vol. 199, col. 444.
[4] Ibid., 28th January 1913, vol. 13, col. 547.

besides being an issue of first-class political importance in its day, it closely concerned the bishops in their capacity as churchmen. Bishops clearly felt no hesitation about intervening in the debates on the subject in a partisan way; some of the episcopal contributions were indeed among the most vigorous attacks on government policy that were heard in the House of Lords even in that troubled time. Some preliminary shots were fired in 1911. In June 1912, some months before the Bill actually came up for second reading in the Lords, Bishop Edwards of St. Asaph rose to call attention to 'misleading statements' made by Mr. McKenna, the Home Secretary, in the second reading debate in the Commons, with regard to the work of the Church in Cardiff as compared with the work of the Calvinistic Methodists there. Mr. McKenna, the Bishop complained, had given wrong figures regarding the relative numbers of places of worship, clergy, ministers, etc., of the two religious bodies concerned; he had improperly belittled the work of the Church in the slum districts of Cardiff, and he had failed to apologize when his errors were pointed out. Lord Strachie, on behalf of the Government, began by asking for a postponement, in order that he might at least see the Home Secretary, as he had had scarcely any notice. When the Bishop refused to accept a postponement Lord Strachie defended the Home Secretary and went on to dispute the figures given by the Bishop in his turn.

When the Bill eventually reached the Lords for second reading both Archbishops and seven bishops, including two of the Welsh bishops, spoke during the three days over which the debate was spread. On the first day the Bishop of St. Asaph spoke immediately after the leading speaker on the Opposition front bench. 'This Bill,' he said, 'if passed, will help no religious body in Wales; it will cripple the Church for many long years; it will leave in the hearts of churchmen the consciousness of a great wrong done, and with this consciousness there will be a stream of bitterness, of the force and volume of which the advocates of this measure have formed no just estimate.' He reinforced his argument with much discussion of the financial losses that the Bill would bring upon the Church, and in this he was followed by Bishop Winnington-Ingram of London, who spoke in the same vein soon afterwards. On the second day the two Archbishops spoke, both of them against the Bill, the Archbishop of Canterbury for an hour and a half. Bishop Percival of Hereford, who consistently supported the Government, spoke in favour of the Bill, as did Bishop Gore, though the latter made some important reservations. On the third day Bishop Jacob of St. Albans concentrated on the unity of the Church. 'I consider it such an outrage on a spiritual body to attempt to sever a part of it from the whole, that I would far rather be a member of a disestablished Church, ... than remain in an established Church with the Church of Wales cut off from that body'. Bishop Owen of St. Davids spoke later, and was the last bishop to contribute before the winding-up speeches from the front benches. In the division both Archbishops and 18 bishops voted, two of them in favour of the Bill.

In 1912 Bishop Percival of Hereford, whose general political views did not correspond with those of his colleagues on the bench, himself brought forward a bill for the restriction of advertisements for the encouragement of gambling. He withdrew his bill when he saw that there was no support for it.[1] The Archbishop of Canterbury spoke against Bishop Percival's bill, and made it clear that he had nothing to do with the bill's introduction. ('I cannot accept this bill as it stands. I did not know anything of it until it was published and circulated. It seems to me to go far in advance of public opinion.')[2] He also spoke and voted in favour of a wrecking amendment moved to the Government's Temperance (Scotland) Bill.[3]

Bishop Talbot of Winchester initiated a discussion of affairs in the Belgian Congo. He attacked the administration of that territory, complained of 'the cynicism with which methods of unexampled cruelty were carried out', and asked that the Foreign Office should delay recognition of the régime until there was proof that the administration was carried on in a humane way. In 1913 Archbishop Davidson spoke in a debate on a motion regarding slavery in Portuguese West Africa. On most of the measures of social reform brought in by the Liberal Government bishops made contributions, generally non-partisan in character.

In the middle 1920s the readiness of bishops to take part in general debates had apparently declined a good deal. In 1922 the two Archbishops spoke on the second reading of the Irish Free State Agreement Bill, but in the whole of the three sessions of 1922, 1924 and 1926 only eleven bishops took part in debates, and four of these spoke only on ecclesiastical measures. Dr. Garbett, who had been appointed Bishop of Southwark in 1919, was already becoming one of the more regular speakers; he was responsible for a quarter of all the bishops' speeches on public affairs (excluding the contributions of the Archbishops) in 1922 and 1924.

By the middle 1930s most bishops had become rare visitors to the

[1] Later he spoke on behalf of another unofficial bill on the same subject, but complained that it did not go far enough, and in Committee moved an amendment to strengthen it (Lords Debs., 4th February 1913, vol. 13, col. 831).

[2] Lords Debs., 11th July 1912, vol. 12, col. 430.

[3] The amendment, whose effect was to increase from five to fifteen years the period that was to elapse before the Bill became effective, was passed by 60 votes to 43.

House. At the same time the quantity of interventions of the Archbishop of Canterbury, instead of decreasing, tended rather to increase. This fact can perhaps be attributed in part to the personality of Archbishop Lang, who had been translated from York in 1928, and in part to the general development of the feelings, both of the bishops and of the nation in general, about the proper function of the episcopate. It is hard to say which factor was the more important; the two factors both tended toward the production of the same results.

In the session of 1934–5 Archbishop Lang spoke so often that he could be classified as one of the few most regular contributors to debate. He spoke on the second reading of the Government of India Bill, and took an active part in the debates on the committee and report stages. He spoke in important debates on government policy towards the League of Nations and Abyssinia, and also in a debate on slavery in Abyssinia. He spoke on defence and on the report of the Special Areas Commission. In 1935–6 he spoke again on Abyssinia, and also several times on the Education Bill. A motion dealing with the Assyrian community in Iraq had a special character, as he was here expressing the opinions of the Church with regard to this small and often persecuted Christian community, for which Christian feeling in Britain has for long felt a special sympathy. He spoke also on a tithe bill, on social services and on redundant public houses.

Apart from Dr. Lang and Dr. Bell, Bishop of Chichester, Dr. Garbett, who had been translated to Winchester in 1932, was the only bishop to speak more than very occasionally, and he continued to be a fairly frequent contributor to important debates for the rest of his life. For the next twenty years he was to be an exponent of the Christian conscience on social questions. It is probably fair to say that, although he nearly always spoke primarily as a Christian, he struck a mean between the two extremes represented on the one hand by the expression of the specific view of the Church of England on matters of particular concern to it, and on the other hand by the statement of purely personal opinions, such as might be expected from an ordinary peer. In 1945 he himself initiated a debate by asking the Government what steps they were taking to provide the large number of houses 'urgently required for the health and happiness of the people', and he gave a detailed and well-informed review of housing problems. Soon afterwards he initiated a debate on road casualties. On the Coal Industry Nationalization Bill he supported Viscount Cecil of Chelwood's amendment advocating the inclusion in the Bill of a guarantee of the workers' right to be consulted on the working of their mines. He made a long speech on behalf of the National Insurance Bill, describing it as a measure 'of which any nation might be proud'. He supported the National Health Service

Bill. In a debate on the international situation he argued that 'the peace of Europe could not be secured until a disarmed Germany was restored to some prosperity and strength'. He initiated a debate on a motion advocating further progress towards the securing of international control of atomic energy. In the session of 1946–7, he spoke on conditions in Austria, on Town and Country Planning, on the Denning Report on Matrimonial Causes, and on the rights of minorities under international agreements (this time on a motion of his own). He discussed the coal shortage and the economic situation. On the second reading of the National Service Bill he spoke at some length, stressing the necessity for care of the moral welfare of young people in the Forces. He contributed to the second reading debate on the Town and Country Planning Bill. During the succeeding sessions he spoke often on Palestine, on many aspects of the international situation and on economic questions, besides debates involving more purely Christian or moral questions.

Dr. Bell, who was appointed Bishop of Chichester in 1929, has acquired a special reputation as an expert on international and particularly on European and German affairs. He has not always eschewed controversy. In the session of 1945–6 he spoke in no less than eight debates on these topics. He initiated a debate on the mass transfers of Germans from Poland, Czechoslovakia and Eastern Germany. Several times he spoke about the distress caused in Germany by the insufficiency of food supplies, and advocated the speedy repatriation of German and other enemy prisoners-of-war still held in Britain and the Commonwealth. He attacked the Potsdam Agreement and warned the House of the dangerous situation arising from it in Central and Eastern Europe. In 1947 he moved a motion calling attention to conditions in Germany and calling for peace to be concluded between Germany, Austria and the Allies. In June 1956 Dr. Bell asked a question on the controversial—and indeed explosive—topic of the deportation of a Greek priest who was said to have been engaged in subversive activities in London. The question led to some rather heated interchanges. In the debate on the Suez Canal in September 1956 he spoke very strongly against any independent British action apart from the United Nations. One of his speeches on the troubles in Cyprus shocked Lord Salisbury.

Dr. Geoffrey Fisher, though he has spoken not infrequently since his appointment as Archbishop of Canterbury in 1943, tended until recently to limit his contributions to subjects which seemed to require a statement of opinion from, and on behalf of, the Church and perhaps organized Christianity in general. He has, however, often spoken vigorously on various Commonwealth questions. In 1947 he disagreed strongly with a motion of Lord Templewood to the effect that the grant of independence was 'likely to imperil the peace and prosperity of India'. He has made outspoken contributions on Central African Federation and on the difficulties in Cyprus. But most of Dr. Fisher's interventions have really been concerned with questions involving public morality. In 1949 he spoke on the problem of artificial insemination and on a private member's bill which proposed to make modifications in the prohibited degrees of relationship in marriage. He said that the Church was neutral, but that he personally opposed the bill for sociological reasons.[1] (Three of his brother bishops also spoke on this bill.) In 1951 he spoke on a motion that the Easter Act, which had been passed 25 years before, should be made operative forthwith. 'I think it is almost the normal procedure,' he said, 'that whenever this topic is raised in this House—as it is at intervals of 10 years or so—the Archbishop of Canterbury for the time being should speak on it.' His personal opinion was, he said, dictated by his liking for anomalies, for he did not want to see the world oversystematized. The Church of England, as such, had no objection provided that there was agreement from the other chief denominations of the Christian world. The main difficulty was that although the Roman Catholic and Orthodox Churches both declared that they had no objection in principle, the Pope seemed unwilling to call a general council of the Church, without which the Roman Catholic Church, as a body, could not make any effective decision.

During 1956 Dr. Fisher made a number of interventions on important political or near-political questions, which brought him nearer to the centre of political controversy. Soon after the introduction of the Government's proposal to issue Premium Bonds, he seized an opportunity, in the form of a debate on a private member's Small Lotteries and Gaming Bill, to attack, not only that Bill, but also the whole principle of the Premium Bonds, which he denounced because they would 'debase the spiritual coinage of the nation at the very time when there was paramount need to restore it'. By his intervention on this matter he drew to himself some rather sharp criticism, both because of what he had said on the proposed bonds, and also because he had introduced the bonds, with doubtful relevance, into the debate at all.[2]

In 1956 he spoke and voted for the second reading of Mr. Silverman's Death Penalty Abolition Bill, though in his speech he expressed

---

[1] Cf. below, p. 206.
[2] Lords Debs., 26th April 1956. As Lord Mancroft said a little later: 'At the Committee stage of this Bill the Archbishop succeeded in making a second reading speech on the Finance Bill which had not yet been published; on the Report stage Lord Lawson made a second reading speech on a Betting Bill which had not yet been drafted' (Lords Debs., 15th May 1956, vol. 197, col. 404).

a hope that if the Bill were given a second reading an attempt would be made by amendment to find a compromise which both Houses would accept. In the debate of September on the Government's policy with regard to the Suez Canal he pleaded for national unity, and persuaded the Government leaders to accept a small amendment to the terms of their motion, in order that he might vote for it. For these rather positive interventions he was criticized in the *Spectator* ('Why he thought it necessary to vote at all is not clear'). On 1st November, in the debate following the British assault in Egypt, he expressed concern about the Government's veto at the Security Council; later he harried the Lord Chancellor with a series of hostile interruptions.

For the rest, the bishops have in recent years rarely gone outside the fields of spiritual, social and moral welfare, on which they have made several valuable and well-informed contributions, such as those of the Bishop of Sheffield (Dr. Hunter) on the well-being of children. In the successive debates on capital punishment several bishops have spoken. On the Bill of 1956 there were four speeches from the bishops' benches, all except one in favour of abolition.

Bishops have also made occasional contributions on administrative matters concerning the local interests of their dioceses. In 1947 Bishop Parsons of Hereford spoke strongly against the proposal to build a power station on the South Bank site of the Thames, which was in his old diocese of Southwark.[1] On 20th July 1955 Dr. Rawlinson, Bishop of Derby, himself initiated a debate on mining subsidence. In December 1956, when there was a debate on the Government's road construction programme, the Bishop of Carlisle spoke about the inadequacy of the roads in his diocese, and of the plans for their improvement. 'It is believed in Cumberland,' he said, 'that the farther away you are from London the more often must you speak and the more loudly must you proclaim your needs. . . . I think there should be in this House opportunity for a speaker to express local concern and also local loyalty within a given rule.'[2]

Many eminent bishops have not spoken in the House of Lords at all. Dr. Ramsey made no contributions to debate while he was Bishop of Durham, and made his maiden speech in July 1956, when he had already been translated to York.

Although it would be wrong to say that any convention has grown up precluding bishops from voting in divisions, it is nevertheless true that nowadays bishops do not often vote. One of the reasons for this, no doubt, is that divisions take place these days on topics of a far more limited type than was previously the case. Controversial private

[1] Lords Debs., 19th May 1947, vol. 147, col. 834.
[2] Ibid., 19th December 1956, vol. 200, cols. 1250-2.

members' bills have almost disappeared, and when motions are introduced into the Lords they are generally withdrawn after the subject has been canvassed. Such few divisions as there are are mostly on the committee stages of bills, with reference to particular points on which the Parties are unable to reach agreement. The purpose of such divisions is generally for the Opposition to register its particular disapproval of a government's intransigence.

The attitude of bishops towards voting in divisions seems to have undergone some change during the pasty fifty years. From 15 to 20 bishops voted against the Liberal Government in each of the crucial divisions in committee on Mr. Birrell's Education Bill of 1906, though Dr. Percival sometimes supported the Government. In 1911, when the outcome of the imminent division on the Parliament Bill was in doubt, Archbishop Davidson gave influential support to Lord Lansdowne's policy of trying to prevent the Bill from being rejected. He told Lord Crewe that he had 'issued a form of enquiry to the episcopal Bench. . . . Though he could not act as a Whip to get the bishops to vote, yet he would help generally as far as he could.'[1] In the event, thirteen prelates voted with the Government and two against it. The Bill would just have been passed even without the bishops' votes, but before the division took place it seemed that they might well hold the balance, as they had in fact held it in the momentous division in which the Reform Bill of 1831 was rejected.

Coming down to the 1920s, we find that in 1926 there were eleven divisions (out of a total of 29) in which bishops voted, and that these related to widely varied topics. Two ecclesiastical measures were contested, and each of them produced a close vote in a well-attended House. The proposal to establish a new diocese of Shrewsbury, which was defeated by 61 votes to 60, found the Archbishop of Canterbury and eight bishops in its favour, and two bishops against it. On the London Church Benefices Union Measure, which was defeated by 84 votes to 71, the Archbishop of Canterbury and five other bishops voted. Archbishop Davidson of Canterbury and Bishop Ingram were in a minority of 44 voting against a motion expressing approval of birth control (57 peers were in favour).

When bishops voted they often found themselves in the company of the more radical element in the House. The Peeresses Bill was defeated by 126 votes to 80, but the minority in favour of allowing peeresses to sit in the House of Lords included five bishops and the

---

[1] J. Pope-Hennessy, *Lord Crewe* (Constable, 1955), p. 125 f. From Dr. Bell's more detailed account (*Randall Davidson*, op. cit., p. 627 ff.), however, it is clear that the Archbishop was in great doubt as to whether he ought to vote at all, and that he finally decided to vote only at the very last minute, when it seemed that the diehards might very probably be in the majority.

majority only one. In the other divisions of 1926, with two exceptions, the only bishop to participate was Dr. Garbett, then Bishop of Southwark. He voted, together with Bishop Pearce of Worcester, against two watering-down amendments to the Wild Birds Protection Bill; on the Lead Paint Bill he voted for a Labour amendment whose purpose was to strengthen the Bill, and against a Conservative amendment whose purpose was to weaken it by making it permissive as far as it concerned women. On the Coal Mining Industry Bill he voted in favour of the second reading, and twice on committee points against the Conservative minority who were opposing such liberal innovations as the Bill contained.

In 1927 Archbishop Davidson and Dr. Garbett voted against the Government on the third reading of the Aliens Bill, which could well be regarded as an illiberal measure. On the Trade Disputes Bill, Bishop Henson of Durham voted for the second reading, but no other bishop voted. On the Peeresses Bill of this session, which was defeated by 80 votes to 78 (a far narrower margin than that which had defeated the Peeresses Bill of the preceding year), Archbishop Lang voted in favour, Archbishop Davidson against. Two questions brought forward in 1927 each brought more than half of the Bench of bishops out to vote. On the Liquor (Popular Control) Bill, whose second reading Bishop David of Liverpool had himself proposed, thirteen bishops voted in favour of the Bill in spite of the Government's hostility, and only one against it. The debate on the proposed new Prayer Book for the Anglican Church naturally brought out a large number of bishops to vote. Both archbishops and twenty bishops voted for it, and Bishops Pollock of Norwich and Pearce of Worcester against it.

In 1928 the Bill to give the vote to women aged 21 and over produced two votes in which bishops took part, in each case in favour of a liberal treatment of women. Bishops Garbett of Southwark and Pearce of Worcester voted for the second reading of the Equal Franchise Bill, and a little later against a committee proposal to raise the voting age for men and women to 25. This time they were joined by the Archbishop of York. On a Shops (Hours of Closing) Bill the Archbishop of Canterbury voted against an amendment whose purpose was to allow a shopkeeper to be exempt from the provisions of the Act, provided that he did not employ anybody else in his shop during the hours of extended opening. In 1928 Dr. Garbett voted for a motion calling upon the Government to ratify the International Labour Office eight hours convention. (The motion, which the Government opposed, was defeated.) He voted against a wrecking amendment on the Preservation of Infant Life Bill, and with the Government against the motion to go into committee on a private member's bill dealing with road vehicles. He voted with the Government to approve the Balfour Memorandum on War Debts.

Although some of the bishops, including Dr. Garbett, voted with the Government on quite a number of occasions, there is no evidence to suggest that at this period any of them felt any special duty to support the Government because it was the Government, or because they owed it anything. When the Labour Government came into office in 1929, there was no evidence of a tendency among the bishops to support the Conservatives, although most of them had received their offices at the hands of Conservative governments. In the session of 1929-30, bishops voted in eleven of the divisions in which the Government took a stand of one sort or another; they voted with the Labour Government in nine of these and against it in two. Dr. Garbett, who voted in most of these divisions, was against the Government on only one occasion; the Bishop of Lincoln voted against the Government for a controversial amendment to the Coal Mines Bill, whose effect was to water down the limitation of working hours. In 1937, on the London Passenger Transport Bill, the Bishop of St. Albans spoke and voted for an amendment which involved the local interests of his diocese.

The last instance of a substantial participation by bishops in a division on a political issue was in 1935, when both archbishops and fifteen bishops voted against Lord Lloyd's amendment to the second reading of the Government of India Bill. Only the Bishop of Exeter voted with the right-wing Conservatives who sponsored the amendment; this was Lord William Cecil.

Since 1945 only a few topics have brought out bishops to vote in divisions, generally in small numbers. In 1948 the Bishop of Chichester was the only bishop to vote for the abolition of capital punishment; Bishop Haigh of Winchester voted against abolition. On the Commons Amendments, Dr. Garbett and two bishops voted against the compromise proposals. In 1956, however, there was a larger turnout of bishops to vote on the same question. Both archbishops and eight bishops voted for the Bill, and one against it. Four bishops voted for the Parliament Bill of 1948, and two against it. Bishops Brook of St. Edmundsbury and Ipswich and Hunter of Sheffield each voted once against the Labour Government on amendments to clauses in the Iron and Steel Bill. In 1953 Bishop Askwith of Blackburn voted against the Government on Central African Federation. In the debate on Suez Canal policy in September 1956 Archbishop Fisher and the Bishop of Sheffield voted with the Government, but only after the Government had satisfied certain conditions. On 1st November 1956, in the debate on the British attack on Egypt, no bishop voted, but Dr. Fisher's abstention, in view of the character of his interventions in the debate, could perhaps be interpreted as an expression of hostility.

These are the only recent instances of bishops voting in purely 'political' divisions. There were, however, five other divisions in 1949, on matters to do with licensing, Justices of the Peace, and improvements to Parliament Square, on each of which one or two bishops voted. In the division on Lord Hailsham's motion on commercial television in 1953, four bishops voted against the Government's plans. When these plans were embodied in a bill, however, only one bishop voted against the Government on the second reading; Dr. Fisher did not vote, although he had spoken in the debate. Bishops Cockin of Bristol and Martin of Liverpool each voted against the Government four times on committee points.

This examination of the voting record of the bishops' bench in recent years suggests that it is unrealistic to grumble, as some commentators have done, at clerical voting in the Legislature. Only on four occasions since 1939 have more than two bishops voted in a division, and bishops have almost universally refrained from voting on party questions. In divisions in which the voting, though technically free, has mainly followed party lines, bishops have been more against the main body of the Conservative Party than with it; this has been so both on commercial television and on capital punishment.

3. THE LAW LORDS AND OTHER LEGAL PEERS

In a narrow sense the term 'Law Lords' covers only the nine Lords of Appeal in Ordinary, who hold life peerages and draw salaries from the Crown for their services as judges. They have been given peerages mainly in order to enable them to perform the work of the House as the highest court of appeal. They are, however, allowed to take part in debates, whether of a political character or otherwise, and as men learned in the law they may have a special contribution to make.

In a broader sense, the term 'Law Lords' may be made to apply also to former Lords of Appeal in Ordinary who have retired from active service, but continue to be peers for the rest of their lives. In addition to these, all the former Lord Chancellors and other peers who have held high judicial office have the right to take part in judicial proceedings.[1]

Although the Law Lords in the strict and narrow sense are not forbidden in any way to take part in the ordinary work of the House, there does appear to be a convention debarring them from participation in political controversy. The convention clearly does not apply

[1] Cf. *Companion to the Standing Orders*, p. 67.

to the Lord Chancellor, but it probably can be said to apply to other holders of high judicial office, such as the Lord Chief Justice, even though they may hold ordinary peerages along with their offices.[1] The origin of this convention is difficult to trace, and its existence, if it does exist at all, became evident only when one of the Law Lords did take it upon himself to intervene in a highly controversial way in questions involving national politics.

During the early years of the century, Edward Carson, as a member of the House of Commons and as a lawyer, became the recognized leader of the Ulstermen, not only in Parliament, but outside it. He was a violent controversialist in Irish affairs. After holding office in Conservative and Coalition Governments, he accepted an appointment as a Lord of Appeal in Ordinary on 24th May 1921. This was rather an unusual appointment; Lords of Appeal are generally men who have distinguished themselves in the rather more narrow fields of the Law than Lord Carson. Carson's biographer suggests that the Government 'had calculated that by making Carson a Lord of Appeal they had procured his silence'.[2]

Soon after Carson's appointment as a Law Lord the Coalition Government negotiated the Articles of Agreement for a Treaty between England and Ireland. Carson, believing that the Government had vilely betrayed the loyalists of Southern Ireland, not only spoke in the House of Lords on this explosive political question, but attacked the Government with invective whose like had rarely been heard.

Lord Carson's conduct was criticized as ill-becoming a judge, and led to protracted discussion,[3] in which precedents were cited and some sort of definition of the limits to Law Lords' freedom emerged. A colleague on the bench, Lord Buckmaster, said that active, salaried judges ought not to engage in acute political controversy, because by doing so they must surely damage the repute of the whole judicial system. Judges ought to be impartial, not only in matters of law, but in politics too. Lord Sumner, another Lord of Appeal, disagreed with Lord Buckmaster's arguments, pointing to the fact that before 1876 many active judges had held ordinary peerages; Lord Chief Justice Ellenborough had actually been in the Cabinet. Lord Chief Justice Denman had spoken on the abolition of the slave trade and had taken part in debates on Sir John Graham's action in opening Mazzini's correspondence. Just before 1876, Cairns, while a judge, had been

[1] It is possible for a Law Lord to be appointed to an ordinary ministerial office. Lord Macmillan was appointed Minister of Information in 1939, but this wartime precedent should not be regarded as of general validity. Cf. below, p. 100.
[2] Cf. Marjoribanks and Colvin, *Life of Lord Carson*, vol. iii, p. 415.
[3] Lords Debs., 22nd, 27th and 29th March 1922. The discussion of 29th March arose out of a personal statement which Lord Carson felt impelled to make in reply to the criticism levelled against him.

given a peerage, before he was made Lord Chancellor, especially in order that he could pilot Disraeli's Reform Bill through the House of Lords for the Government. Since 1876, he said, at least four Law Lords had taken part in controversial debates and no one had complained. Lord Haldane, on the other hand, rejected Lord Sumner's contentions; Lord Ellenborough's presence in the Cabinet had been sharply criticized, and no Lord Chief Justice had ever sat in the Cabinet again. Lord McNaghton, he said, had deliberately refrained from speaking on controversial matters because delicacy prevented him from doing so.

The practice of the last half-century had, according to Lord Haldane, virtually established a convention of the constitution 'that the six judges' (there were only six at that time) 'who have been introduced into your Lordship's House as judges, made peers in order to enable them to be judges, should be most sparing in the exercise of their freedom as legislators.' If this were not so, a Government in appointing Law Lords would be compelled to ask, 'is this man our supporter, or is he going to be our antagonist?' The position of Lord Chancellors and ex-Lord Chancellors was clearly quite different.

The Lord Chancellor, Lord Birkenhead, agreed that such a convention did exist, and suggested that since 1876 it had never really been broken except on certain unfortunate occasions. Lord Robertson had been active as a Tariff Reformer, but he had been much criticized, both at the Bar and in political circles, for his political activities. There was an instance in which a former Lord Chancellor, having spoken in an Irish debate, had said that for this reason he could not sit on an Irish Appeal. That was all right, said Lord Birkenhead, for an ex-Lord Chancellor, but not for a Law Lord, because a Law Lord had no right to disqualify himself from doing that which he was paid to do. Furthermore, there was a considerable danger that if judges took part in politics, political opposition to the bench as a whole might result. It was true that Carson's personal position was exceptional, and that silence on his part would inevitably be regarded in Ulster as treason. But even if Lord Carson had a special freedom belonging to him personally, that freedom did not entitle him, as Carson clearly supposed, to go on to a public platform in order 'to make bitter, if dull, taunts against individual members of His Majesty's Government, and deliver what is in every respect and in all its aspects a crude partisan political attack upon the policy of the Government'.

In spite of these strictures Lord Carson continued to hold his office, but the general rules seemed to have been given a definition which had not been required before. Problems such as this have never arisen again. Law Lords have indeed made fairly frequent contributions to debate, but nearly always in their special capacity as men learned in the law.

Parts of many ordinary bills are concerned with strictly legal questions, and on these the Law Lords have a considerable contribution to make. In the Commons there are, apart from the Law Officers of the Crown, many barristers who are private members, and who are very ready to take part in discussion of the technical legal points in bills. In the Lords, however, legal learning is represented mainly by the judges and by the Lord Chancellor and his predecessors still living. If Law Lords could not speak in debates on bills, the burden falling on the Lord Chancellor would be even heavier than it is. When the Law Lords do speak on legal questions, they can be regarded as counsellors of great authority.

The convention that Law Lords should not talk on political questions does not debar them from contributing on legal points in bills involving controversy both political and of other kinds. In the session of 1936-7, for instance, judges made substantial contributions to the debates on Sir Alan Herbert's Matrimonial Causes Bill. Lord Atkin was particularly prominent. In the session of 1946-7 Lord Simonds made several contributions on the Crown Proceedings Bill and on the Companies Bill. The judges' contributions even on technical legal matters may verge on the political in some cases, as with the Defamation Bill of 1951-2; Law Lords not only spoke, but disagreed with each other, on the proposal to assimilate the law of libel and slander.

Naturally enough, when measures are before the House concerned with the organization of the Courts, or of the legal profession as a whole, the Law Lords have a great deal to contribute. In 1934-5, Lord Wright contributed a speech on the second reading of the Supreme Court of Judicature (Amendment) Bill, and in the following session Lord Atkin spoke on a proposal to abolish the right of peers to be tried by the House of Lords. He spoke also on bills dealing with the law of evidence, and on a bill dealing with the organization of the Courts.

A good example of a recent debate in which Law Lords, with their wide experience in the Courts, had an evident contribution to make was the discussion on capital punishment and juries on 16th December 1953. The debate concerned a proposal, arising out of the report of the Royal Commission on capital punishment, that juries might have the power to decide between degrees of murder, and themselves to recommend whether or not particular murderers should be made subject to the death penalty. Lord Chief Justice Goddard and two Law Lords took part.

If we compare the experience of the last few years with that of a dozen years ago, we find that the amount of intervention in debate by Law Lords has tended to decline. In the four years 1934–8 there were no less than 38 separate interventions by Law Lords on different subjects, apart from contributions to committee stages of bills, which in their turn were extremely numerous. Lord Atkin spoke no less than thirty times in committee on Sir Alan Herbert's Matrimonial Causes Bill of 1937, and on several other bills there were many interventions in committee by judges. Only Lords Tomlin and Blanesburgh, neither of whom survived the period, remained silent throughout.

During the five years 1950–5, five of the Law Lords, including two who held office throughout the period, did not intervene in debate at all. After he had ceased to be Lord Chancellor, Lord Simonds spoke only once during the two sessions 1954–6, and that was on the proposed Oxford by-pass. In the whole of these five years there were only thirteen individual interventions by Law Lords apart from the Lord Chief Justice and Lord Chancellor. Lord Chief Justice Goddard was an exception to the general rule; in 1950–5 he intervened on eleven separate matters, and in addition contributed substantially to debate in committee and on report on two bills, the Courts-Martial (Appeals) Bill of 1950–1 and the Road Traffic Bill of 1954–5.

Even in very recent times some Law Lords have continued to contribute to debates on proposals for reform of the penalties imposed by the criminal law. On some occasions their interventions have brought them near to the centre of political controversy.

During the passage through the House of Lords of the Criminal Justice Bill in 1947–8, several Law Lords took part in the debates and Lord Chief Justice Goddard spoke vehemently against the proposal to abolish the death penalty. In the division he and Lords Du Parcq and Oaksey voted against abolition. The speeches and votes of the Law Lords on this subject were all in agreement with the opinions of the Lord Chancellor and of the Government itself. Lord Goddard's proposal to retain the power of courts to order corporal punishment was, however, on a rather different plane. His amendment was moved against the opinion, firmly and confidently held, of the Home Office, and he nevertheless pressed it to a division in which, in a rather thinly attended House, the amendment was carried by 29 votes to 17. In this division Lord Goddard was joined by Lord Oaksey, but Lord Du Parcq voted against the amendment and with the Government. When the Bill returned to the House of Lords with the Government's new compromise death penalty abolition clause, the Lord Chief Justice and other Law Lords again spoke and voted against any modification of the existing law.

In 1952 Law Lords contributed to two debates on the penalties for particular kinds of crime. Lord Goddard spoke on a motion calling for action to stem cases of cruelty to children. In October of the same year Lords Goddard, Oaksey and Tucker spoke in favour of an increase of penalties for crimes of violence. Lord Goddard wished to see corporal punishment reintroduced; indeed he appeared to go further than he had gone in 1948.[1] Lord Oaksey went out of his way to criticize the Home Office for not seeing criminals as criminals, and for not paying enough attention to the State's duty to protect the law-abiding public; punishment should be of such a kind as to deter would-be criminals from wrong-doing.

Lord Goddard spoke also on the second reading of the Prevention of Crime Bill in the following session, and he and Lord Oaksey spoke and voted against the death penalty abolition Bill of 1956.

It may be suggested that Law Lords who participate in debates of this kind lay themselves open to public criticism of a sort which it is preferable that judges should not incur. Capital punishment and corporal punishment are subjects of fairly acute controversy and have over many years been debated with some heat in the country, in public and in private; arguments such as those put forward by Lord Goddard in particular, and by one or two of the other judges also, are bound to incur the disapproval of many honest citizens. Furthermore, the criminal law is now much concerned with the social purposes and consequences of the penalties imposed on offenders. The experience which judges obtain in court, through the hearing of cases and pronouncing of sentences, does not necessarily qualify them to be the interpreters of the will of society with regard to the deterrent and reformative effects of punishment.

4. MILITARY COMMANDERS

So far in discussing the rôle of peers with special qualifications in the debates of the Lords we have concerned ourselves with only two classes, both of which, the bishops and the Law Lords, hold a special constitutional position, in so far as the bishops hold their peerages normally for their time in office only, and the Law Lords for life. We may now pass to an examination of the contributions of a special class of peers not holding any peculiar constitutional position. Ordinary hereditary peerages are regularly given to the most prominent men in many walks of life, and among these are men who have risen to the highest ranks in the Navy, Army and Air Force. During the period 1948–55, which has been made the subject of examination for the purposes of this study, the House contained 21 peers who had received their peerages as rewards for their services as military commanders, generally during the War, although one of these, Lord Chatfield, had received his peerage in 1937.

[1] Lords Debs., 22nd October 1952, vol. 178, cols. 849–60.

MILITARY COMMANDERS

In addition we must mention two other peers who do not properly fall into this strictly 'specialist' category, though they were on its fringe. Lord Jeffreys, who had retired from the army with the rank of General in 1938, had been in the House of Commons for 14 years until he was made a peer in 1952. The Earl of Cork and Orrery had inherited his peerage, but would probably otherwise have received a peerage as a reward for his services as Admiral of the Fleet.

If we exclude Lord Jeffreys, and also Lords Ismay and Alexander for the period during which they were ministers of the Crown, and therefore obliged to speak on behalf of the Government, we find that with hardly any exceptions the military commanders spoke on no subjects other than defence and matters to do with it. Lord Douglas of Kirtleside spoke on the contractual arrangements with Germany in 1952. In 1951 Lord Tovey took charge in the House of Lords of the Leasehold Property (Temporary Provisions) Bill, and Lord Trenchard, who had special experience of the police service, asked a question to do with the police. In 1949 Lord Mountevans spoke on Malaya. In 1952 Lord Dowding spoke on experiments on animals and on spiritualism in the Forces. In 1953 Lord Chatfield spoke on the Life Peers Bill, and Lord Tedder, who had become a special authority on university matters since his appointment, in 1950, as Chancellor of Cambridge University, took part in the second reading, committee and report stages of the University of St. Andrews Bill. In 1954 Lord Freyberg spoke on the National Gallery Bill.

These were apparently the only instances in the five years 1950–5 in which military peers took part in discussion in the Lords of subjects unconnected with the Services, defence or foreign affairs. Even on these matters the military peers did not contribute a great deal. Several of them did not speak at all; others spoke once or twice a year each, generally in debates concerned with the broad lines of Service or defence policy.

Even in defence debates the generals, admirals and air-marshals do not by any means monopolize the time. One service chief spoke on the Air Estimates on 16th May 1956, none in the long defence debate of 21st March 1956, to which 17 speakers in all contributed. Usually, however, a debate of this character can be expected to attract one or two contributions from the professional element, though there are usually ten speeches from other peers for every speech from a military commander. Ten years ago, however, service peers spoke rather more frequently in defence debates. Two admirals and two air marshals were among the 16 speakers on 28th October 1947, and commanders took a similar share five months later.

Commanders do not always speak in harmony together. Lord Brabazon has written of a debate in which there was 'a concerted movement by the Admirals ... to attack Lord Trenchard's air policy'.[1] Defence debates in the Lords are not usually, however, made occasions for arguments between the Services, although admirals, for example, have been known, even in recent times, to press for more attention to be paid to naval building. On 2nd December 1954, Lord Chatfield moved an amendment to the Queen's speech to 'regret the absence of any statement indicating the immediate commencement of a building programme to strengthen the Royal Navy'.

On 14th May 1952, Lord Cork himself initiated a debate on a chapter of the new manual of military law. He complained that in the form in which it had been written it was inimical to discipline in so far as it provided that soldiers on duty should not have the absolute protection of a plea of obedience to superior orders. He proposed that a tribunal should be set up to consider this chapter before the publication of the revised edition. Lords Wilson and Chatfield also took part in the debate, supporting Lord Cork's view; the debate turned out, in fact, to be a contest between military men and lawyers. The view of the lawyers was expressed by Lord Jowitt: 'The manual is a textbook and must say what the law is. If it said that "superior orders" was a hundred per cent defence, it would be wrong. I could show your Lordships opinions of distinguished judges for centuries past demonstrating that this is not the law.' The Lord Chancellor, in summing up, said that this chapter would in any case go to the War Office for comment before the publication of the manual, and he was sure that the War Office would take note of what had been said during the course of the debate.

During 1950–6 the matter of officers' pensions was discussed often and with some acrimony. The only military peers to take part in these proceedings were Lord Jeffreys and Lord Chatfield, both of whom had retired from ordinary active service before 1939; the former made vigorous and fairly numerous interventions in favour of better treatment of the retired officers of an earlier generation. His efforts here were in the nature of the contributions of a parliamentarian speaking on behalf of constituents, rather than of a military expert on military matters.

Ennobled military commanders, even when they have retired from active service, generally prefer not to avow allegiance to any political party. Earl Alexander of Tunis and Lord Ismay accepted office in a Conservative Cabinet in 1952, but did not join the Conservative Party. Of the 19 commanders in the House in 1955 (excluding the Conservative Lord Jeffreys), two are described in *Vacher* as Conservatives and two as members of the Labour Party. It would be unwise to suggest that this implies that the sympathy of the military men as

[1] Lord Brabazon, *The Brabazon Story* (Heinemann, 1956), p. 214.

a whole is distributed equally among the two parties; on the other hand, the military men very rarely vote in party divisions. In the 22 divisions of the session of 1955-6 (apart from the three of exceptional importance), there were eight instances of military commanders voting. Lord Freyberg voted five times, twice on free votes but always on the same side as the ministers. Lord Alexander of Tunis supported the two Front Benches against a Conservative back-bench onslaught on a private bill; Lord Dowding voted for a Performing Animals Bill, Lord Douglas of Kirtleside (one of the Labour Party's supporters) for an amendment to the Copyright Bill. In the division on the Government's Egyptian policy on 12th December 1956 Lords Fraser of North Cape, Newall and Dowding voted against the Labour amendment; Lord Tedder, the only ennobled military commander to speak in the debate, condemned the Government but did not vote in the division.

5. CIVILIAN PUBLIC SERVANTS, DOCTORS, ETC.

With ordinary civil servants, whose work has been in the United Kingdom, the fountain of honour has been as sparing in its grant of peerages as it has been liberal in its grant of knighthoods. Lord Waverley, who was for ten years (1922 to 1932) Permanent Under-Secretary of State at the Home Department, played his part in the House of Lords, but it was only after he had served as Governor of Bengal, sat for many years in the Commons, and held high ministerial office, that he was created a peer in 1952. Peerages have been given far more liberally on the other hand to colonial civil servants who have become Governors, and to members of the Foreign Service who have served as Ambassadors. A study of the rôle of these men as peers in the House of Lords produces results fairly closely parallel with those which we have found in our study of the work of the ennobled military commanders. Most of them have avoided voting on party questions, and have intervened in debate rarely and only on their own subjects. There have been important exceptions, however. Lord Hankey, the former Secretary to the Cabinet, and Lord Vansittart, who came from the Foreign Office, have both been frequent contributors to debate. Neither has joined a political party, but both have often supported the Conservatives with their votes. Lord Vansittart often spoke strongly in favour of a particular kind of foreign policy. Lord Hankey in 1949 'launched a major attack on the origin, principles and policy of the war crimes trials'.[1] Lord Killearn, whom *Vacher* lists as a Unionist, has been a frequent contributor on Middle East questions.

[1] Lord Hankey, *Politics, Trials and Errors* (Pen-in-Hand, 1950), p. xiii.

Some permanent officers of the Houses of Parliament have received peerages after retiring from office, and they too have tended to speak only on matters for which their experience gives them special qualifications. Lord Badeley, for example, who resigned from his office as Clerk of the Parliaments in 1949, was able to make a valuable contribution to a debate on the admission of women to the House of Lords. He gave the House useful information about the constitutional position with regard to the right to a writ of summons, and also about the difficulty of knowing just what was the potential total number of peeresses in their own right.[1]

It is not strictly correct to call a former Speaker of the House of Commons a public servant. Acceptance of the office of Speaker is, however, supposed to involve the abandonment of any right or desire to take any further part in politics, at least in a party sense, so a former Speaker of the House of Commons, when he receives a peerage, seems to hold a position in some ways akin to that held by a former Clerk. Lord Ullswater, who (as Mr. Lowther) had been Speaker of the House of Commons, was during his career in the upper House a frequent contributor to debates. He did not speak in a controversial vein, but voted in many divisions, sometimes with the Government and sometimes against it. Former Speakers may be regarded as elder statesmen of parliamentary business.

A number of doctors have received peerages; in recent years the two or three most prominent men in the medical profession have generally been members of the House of Lords. When we examine the contributions to debate of Lords Dawson of Penn and Moynihan in the 1930s, or of Lords Horder, Moran and Webb Johnson in more recent times, we find that they too all spoke infrequently and only on matters about which they were specially qualified to speak. In 1933–4, Lord Dawson of Penn himself introduced into the upper House a Contraceptives Regulation Bill and steered it through the House. In the same session Lord Moynihan introduced a Road Traffic (Emergency Treatment) Bill, whose purpose was to improve the position of doctors who gave treatment to people injured in road accidents, and often received no payment for their services. In the next session Lord Moynihan himself moved the rejection of the Osteopaths Bill, and he seized the occasion to make a strong attack on the practice of osteopathy. Lord Dawson of Penn also spoke on much the same lines. Since 1950 we find Lord Horder speaking on euthanasia and on processed foods; Lord Webb Johnson speaking on euthanasia, on the National Health Service Bill of 1950–1, on the administration and finance of hospitals, on an Education Bill at the committee stage (in which he concerned himself particularly with

[1] Cf. below, pp. 255 f.

medical education), and on a Therapeutic Substances (Prevention of Misuse) Bill in Committee. Lord Moran spoke in 1953 on hospital nursing services, and—a rather exceptional instance—on the Life Peers Bill of the same session.[1]

The House has been particularly glad to hear speeches from its eminent scientists and economists, such as Lords Adrian, Boyd-Orr, Cherwell, Keynes and Beveridge. Some of these great experts have, at times, contributed fairly frequently to debate; Lord Beveridge, as befits a man of his wide experience, has spoken on many subjects, and has been one of the leading spokesmen of the Liberal Party.

This summary of the contributions to debate of some classes of peers who hold special expert qualifications, suggests that a House of Lords composed entirely of such men, as it has sometimes been proposed that it should be, might seriously lack continuity. Men of the highest distinction in particular walks of life, such as military service, the public service, the arts and the professions, can hardly be expected to have the inclination for regular attendance at a parliamentary assembly, even if it meets only on three afternoons a week. Those who are still active have not the time either. They have too many interests and commitments elsewhere, and quite apart from this their particular talents would hardly be used to the best advantage if they were in constant attendance at a parliamentary assembly which in the course of the session has to discuss matters of very many and widely varying types.

This fact does not, however, diminish the great advantage which the House of Lords obtains from the presence of such people among its members. Lord Halifax said in 1936, 'It is the accustomed boast of this House that we can command the services of experts in relation to whatever topic may from time to time engage our attention.'[2] Lord Halifax was undoubtedly right. The great virtue of the House of Lords as it is at present constituted is that whatever subject is debated, there are not only the experts who have something special to contribute, on the basis of their own experience, to that particular debate, but also the nucleus of politicians who regularly attend the House as their day-to-day business. This mixture of experts and politicians is extremely valuable.

---

[1] His speech on this occasion was based on extensive research. Cf. above, pp. 33, 49.
[2] Lords Debs., 22nd July 1936, vol. 100, col. 151.

PART II

THE ORGANIZATION OF THE HOUSE

Chapter V

PROCEDURE AND ORGANIZATION OF BUSINESS

1. GENERAL PRINCIPLES

IT would be hard to imagine a modern assembly less trammelled with procedural rules than the House of Lords. Its presiding officer 'has no authority beyond that of any other member in matters of order';[1] there is no provision for closure or allocation of time orders, no formal restriction on the right of any peer to initiate a debate on any subject at any time, or to speak at any length in any debate. The lack of rigidity or formality is to be attributed to the behaviour of the House, in which disorder and obstruction are unknown.

The House of Lords is often said to have more time than the House of Commons, and to be well placed for reconsidering at leisure matters which have been dealt with too hurriedly in the lower House. It is sometimes suggested that the main reason why the upper House appears to have more time is its freedom from financial business, but this argument is only partly acceptable. It is true that the upper House does not have to devote any time at all to the Estimates or the Consolidated Fund Bills, and that it normally refrains from debating the details of the Finance Bill in Committee.[2] As a result of this it may be said to gain about fifty days a year as compared with the Commons, but almost thirty of the days which appear to be 'saved' are

---

[1] Erskine May, *Treatise* (Butterworth, 15th (1950) ed.), p. 229.

[2] If the Finance Bill is technically a money bill, the Lords do not discuss it in committee. Oddly enough, the content of the main Finance Bill of a year is sometimes such as to prevent the Speaker of the House of Commons from certifying it as a money bill. Even so, the Lords still refrain from exercising their technical right of examining the Bill in Committee.

days spent by the Commons on business of Supply. The Commons in fact devote those days, not really to the Estimates themselves, but to general questions, such as are in fact discussed in the Lords under other forms of procedure.

If the Lords appear to have more time than the Commons, it is mainly because debate is conducted more expeditiously in the upper House than in the lower. Speeches tend to be shorter, and on matters of minor importance there are usually fewer peers who want to speak.[1] It has never become necessary to provide for fixed closing times for debates in the Lords, and in some sessions, when questions of great interest are before the House, debates of considerable length may greatly swell the total length of sitting time. Thus the time spent in session, as indicated by the number of columns occupied by the official report of the proceedings in *Hansard*, was twice as great in 1920 as in 1923 or 1928. Again, the sitting time in the session of 1946-7 was nearly twice as great as in that of 1950-1, which covered a period of similar duration.

There has, however, been a tendency for the House to sit for far longer in recent years than was previously the case. The four years, 1945-9, during which the Labour Government was introducing its long and complicated legislative programme, caused the House to sit for considerably longer than it has sat since 1949, but the session 1953-4 rivalled the sessions under the Labour Government in the length of the sittings. In general, when we consider recent sessions in comparison with those before the war, we find that since 1945 the average length of time spent in session each year has been about twice as great as between 1920 and 1940.

The days of meeting are not altogether fixed. While Parliament is in session the House normally meets on Tuesdays, Wednesdays and Thursdays. Sometimes, if it is being found inconvenient to fit all the business into three days a week, additional sittings are called on Mondays and, very rarely, on Fridays. There were three Monday sittings for debate in the session of 1935-6, one in 1953-4 and four in 1955-6. In 1946-7, however, there were no fewer than sixteen, of which all but two were devoted to government bills. Friday sittings are nearly always formal, and of barely five minutes' duration. Thus on Friday,

---

[1] A striking illustration of the greater conciseness of peers' speeches is provided by the proceedings on the second reading of the Road Traffic Bill of the session 1954-5. The Bill went through the Lords first, and the eleven peers who spoke on the second reading, apart from the four front-bench spokesmen who opened and closed the debate, took on the average ten minutes each. The Bill duly went to the Commons, where, although the main arguments had already been rehearsed in the Lords, the fourteen back-bench members who spoke took on the average seventeen minutes each. (Cf. Lords Debs., 21st December 1954, and Commons Debs., 5th April 1955).

23rd October 1953, a few days before the end of the session, the House sat in order to receive (but not to debate) the Commons amendments to the Enemy Property Bill. The amendments were then dealt with on the first sitting day (Tuesday) of the next week.[1]

The House has now abandoned its old habit of not sitting on the days of the Derby and the Ascot Gold Cup, when it was once assumed that all sane peers would wish to be occupied elsewhere than in the Palace of Westminster. Even now the House sometimes takes a day off when there is some other kind of special occasion, such as a review of the Royal Air Force.[2] It is also the custom of the House to adjourn, if necessary, for an appropriate interval on a day on which there is a royal Garden Party.[3] Test Matches at Lords and the tennis championships at Wimbledon are not considered sufficient pretexts for adjournment, but peers contributing to debate sometimes begin by deploring their absence from these more entertaining functions outside, and by commiserating with the other noble Lords who are similarly incarcerated by their assiduity.

2. TIMES OF SITTING

Until 1948 the times of meeting had to be made to fit in with the demands of judicial business, because the Lords' debating Chamber was used by the House also for the purpose of conducting its business as the highest court in the land. The judicial sittings in their turn had to be concluded in time to allow legislative business to begin at the appointed hour. In theory the Chamber should apparently still be used for the judicial sittings, and indeed still is so used on occasion. There is in reality little in common between the ordinary House of Lords when it is sitting as a legislating and debating body and the House of Lords when it is sitting as a court. The judicial sittings are conducted by the peers who have the legal qualifications prescribed by the Appellate Jurisdiction Act of 1876—the Lords of Appeal in Ordinary and other peers who have held high judicial office. Usually five of them sit together to constitute the House. Ordinary peers may attend judicial sittings, but by convention may not speak. According

---

[1] Lords Debs., 22nd and 27th October 1953, vol. 183, cols. 1313, 1393–6. In the session of 1955–6 there were formal sittings on three Fridays, all in June. At the short emergency sitting of Parliament during the summer recess, in September 1956, the last of the three sitting days was on a Friday.

[2] Wednesday, 15th July 1953, was taken as a holiday because of an Air Force review (Lords Debs., 9th July 1953, vol. 183, col. 429). The House of Commons sat as usual on that day.

[3] Lords Debs., 9th July 1953, vol. 183, col. 429. On the day of the Garden Party on this occasion, however, the House completed all its business by 3.48 p.m., so there was no need for a resumption later in the afternoon.

to Lord Simon, when non-legal peers have wanted to make observations they have been 'suitable suppressed'.[1]

According to the long-established practice of the House the judicial sittings begin in the morning, at 10.30 or 11 a.m., and continue until the early afternoon. When the judicial sittings are held in the debating chamber the hour of meeting for ordinary business is 4 p.m. Before 1939 there was some irritation at the lateness of the hour of sitting. Attempts were made, unsuccessfully, to have the judicial sittings held outside, simultaneously with the legislative sittings. At first these attempts were strongly resisted, and the difficulties involved in the proposal for an appellate committee were found to be insuperable; later, however, extraneous circumstances compelled the House to overcome the difficulties. The appellate committee was set up for a time as a temporary measure, and for the past five years has continued to operate although the original circumstances which led to its establishment are no longer present.

The story of its inception deserves to be told in some detail, as it well illustrates the processes of development of British constitutional practice. In 1938 there was a debate on the question of the organization of the work of the Lords as a court.[2] Lord Newton suggested that the judicial sittings should be held in a committee room. If this were done, he said, it would be possible for the House to meet at 2.30 p.m. even on the days on which the judicial sittings might continue beyond that hour. He referred to the extreme unsuitability of the physical arrangements of the Lords' debating chamber for the business of a court. 'The Lord Chancellor,' he said, 'sits flanked by two colleagues, and the others, for whom there is no room at the table, are accommodated with a sort of miniature tea-table . . . the sort of thing you would see outside a second rate café in Paris. There is no place for their papers, no convenience of any kind whatever.' The process of shifting the scene and preparing for the ordinary debate took as much as twenty minutes of wholly unnecessary labour. Lord Rankeillour agreed, and referred also to the extreme inconvenience to all litigants and counsel of the so-called 'pig-pen', where they were 'all herded together with very scanty opportunity for making notes or for consultations without the other side hearing all that passes'.

The suggestion that legal sittings should be held in a committee room, and that their timing might overlap with the ordinary sittings, raised constitutional difficulties. Lord Newton's scheme, in spite of its evident practical advantages, was, as might be expected, vigorously opposed by the traditionalists. Lord Atkin, a Law Lord, pointed out

[1] Lords Debs., 11th May 1948, vol. 155, col. 743.
[2] Ibid., 13th July 1938, vol. 108, cols. 792–820.

that, although the House of Lords in its judicial capacity was composed of only a very small part of the whole House, and of peers enjoying a special status, it nevertheless preserved its legal and constitutional identity as the House of Lords. The House of Lords in its judicial capacity was not a committee of the House of Lords, but the House itself. To hold legislative and judicial sittings simultaneously would involve a fundamental breach of the constitution. It would certainly need an Act of Parliament to make this possible. Even the use of a committee room, or of any place other than the Lords' chamber, without simultaneous sittings, would involve considerable impropriety.

This constitutional objection was seen by the Lord Chancellor, and by others, to present insuperable obstacles to Lord Newton's proposal. There were practical objections, too. If an appellate committee were set up the Lord Chancellor would sometimes be unable to take part in its proceedings and the judges would have to miss some of the debates in the House.

In recent years, however, the House has accepted a solution much on the lines suggested by Lord Newton; at the beginning of each session an Appellate Committee has been set up. The origin of the actual institution of this rational change was not, however, a positive desire to achieve the objectives at which Lord Newton's earlier motion was aimed; the change arose out of fortuitous circumstances. During the war the desirability of adjourning early, before the beginning of air raids, forced the House to accept a temporary change in its practice. Soon after the war a new pretext arose. In 1948 progress with the rebuilding operations in the Palace of Westminster would have been impossible unless the builders had been able to work during the mornings, and for this reason the House accepted a motion for the establishment of an appellate committee for the hearing of appeals. The committee was to include all Lords qualified under the Appellate Jurisdiction Act of 1876, as amended, it was to hear the appeals when and where the Lord Chancellor should determine, and it was to report to the House the result of its deliberations.

Lord Jowitt moved his motion with regret, and in the debate there was no lack of expressions of the wish that the committee would really be a temporary expedient. Three years later, however, when the building operations were completed, the Appellate Committee was again set up at the beginning of the new session, because, in the words of the Lord Chancellor, 'the public interest was thus best served'. At the beginning of each session since 1951 the appellate committee has been set up as a matter of course and without discussion. For a time there was some half-hearted attempt to preserve the fiction that the device was still a temporary expedient. In December 1954 the Lord

Chancellor justified the motion as follows: 'I think all your Lordships will agree that so long as the present pressure of business requires that the House should meet at 2.30, then the procedure contained in this motion is necessary.' But nobody thought fit to suggest that there was anything temporary about the pressure of business. At the beginning of the session of 1955–6 the motion for the Appellate Committee was introduced and agreed to without explanation or discussion,[1] as though it were a routine matter. The reports, to which the House agrees formally, are entered in the Journals of the House.

It is probably safe to assume that this sensible modification in practice, having been indignantly rejected at first, then accepted with regret as a temporary expedient imposed by passing circumstances, has now become part of the permanent procedure of the House. When judicial hearings take place outside the times of parliamentary sittings, the peers (usually five in number) constituting the Court sit as the House of Lords in the old way, and not as a committee.[2]

Like the Commons, the Lords have tended to bring their times of meeting earlier in the day during the past century. The sittings for ordinary business now begin, like those of the House of Commons, at 2.30 p.m., except on Thursdays, when the usual time is 3 p.m.[3] Occasionally, in order to prevent a debate from continuing too late in the evening, the House agrees to meet at 2 p.m. More rarely still it meets before lunch. It met, for example, at 11 a.m. on 2nd April 1953, the last day before the Easter recess, and adjourned early in the afternoon. On 1st and 8th November 1956, during the Egyptian crisis, it met at noon. The debate very often ends by 6 p.m., and rarely continues for long after 7 p.m. On an ordinary day, when the debate is not being continued after dinner, it is not unusual for a peer who makes a speech at any time after 5.30 p.m. to begin by apologizing for detaining their Lordships 'at this late hour'. If the state of business is such that it seems necessary to continue the sitting for longer into the evening, the House sometimes adjourns at 7 p.m. for an hour and a half for dinner, and reassembles at 8.30 p.m., continuing generally not later than 11 p.m. During the past two or three years the House has sometimes followed the practice of the House of Commons and sat right through the dinner hour without adjourning.

[1] Lords Debs., 13th June 1955, vol. 193, col. 34.
[2] The Lords Journals record such sittings on the Mondays, Tuesdays, Wednesdays and Thursdays of January 1955 until the end of the recess. On one day the House sat until 5.30 p.m.
[3] Cf. Erskine May, p. 305. These times of meeting are not laid down in the Standing Orders; in the words of Erskine May, 'the House may meet at any hour to which it had been adjourned at the preceding meeting'. The opening at 3 p.m. on Thursday reflects a desire, even now, to avoid overlapping between the ordinary and the judicial sittings.

Many modern peers would rather miss some back-bench speeches in order to have the debate finished by 9 or 10, than stay on at the House until it is too late to get back to Sussex in comfort. The decision whether or not to adjourn for dinner in any particular debate is made informally through the usual channels and announced to the House by a Government Whip.[1]

There is no suggestion of a 10 p.m. rule; the House merely adjourns when everyone who wishes to speak in the current debate has finished. It is in practice very rare indeed for the sittings to continue after 11, and sittings into the small hours of the morning are nowadays unknown.

During the summer of 1947, when the House was particularly busy because of the Labour Government's heavy legislative programme, Lord Addison, the Leader of the House, proposed that there should be some kind of time-table for the remainder of the session, and that the House should meet from 2.30 to 11 p.m. on Tuesdays and Wednesdays, and from 4 to 11 p.m. on Mondays and Thursdays. These purely *ad hoc* proposals were made the subject of a brief discussion, at the end of which Lord Addison agreed to Lord Salisbury's suggestion, on behalf of the Opposition peers, that the hour of adjournment should be 10.30 p.m. instead of 11, because of the difficulties with public transport after a quarter to eleven. In fact the House sat after 10 p.m. on 26 of the 62 sitting days after Whitsun, and on nearly all of these days adjourned within a few minutes of 11 o'clock. One sitting continued until just after midnight.

In 1954 the Conservative Government found it necessary to keep the Lords in session rather late on one evening of the debate on their Television Bill. They were met with the most vigorous protests from the Labour benches. At 10.16 p.m. Lord Jowitt, speaking for the Labour peers, asked the Leader of the House to adjourn as soon as possible. Later on he made further appeals, and in particular complained that there had been no warning. 'I cannot keep the Lords of my own party here after 11 p.m.,' he said. 'Members of this House are not so young as they used to be and they are paid absolutely nothing, and it is very difficult to get people to stay in these circumstances without any warning.'[2] Lord Salisbury insisted that the debate should continue, as many peers had come great distances to attend on this particular day, and some would not be able to attend so easily on other days. He pointed out that the Conservative

---

[1] Thus on 21st July 1953, as nineteen peers had put their names down to speak on the next day's debate on charitable trusts, Earl Fortescue announced that it had been agreed through the normal channels that there would be no adjournment for dinner. The debate lasted until nearly 9 p.m.

[2] Lords Debs., 12th July 1954, vol. 188, cols. 777 f.

Government had in the past three years not once asked the House to sit later than 11 p.m. On this occasion the sitting came to an end at half an hour after midnight.

The following table indicates the times at which the House brought its business to a close on the 85 sitting days (excluding formal sittings) during the period August 1955 to August 1956.

Number of days on which the evening adjournment was

	Before 5 p.m.	5 to 6 p.m.	6 to 7 p.m.	7 to 8 p.m.	8 to 10 p.m.	After 10 p.m.
Up to Easter 1956	9	15	14	11	2	1
After Easter 1956	8	8	7	6	2	2
Total	17	23	21	17	4	3

One advantage that the Lords have over the Commons is that in the upper House there is no need for peers to catch the Speaker's eye before they can be called upon to speak. Peers who come down to the House with carefully prepared speeches do not need to fear that they may never have the good fortune to be called. For each debate that is to take place those peers who intend to speak have simply to hand in their names beforehand. An order of speaking is drawn up and supplied to people attending the debate, like a programme, along with the formal Order Paper. The length of the debate will depend on the number of peers who want to speak on the particular matter in question. Thus it will usually be known in advance if a debate is likely to continue fairly late in the evening. The order of speaking is not rigid. It may be varied by informal arrangement, and a peer who has not put his name down in advance is not debarred from making an intervention even if he only decides to speak as the debate progresses.

Upholders of the practice of the House of Commons, where the Speaker decides whom to call next as the debate proceeds, may criticize the system of the 'batting order' in the Lords, on the ground that it produces a series of unrelated harangues rather than a debate. There has, indeed, been some complaint recently that peers are too much inclined to depart after making their speeches, and to be absent when later speakers wish to answer arguments which they have put forward.[1]

The preparation of the order of speaking may not always be easy, because peers prefer to be put down to speak at a time when the House is likely to be reasonably well filled. Bishop Percival was very angry in 1909 when 'the Government Whip would only give him the

---

[1] Cf. Lords Debs., 14th November 1956, vol. 200, cols. 300-10.

time of empty benches just after dinner, and told him to take no more than ten to fifteen minutes'.[1]

3. TYPES OF BUSINESS AND ARRANGEMENT OF TIME

Although there is no rigid organization of the time-table of the House of Lords such as we find in the Commons, there is the same kind of classification of types of business in the upper House as in the lower. (Cf. S.O. 35.) Erskine May (pages 323–31) analyses these and shows the order in which the specific items may be taken. It is not necessary here to repeat the formal rules. Most of the items in Erskine May's list occupy negligible amounts of time. Essentially there are two main types of business—bills and general debates; mention must be made also of starred questions, which peers may ask like the members of the lower House.[2]

A rule of some importance is S.O. 35(5), which provides that on Tuesdays and Thursdays the proceedings on public bills have precedence over questions, motions or resolutions. Even this does not imply that Tuesdays and Thursdays are necessarily to be regarded as government days; private members' bills may be taken on those days as well as government bills. Furthermore, the precedence given to bills does not necessarily squeeze out other business. Very often the proceedings on bills are completed very quickly, and a debate on a private member's motion begins well before 4 p.m.

In the arrangement of the order of business the House of Lords differs fundamentally from the Commons in one important respect. During the past hundred years the lower House has been obliged to give precedence to 'government business' for ever-larger proportions of its sitting time—though in practice the Opposition has much influence in the allocation of government time to different topics. In recent years government business has had precedence in the Commons on every sitting day except for the twenty private members' Fridays in each session. In the Lords, on the other hand, there is no part of the time during which precedence is regularly given to government business, and consequently the arrangement of types of private members' business has not been formalized.

There is no distinction between government time and private members' time; no daily Question time of fixed duration, no days regularly reserved for private members' bills or motions, no guaranteed half-hour adjournment debate at the end of the day's business. In spite of the great increase in the quantity of business in the past

---

[1] Quoted in William Temple, *Life of Bishop Percival*, op. cit., p. 241.

[2] The technical procedure regarding bills is discussed in detail in chapters VIII, XIV and XV, below, and that regarding questions and general debates in chapter XVII.

few years, there is still normally little serious pressure on the available time, and the arrangements are still as flexible as were the arrangements in the Commons a hundred years ago. It is true that a great part of the Lords' sitting time is occupied with the discussion of bills, and occasionally of other measures, brought forward by the Government, but there is still plenty of opportunity for fitting in debates on all kinds of subjects according to the wishes of individual peers or groups or of the official Opposition. Private members' debates do not need to depend on the chances of a ballot, and on other debates, however important, the imposition of rigid time-tables never becomes necessary. Peers have, then, an almost unrestricted freedom to initiate debates. Considering that so many people enjoy this freedom, it is perhaps surprising that it is not abused or even over-used. Indeed, in some ways, and particularly in the matter of proposing bills, it might be suggested that the freedom could well be used more than it is. The House gives little encouragement to a peer who persists in raising a topic which is of little interest; he will soon find himself talking to empty benches.

The fact that Government and official Opposition have been so moderate in their demands on the time of the House does not imply any special tenderness on their part towards back-bench peers, or any self-abnegation. On the contrary, it is rather because of the moderation of the demands of the back-bench peers for time that their technical 'rights' with regard to the use of time have been left so largely unrestricted. In practice, the leaders on both sides of the House are able to ensure, by means of persuasion (and, if necessary, pressure) that their wishes with regard to the management of business are not interfered with by the demands of private members. If a back-bench peer has a motion down for a particular day, and the Whips find that it is standing in the way of some subject that they wish to have discussed, they can usually persuade him without much difficulty to hold his motion over for the time being, so that the Party's requirements may have priority. Furthermore, a private member peer, before putting down a motion, will probably discuss his intention with the Whips, or he may even have been prompted by them. Thus the 'usual channels' have in fact a considerable influence over the order and content of the time-table of business, although that influence may be exercised in a rather subtle way.

A general debate in the House of Lords is very often based on a question or a motion to express an opinion or to call attention to some situation and ending with the somewhat cryptic motion for 'papers'. This term has, according to Erskine May, no specific meaning, but is related to a procedural fiction. By adding 'and to move for papers' to his motion, a peer reserves to himself a clear right to reply to the debate. As the House of Lords has the same rule as the House of Commons to the effect that the same person may not speak twice on the same question, the device of moving for papers is in fact no more than a useful piece of procedure for getting round a rule which may sometimes be awkward.

When a debate has been founded on a motion for papers the motion is generally withdrawn at the end of the debate. If it is not withdrawn the House has to decide whether to ask for papers or not. If a motion for papers is carried, the Government is (in theory) obliged to supply the papers, whatever they may be, though their nature is neither specified in the motion nor defined under any convention.

Although, looked at from the point of view of formal procedure, debates of this type appear to be the Lords' equivalent of the Commons debates on private members' motions on Fridays, the analogy is not altogether satisfactory. In substance these debates often serve much the same purpose as those on Supply days in the Commons. Because of the rule that Supply is a matter for the Commons, the Lords are precluded from debating it, but this is not really a serious disability. Supply debates in the Commons rarely have anything to do with the actual votes of money to which they are formally related, and most of the subjects debated in the Commons in Committee of Supply can equally well be debated in the Lords on the basis of ordinary motions. It must again be emphasized that, as the Lords have not found it necessary to limit 'private members' time' to specific days, the distinction between private members' debates and other debates scarcely exists in the upper House. The whole programme of debates is drawn up according to the wishes of the two front benches and of the individual members of the House.

Any peer who wishes to initiate a debate can hand in his motion or question at the Table, and can make arrangements with the clerks for the fixing of a date, which, under S.O. No. 38 (1934), may not be more than one month of sitting time ahead. He may wish to put the motion down without at first fixing a date; the Minutes generally mention several motions for which no date has yet been fixed. Before agreeing to the fixing of a particular date, the mover of the motion may find it useful to consult his Party leaders and Whips, and perhaps also representatives of the opposite Party.

Naturally many subjects for debate are put down by peers on the Opposition Front Bench, or by leaders of the Liberal Party. Some debates are clearly front-bench occasions and others are back-benchers' occasions; a great many others, however, fall somewhere between the two. The lack of rigidity in this matter is a great advantage.

PROCEDURE AND ORGANIZATION OF BUSINESS

There is no weekly announcement of forthcoming business as in the Commons, but the printed Minutes of each Thursday's proceedings normally mention the whole of the business for the next week (and some of the business for later weeks also). It is, however, often found desirable to make alterations in the programme at fairly short notice, usually to suit the needs of government business, and changes are often made by mutual agreement.

There have on occasion been complaints that this flexibility has caused inconvenience to peers who have missed a debate against their will, because they have not known that it was coming on. Some steps have been taken to remedy the trouble. Early in 1953 the House agreed to a motion, put forward by Lord Teynham, to the effect that, save in circumstances of urgency, notice of the date of any motion should be given to the Table by the Thursday before it was to be moved. It is typical of the way the House manages its business that nobody suggested introducing a Standing Order to this effect; the resolution that was passed was merely in the form of an expression of opinion.[1]

Changes in the time-table can often be made smoothly and with adequate notice. On 22nd November 1951, for example, a fortnight before the Christmas recess was to begin, the Government decided that the needs of its legislative programme demanded that two of its bills should be debated on the 29th. But a private member's bill was already down for that day. It was agreed, therefore, to advance the debate on this bill to the 28th, and to defer until after the recess a debate on housing which had at first been put down for the 28th.[2]

A rearrangement of the time-table often becomes necessary at fairly short notice. If an unexpectedly large number of peers put their names down to speak in a forthcoming debate, for example, it may be decided to give a second day to the debate. A Monday is sometimes used for this purpose, but at other times adjustments are made in the plans for the normal sitting days.

Occasionally misunderstandings arise over the arrangement of business. On 13th May 1952, when fourteen peers had put their names down to speak on a forthcoming motion on transport, a rearrangement was considered necessary. Earl Fortescue, speaking for the Government, proposed that the transport debate should begin on the following day, Wednesday, at about 5 p.m., after a debate on a motion put down by Lord Cork, and continue after dinner that even-

---

[1] Lords Debs., 22nd January 1953, vol. 179, cols. 1196–1208.
[2] Ibid., 22nd November 1951, vol. 174, col. 503. The change was announced in the House, in accordance with the normal practice, by the Government Chief Whip. It is unusual to advance a debate in this way. Cf. *Companion to the Standing Orders* (1946), p. 22.

ing, and that it should be resumed a week later. Earl Jowitt, replying for the Labour peers, said: 'The noble Earl says that it has been agreed through the usual channels. Is he sure that he is right? My noble friend Lord Shepherd came to me and told me of this proposal and asked me what we thought of it. After seeing those concerned with the transport motion it was obvious that they were reluctant to do this. Therefore I said that I would not agree. The machinery seems to have broken down. Would noble Lords consent to the matter being mentioned again tomorrow, and in the meantime we will get busy through the usual channels to try to make an arrangement that will satisfy everybody?' A little later, Earl Fortescue rose to announce revised arrangements for the transport debate. On Wednesday 14th Lord Cork's motion came on first, as had originally been proposed, but did not finish until nearly 6 p.m. This was a good deal later than had been expected, and Earl Fortescue rose to propose a further alteration, by which the transport debate was to take place on one day, instead of beginning during the last part of the sitting then in progress.

On certain occasions the Lords have to suffer some inconvenience in order to make their business fit in with that of the Commons. The timing of ministerial statements is an instance. In the Commons there is a recognized point in the parliamentary day at which such statements are made, namely at the end of Question Time, at 3.30 p.m. or a little later. On occasions on which it is appropriate for parallel statements to be made in the two Houses, the business of the Lords is interrupted, so as to allow the statement there to be made at the same time as that in the Commons.[1] The interruption of the debate is accepted without complaint; there have, however, been complaints about statements being made without adequate notice.[2] As in the Commons, members may ask questions for the sake of elucidation immediately after a ministerial statement has been made, but there can be no debate so long as there is no motion before the House (S.O. 31.)

4. THE PHYSICAL ARRANGEMENTS OF THE HOUSE OF LORDS

In shape the debating chamber of the House of Lords (though its colour-scheme is red, not green) closely resembles the nearby House

---

[1] Thus on 19th December 1956 a debate on roads was interrupted at 3.32 p.m., at the end of a speech, for two statements, one on troubles in Northern Ireland and the other on the publication of constitutional proposals for Cyprus. On the second, five peers made comments or asked questions, and the Government spokesman briefly replied. The debate on roads was resumed after an interruption of twenty minutes in all.

[2] Lords Debs., 27th January 1954, vol. 185, cols. 487 ff.

of Commons. The Government and Opposition benches face one another across the clerks' table, which is furnished with two dispatch boxes, one immediately in front of each of the two Front Benches. The Table itself, like that of the House of Commons, provides a convenient resting-place for the feet of the ministers and Opposition leaders. The seats on each side are arranged in three blocks instead of two. The Front Benches are in the middle block. The first two benches on the Government side in the block opposite the Woolsack are reserved for the bishops.[1] Facing the Woolsack below the Table are the cross-benches, which are used by peers who adhere to the main Parties.

The benches on the floor of the House provide seats for some 250 peers—a number small in relation to the total membership, but large in relation to the active membership. The public gallery is sometimes rather sparsely filled, and some of its occupants may be people who have come in only to console themselves for failure to gain admission to the gallery of the nearby House of Commons.

Every new peer, on elevation to the peerage or on succession to a title, becomes a member of the House of Lords after attending to the necessary formalities, and is entitled to share in privileges appropriate to a member of the Legislature. Until the beginning of 1957 no provision for payment of salaries or allowances in any form had been made. In 1946, however, provision was made for payment of travelling expenses to peers who attended at the House, and since July 1957 an allowance up to £3 3s. has been payable in respect of each day's attendance, to cover expenses actually incurred.

Papers relating to the business of the House, such as *Hansard* and the Minutes, which include a statement of impending business, are not sent automatically to all peers, but only to those peers who intimate that they wish to receive them. In order to do this they must fill in a form, specifying which classes of papers they wish to receive.

The Standing Orders and the custom of the House prescribe rules of debate, most of which are dictated by convenience or common sense. S.O. 25, which dates back to 1621, says, 'When any Lords speak, they are to address their speech to the rest of the Lords in general.' A peer referring to another peer does so in the third person, calling him 'the noble earl' (viscount, etc.). As in the Commons, military members are also 'gallant', and barristers or judges are 'learned'. S.O. 29, of 1626 ('all personal, sharp or taxing speeches be forborn') already illustrates the lack of any disciplinary powers in the hands of the presiding officer: 'If any offence be given in that kind, as

---

[1] Temporal peers may sit on the bishops' benches if bishops are not using them, but they may not speak from them. For the rest, individual peers do not sit in prescribed places. Cf. *Companion to Standing Orders*, p. 28.

the House itself will be very sensible thereof, so it will sharply censure the offender.' The House of Commons is always called 'another place'.

Divisions are taken as in the Commons, but a little more expeditiously. (S.O. 46.) Peers voting walk through the 'aye' or 'no' lobbies and are counted by tellers, two from each side in each lobby. The votes of the tellers are counted. The names of the peers voting are taken down by the clerks, and published in *Hansard* and in the *Journal*.

As a result of a decision made in February 1957 the interval between the putting of a Question and the locking of the doors into the division lobbies was increased from three minutes to four minutes, in order to allow peers more time to make their way down from committee rooms, etc.[1] The 'ancient and inalienable right' of peers to cast their votes by proxy was effectively abolished in 1868, when a Standing Order was introduced to render the right of no effect.[2]

5. OFFICERS OF THE HOUSE

Like the House of Commons the House of Lords entrusts to some of its members functions concerned with the management of business. The equivalent of the Speaker is the Lord Chancellor,[3] who takes his place on the Woolsack and presides over debates when the House is in ordinary session, though his place may be taken by a deputy when occasion demands it. When the House goes into committee the chair is taken by the Chairman of Committees or his deputy; the Lord Chancellor removes his wig and sits on the Government front bench.

The anomalous nature of the Lord Chancellor's office is notorious. The character of his duties is such that all the most sacrosanct rules regarding the separation of powers are broken. Although he is technically 'Speaker' of the House of Lords and its presiding officer (cf. Erskine May, p. 228) he is not debarred from voting in divisions or participating in debates like any other peer. Both when the House is

[1] Lords Debs., 5th February 1957, vol. 201, cols. 418–22.

[2] Cf. Francis Holland, *The Constitutional History of England* (vol. iii of May's *Constitutional History*), Longmans, 1912, p. 14 f.; and Report of the Select Committee of the House in relation to the Attendance of its Members, 1956, para. 4 and Minutes of Evidence, pp. 10 and 40, and Q. 286–99 and 342–3.

[3] In early times several Chancellors attended without having received writs of summons. (Cf. Pike, op cit., pp. 351 ff.) Technically it would still be possible for a person who was not a peer to act as Speaker of the House of Lords, and even in recent times a newly-appointed Lord Chancellor has acted as Speaker before his patent of creation as a peer has been made out. This is possible because the Woolsack is considered to be outside the limits of the House. When the Lord Chancellor speaks in a debate, he rises from the Woolsack and moves a few feet to the left, so that he may be technically 'in' the House. Cf. Erskine May, p. 229; S.O. 17, as revised in 1954, says, 'If the Lord Chancellor will speak to any thing particularly, he is to go to his place as a Peer'.

in committee and when he is on the Woolsack as the presiding officer, the Lord Chancellor regularly acts as one of the principal spokesmen for the Government. With the Speaker of the House of Commons, a large body of conventions has grown up, designed to ensure that the presiding officer shall be absolutely and irrevocably separated from party politics. With the Lord Chancellor, on the other hand, there is no suggestion of a requirement of impartiality. He speaks and votes as a member of his party and as a member of the Government. He defends the Government's policy and replies to the Opposition's attacks.

In a more formal sense, and more seriously perhaps, his position breaks the rule of the separation of judicial powers from legislative and executive powers. Besides being an ordinary member of the House of Lords as well as its presiding officer, and a member of the Cabinet, the Lord Chancellor is not only the head of the judiciary but also a judge concerned in the actual administration of justice and in the deciding of cases. Sometimes the Lord Chancellor is a Law Lord. When the House of Lords is sitting as a judicial court the Lord Chancellor sits regularly among the peers who are performing that function. He also has duties concerned with the supervision of the Justices of the Peace and of the administration of justice in general.

Perhaps the most interesting and the most significant peculiarity about the office of Lord Chancellor is one that has nothing to do with these well-known formal incompatibilities. With the House of Commons, and with most other legislative assemblies, the first qualification for the office of Speaker or President is a fairly long period of membership; a good familiarity with procedure and rules, such as can only be gained through some years of experience, is generally considered to be indispensable. Yet not merely a few, but most, recent Lord Chancellors have been new peers, appointed to their office straight from the House of Commons. This fact illustrates the nature of the office. Lack of experience of the House of Lords is no disability in a Lord Chancellor, just because his functions as Speaker, his powers of keeping order and managing procedure and so on, are almost non-existent. The House of Lords contrives to run its debates without the need of a presiding officer in the normal sense.

It is also noteworthy that the House as such has no say in the appointment of the Lord Chancellor. The office is filled, like other posts in the Cabinet, by the Prime Minister, who is not expected to consult the wishes of the House of Lords in any way before deciding whom to appoint. If there is any body of people whose feelings and wishes the Prime Minister must consider in making his choice, it is the legal profession. The Lord Chancellor must be a man whose standing and reputation in the law make him acceptable to the profession as a whole. Usually he is a barrister who has spent some years in the House of Commons and who has been prominent enough in his Party to hold ministerial office; sometimes he is appointed from the judicial bench and has no background of party politics.

The Chairman and deputy-Chairmen of Committees are chosen by the House itself, as are their opposite numbers in the House of Commons. Although the Lord Chancellor is not expected to cease to be a partisan, the Chairman of Committees takes no part in debates on ordinary topics.

The Lord Chairman of Committees, who receives a salary, came long ago to have extremely important functions to perform in relation to private bills.[1] The Government as such has no responsibility for private bills. Parliament can normally deal with them on their merits, and the rôle of the House of Lords is of at least equal importance with that of the Commons in this field of activity which has little to do with national party politics. Much of the task of managing the business connected with private bills falls on the Lord Chairman of Committees, and as his work in this field is highly technical there are many advantages in avoiding frequent changes in the chairmanship. The appointment of the Lord Chairman is always for the current session only, but in practice, like the Speaker of the House of Commons, he normally remains in his office until he chooses to resign. The Earl of Donoughmore held the office from 1911 to 1931, the Earl of Onslow from 1931 to 1944, and the Earl of Drogheda from 1946 until his death in 1957.

The deputy-Chairmen of Committees correspond, in a way, to the members of the chairmen's panel in the House of Commons. They are appointed at the beginning of each session, and are not expected to renounce ordinary partisan activity. Lord Mersey was for some years, until 1949, simultaneously a deputy-chairman and the Liberal Chief Whip. Of the eleven peers appointed as deputy-chairmen for the session of 1955–6, five were Conservatives, three Labour and three Liberals.

The work of planning the debates, being essentially 'political' in character, is performed mainly by the Leaders of the House and of the Opposition, together with the Whips. The Whips in the House of Lords, unlike those in the House of Commons, also act as party spokesmen in debates, and for this reason it seems appropriate to discuss their work, not here, but in the chapter dealing with the relations between the House and the Government.

The House of Lords has its permanent staff under the Clerk of the Parliaments, whose title indicates the priority of the Lords over the

[1] Cf. O. C. Williams, *History of Private Bill Procedure* (H.M.S.O., 1948), vol. i, pp. 56, 103, etc.

Commons in the historical development of Parliament. It appears that in the time of Edward I the official whose first task was to act as clerk to the permanent council also performed similar duties in relation to meetings of Parliament. The surviving Rolls of Parliament date back to the year 1290, when Gilbert of Rothbury was appointed; the title 'Clerk of the Parliaments' was instituted in 1510, and still survives. It is also in 1510 that the printed series of Lords Journals begins, though fragments of earlier journals still survive.

In modern times the arrangement of business has come to require the services of a fairly large expert professional body of officers of the House. The fact that the business of the House can proceed so smoothly with so little need for exact definitions indicates the value of their services.

Chapter VI

THE REPRESENTATION OF THE GOVERNMENT IN THE HOUSE OF LORDS

IN the House of Lords as in the Commons, the Government and Opposition Front Benches face one another across the Table, and the front-bench spokesmen play an important and recognized part in the proceedings. A debate on the second reading of an important bill is opened and closed by front-bench speakers, who speak on behalf of the Government and of the official Opposition, whose views they express rather than their own. When a motion is moved from the floor of the House, a reply from the Government Front Bench is expected. Government spokesmen are provided with departmental briefs. During a debate civil servants from the department concerned sit in the box, close to the Government benches, where they may be discreetly consulted, generally through an intermediary, by the peer who is to reply to the debate on the Government's behalf.

The British conception of parliamentary debate presupposes a special kind of relationship between ministers, members of the Opposition Front Bench, and ordinary members in all debates except those of interest entirely to private members. Even on subjects which are outside the direct responsibility of the Government it is normally expected that a minister or other office-holder should state the Government's point of view. It is therefore necessary for the Government to have its representatives to speak on its behalf in the House of Lords.

The task of securing the proper representation of the Government in the House of Lords is a somewhat complicated one. In most European countries where there are two Houses of the Legislature, all ministers are entitled to speak in either House.[1] In Britain on the

---

[1] In some countries it is quite common for ministers to be appointed who are not members of the Legislature at all. In France, indeed, because of the French

other hand ministers continue to be ordinary members of the House of Parliament to which they belong. It has often been proposed that ministers should be permitted to speak in either House, but there are two principal objections to such a proposal, one theoretical and the other practical. The theoretical objection is that such an innovation would fundamentally alter the status of ministers within their Houses of Parliament; the practical argument is that ministers are already overburdened with work. If they were made liable to be called upon to speak in either House the burden on them would, it is said, be almost intolerable.[1]

By now convention has come to require that every ministry should have a representative to speak for it in the House of Commons. With the major departments, this representative must normally be the Minister himself; with a ministry of secondary importance, or which spends little public money, it may be enough to have a Parliamentary Secretary or Under-Secretary of State in the House of Commons.

We do not need to go very far back in history to find precedents for Prime Ministers and Foreign Secretaries in the House of Lords. Indeed Lord Halifax sat in the House of Lords while Foreign Secretary as recently as 1937–40. The changed circumstances of modern times, however, have come to require the presence of the heads of the chief departments in the Commons. With all the more important ministries, notably the Home Office, Exchequer, Board of Trade, Foreign Office, Ministry of Labour and some others, it would by now be almost inconceivable for the Minister not to sit in the Commons. This rule has been established gradually, and under the influence of events. In 1939 Mr. Chamberlain gave the office of Minister of Information to a peer, but before long was forced, by the volume of complaint in the Commons, to ask the Minister to resign, and to appoint a member of the House of Commons in his place.[2] By now, as a result of these developments, it is impossible for most of the main Departments of State to be represented in the Lords by their chiefs; the upper House can only have, at best, departmental assistants from such ministries.

In this matter there have been great changes of opinion during the

conception of the separation of powers, the Government can be regarded as having a separate existence from the two Houses of the Legislature. This is clearly expressed by the fact that no minister in France can be a member either of any standing committee or of the organizational leadership of any party in either House.

[1] E.g. Lord Darling's motion of 24th July 1929 (Lords Debs., vol. 75, cols. 226–70). The Government put the Whips on against the motion, which was defeated by 43 votes to 31. A number of other not very convincing objections were framed in the debate.

[2] Cf. Lord Macmillan, *A Man of Law's Tale*, Macmillan, 1952, p. 178.

present century. Sir Sidney Low, writing fifty years ago, quoted with approval Balfour's dictum that the Foreign Secretary could not perform the functions of his office adequately if he were in the House of Commons—unless he neglected his duties in that House.[1] Even today it is not uncommon to hear expressions of a wish that the Foreign Secretary could escape from the House of Commons. Lord Strang, after many years of experience at the Foreign Office down to 1954, wrote in 1956: 'If the Foreign Secretary could be in the Lords it would certainly be an advantage, though in modern conditions this is perhaps asking the impossible.'[2]

If the House of Lords were of equal status with the House of Commons we might expect to find some arrangement whereby if a minister sat in the Commons, his deputy, or at least one of his deputies, would be in the Lords; and contrariwise that if the minister were in the Lords his deputy would be in the Commons. There would however be several inconveniences to such an arrangement. With the chief ministries it would scarcely be possible for the minister to deal with his work in the Commons without a deputy there, and although several ministers have two or even three deputies each, some limit must be set to the number of ministerial posts. Furthermore, it is doubtful whether there would be enough peers available to provide each department with its own representative in the Lords. Most of the posts of office-holders in the Lords would require to be junior posts, and the number of peers on the Government side, even when a Conservative Government is in power, who would be prepared to serve as junior ministers is not large enough to supply the necessary 30 or 40 people.

As long ago as 1868 'any young Liberal peer who gave any indication of ability was warmly welcomed and almost certain to secure' a minor government post.[3] The fifth Marquess of Lansdowne was given a government post at the age of 23, as soon as he had left Oxford. In 1886 Lord Houghton (later Lord Crewe) was made a Lord in Waiting within a few months of succeeding to a peerage at the age of 28. It has often been remarked that acceptance of a minor government appointment, carrying a salary of £1,200 or £1,500 a year, involves great financial sacrifice for a man who has been earning more than that amount in his business or profession, and who is

[1] *The Governance of England*, 1904, p. 252.
[2] Lord Strang, *Home and Abroad* (André Deutsch, 1956), p. 300. Lord Strang remarks that the Foreign Secretary sat in the Lords from 1868 to 1905, and that 'when Sir Edward Grey became Foreign Secretary in 1905, there was some doubt whether he could combine the departmental duties with the parliamentary duties'. Yet it would probably be true to say that today both sides of the Foreign Secretary's duties are more arduous than in 1905.
[3] Lord Newton, *Lord Lansdowne* (Macmillan, 1929), p. 13.

compelled to resign his directorships and keep away from the television cameras.[1] A member of the House of Commons may make the sacrifice gladly for the sake of the prospects of promotion; a peer with an established professional or commercial position may find the sacrifice less attractive. In modern conditions a government has to rely on the services of peers who are prepared to forgo earnings outside Parliament, and who demand little by way of recompense. (They cannot even be rewarded with peerages.) So the Lords have to be content with the situation in which many ministries are unrepresented in their House.

Convention, or at any rate practice, requires that there should be representatives of the Foreign Office and Ministry of Agriculture in the upper House. In 1936 the Ministry of Agriculture was for a time unrepresented in the House of Lords, and Lord Strachie proposed a motion, 'that in the opinion of this House it is to be deprecated that neither the Minister nor the Parliamentary Secretary of the Ministry of Agriculture is a member of the House, whereby the agricultural interest is injuriously affected'. There was much complaint in various parts of the House, and in response the Government soon appointed a peer as Parliamentary Secretary to the Ministry of Agriculture.[2] At about the same time there was a similar complaint in relation to the Foreign Office.[3]

In recent years it has been usual for the House of Lords to include about fifteen office-holders, including the Household officers who act both as Whips and as spokesmen on behalf of the Government.[4] There are usually three or four members of the Cabinet who sit in the House of Lords, sometimes more,[5] and usually two or three other

[1] In July 1957, however, junior ministers' salaries were increased.

[2] Lords Debs., 22nd July 1936, vol. 102, cols. 142–56. The office of Parliamentary Secretary to the Ministry of Agriculture had originally been established in 1912, in response to demands that that Ministry should be represented in each House. By 1936, as Lord Halifax said, the Minister needed to have a deputy in the Commons, so the establishment of a second parliamentary secretaryship was the only solution.   [3] Lords Debs., 27th July 1936, vol. 102, cols. 269–76.

[4] The offices of the Government Whips are allied, rather anachronistically perhaps, with salaried offices connected with the Royal Household. The Chief Whip on the Government side holds office as Captain of the Honourable Corps of the Gentlemen-at-Arms, and his deputy is the Captain of the Yeomen of the Guard. (It is incidentally only the captains of these bodies that hold strictly political appointments. The ordinary members receive their membership for quite other reasons.) Similarly the other Government Whips hold office in the Royal Household, as (political) Lords in Waiting.

[5] In 1952, when Mr. Churchill's Cabinet included seven peers, the Opposition complained that the proportion of peers was excessive. Their main strictures were, however, directed not against the number of peers in the Cabinet, but against the fact that several of the peers, the 'overlords', had rather obscurely-defined responsibilities for co-ordinating the work of groups of ministries.

ministers without seats in the Cabinet. Then there are generally a few Under-Secretaries of State or Parliamentary Secretaries to Departments, and in addition to these there are the three political Lords in Waiting. All these office-holders receive salaries and share in the collective responsibility of the Government. Normally they all belong to the Party in power, but there have been exceptions. In 1951 and 1952 Sir Winston Churchill gave office to some non-party peers from choice; in 1924 Mr. Ramsay MacDonald did so from necessity, because the Labour Government was almost unrepresented in the upper House. It should be noticed, though, that Sir Winston Churchill's non-party peers took little part in the proceedings of the House.

The functions of the Leader of the House and of the Whips are concerned mainly with the organization of business so as to satisfy the demands of the Government, the Opposition and private members. For the reasons set out in Chapter V, above, their task is considerably easier than that of the equivalent 'usual channels' in the House of Commons. The Whips may sometimes be concerned with trying to secure a vote favourable to the Government, particularly the Conservative Whips when their Party is in office. Under a Labour Government almost any division on party lines can be expected to go against the ministry, so it is not of very great importance to the Labour minister how many Labour peers vote on the Government side. But a Conservative administration does not take defeat in the Lords so lightly, and may on occasion be afraid of rebellion from among its own back-benchers which may cause it, to say the least, a certain amount of embarrassment.

The peers who hold office as government Whips, unlike their opposite numbers in the House of Commons, act when necessary as government spokesmen in debate. The difference in practice between the two Houses in this respect appears to have a twofold foundation. In the Commons the duties of the Whips as such, in acting as channels of communication between the Parties and between leaders and back-benchers, and in attending to their organizational work, besides being extensive and time-consuming, are of such a character as to set the Whips somewhat apart from the ordinary members. In the Lords, just because there is so much less in the way of 'organizational' work, there are not the same grounds for setting the Whips apart. Secondly, in the Commons each Department has its own representative, and there is no need for non-departmental government spokesmen. In the Lords on the other hand, the Government needs to have some peers available to speak for departments which are unrepresented in the House. The Lords in Waiting are handy to fill in the gaps, and are extensively used for that purpose. This part of their work is more important than their work as Whips, which is often analogous rather than to that of parliamentary private secretaries in the Commons. Sometimes indeed they are not regarded as Whips at all.

Some continuity in the representation of departments is clearly desirable, and every department has one peer allocated to it as a spokesman in the House; each of the more important departments has a peer of ministerial rank and an assistant, who may be a Lord in Waiting or a departmental Under-Secretary of State or Parliamentary Secretary. Under this system it can usually be expected that each of the Lords in Waiting will be a spokesman for three or four or even five departments; in some cases a great part of the burden falls on the 'assistant' rather than the senior minister who is principally responsible.

A peer who is a spokesman in the House for a particular department has no status in the department, no part in its administrative working, no personal responsibility for its actions; he merely speaks on its behalf within the limit of the instructions which he has received. An attempt is sometimes made, however, to give a peer some sense of belonging to a department for which he speaks in the House. He may be given a room there, and will very probably be invited to attend meetings at which departmental policy is discussed, in order that he may gain some insight into the general workings, beyond the mere receipt of instructions or 'briefs' related to particular topics which are about to be raised in the House.

The allocation of duties is generally not very rigid, and there is often some overlapping between the functions of the office-holders in the House of Lords. The Lord Chancellor often acts as the leading government spokesman in important debates, but in addition he generally speaks on the Government's behalf on any matter raising a legal issue, and his high office does not prevent him from dealing with relatively minor committee points. The task of speaking for unrepresented ministries is not performed only by the non-departmental office-holders. Heads of administrative departments and Parliamentary Secretaries may also have to speak for ministries other than their own. When Lord Hall was First Lord of the Admiralty in the Labour Government he also spoke for other departments, in particular the Colonial Office. In the session 1947–8 he spoke in committee on the following subjects: the independence of Ceylon, cinematograph films, the development of inventions, employment and training, factories, the Gas Bill, mandated and trust territories, the Monopolies (Enquiry and Control) Bill, the Parliament Bill, the Pensions Bill and a bill dealing with the Royal Marines. Lord Chorley, a Lord in Waiting, spoke on the second reading of four bills and took part in the committee stage of four, including the Criminal

THE REPRESENTATION OF THE GOVERNMENT

Justice Bill, on which, being a lawyer, he had a good deal to do. On the Gas Bill he concentrated particularly on points which had to do with coal and petrol.

On a long and complicated bill the task of representing the Government may sometimes be distributed among a rather large number of ministers; thus on the Transport Bill of 1946-7 no less than seven office-holders spoke for the Government in committee. They were Lord Addison, Secretary for the Dominions and Leader of the House; Lord Nathan, Minister of Civil Aviation; the Lord Chancellor; the Government Chief Whip and the three Lords in Waiting. In addition, Lord Pakenham, Chancellor of the Duchy of Lancaster, made a long speech on the second reading.

Sometimes one or two of the ministers in the House of Lords are kept free of routine work in the House, in order that they may be able to attend to their work outside. Some of Sir W. Churchill's 'overlords' made little contribution to debate. In the session of 1952-3 Lord Cherwell spoke on only four occasions; Lord Leathers, the Minister for the co-ordination of Transport, Fuel and Power, was called upon to speak rarely, and never outside his field. On the bill denationalizing road haulage, although it apparently was a matter within his field, he spoke only on the second and third readings and on the Commons amendments, but not on the committee stage. (Most of the work of dealing with committee points on the 1953 Transport Bill was done by the Earl of Selkirk, then a Lord in Waiting, and by Lord Swinton, then Chancellor of the Duchy of Lancaster.) When Lord Alexander of Tunis was Minister of Defence he had to speak fairly frequently on defence questions, but was never required to deal with other matters.

Sir Winston Churchill seems to have had a deliberate intention of making the House of Lords a home for a few ministers who ought, while being members of Parliament, to be shielded as far as possible from parliamentary duties. His institution of the office of Minister of State for Scotland is a good illustration of this policy. This office was created in order that its holder might spend much of his time in Scotland, and its holder has until now always been a peer. When he is available in London the Minister of State deals with Scottish matters in the House of Lords, but no holder of the office has yet said much in debates on other questions. In the session of 1952-3 the Earl of Home looked after two Scottish bills and two Statutory Instruments, dealt with a Scottish question arising on the Transport Bill, and answered three questions on Scottish matters. Otherwise he did not speak in the Lords in that session. When Lord Home was not available, Scottish questions were generally dealt with by Lord Selkirk, a Lord in Waiting.

THE REPRESENTATION OF THE GOVERNMENT

Some peers holding departmental offices may keep to their own subjects; in the session of 1952–3, for example, Lord De L'Isle and Dudley, Secretary of State for Air, spoke only on Air Force matters. Lord Carrington, Parliamentary Secretary to the Ministry of Agriculture, dealt only with matters concerning his department (of which there were many), and the Earl of Munster, Under-Secretary of State at the Colonial Office, went outside the scope of his department only to deal with the arrangements for the Coronation.

With some of the office-holding peers keeping strictly to their own fields, the peers who look after the general interests of the Government have still, since 1951, had to cover wide varieties of topics. The fact that much of the work of speaking for the Government has to be entrusted in the House of Lords to peers who do not belong to the department concerned does cause some complications with regard to the whole organization of governmental responsibility. When a peer who is not inside a department is to be required to represent it for the committee stage of a complicated bill, the task of coaching him in order that he may deal with the amendments involves a good deal of work both for the peer concerned and for the civil servants who have to provide him with his arguments. It is almost inevitable that a peer in such a position must stick rather closely to his brief, and it is not easy for him to make concessions on his own authority. He must constantly say, 'I must consult my right Honourable friend.'

Some rather amusing incidents have been caused by the contributions of non-departmental office-holders to the proceedings in the Lords. On a day not long since a government spokesman, attempting to deal with an interruption, was seen feverishly but silently flipping through his papers in an unsuccessful search for the answer, then sending a colleague off to the civil servants in the box to ask for help, and finally, after speaking of other matters for a time, looking at the piece of paper sent up by the officials and muttering, for all present to hear, 'I can't understand what the devil it means.' There is one story, probably apocryphal, of a Minister who was following his brief so closely that, having read out what the civil servant had written on the paper for him to read, he continued with an *obiter dictum*, 'this argument is a pretty poor one I am afraid, but it should be good enough for the Lords'. It is by no means unknown for a government spokesman to get his papers mixed up, and to read out the reply relating to the wrong amendment. Recently a prominent Labour peer, in comforting a Conservative minister who had made this mistake, admitted that he had done the same thing himself when he had been in office—but on that occasion nobody had noticed.

On the whole ministers and other office-holders with seats in the House of Lords seem to be rather more assiduous in their attendance at debates than do ministers in the Commons, particularly at times when the Government has a good majority in the Commons. During the years 1945–50, when the Labour Government had a majority of about two to one in the Commons, the number of ministers voting in the divisions taking place in the lower House was often rather small, and was rarely as many as half of all office-holders. In the Lords, on the other hand, most of the peers who held office were present at nearly every division.

Ministers who sit in the Lords are subject, in the same way as are ministers in the Commons, to the rule of collective responsibility. They must always act together and certainly never oppose each other on any matter for which the Government is taking responsibility. In recent years, in both Houses of Parliament, the rule seems to have become almost all-embracing; ministers have hardly ever voted against each other in any circumstances whatever. If we go back twenty or thirty years, however, instances of cross-voting among ministers were much less infrequent, particularly in the Lords. In 1922 the members of the Government who were in the House of Lords were almost equally divided over the Exportation of Horses Bill, and again over a proposal to remove restrictions on the import of cattle. In 1927 ministers voted on different sides on the Prayer Book measure, and on two private members' bills, one dealing with betting, and one which provided for the protection of performing animals.

In the middle 1930s there were several cases of cross-voting among office holders in the Lords over questions concerning the reform of the House. On Lord Rockley's Life Peers Bill of 1935 (to provide that five life peers should be created each year), Lord Rochester, the Paymaster-General, who was a member of the MacDonaldite group, voted with the minority of 14, against the majority which included other members of the Government. In 1934, however, on Lord Salisbury's bill for the reform of the Lords, although the number voting was very large (171–82), all the ministers abstained.[1] In 1935 ministers voted on opposite sides on a private member's bill for the abolition of gin-traps for the catching of rabbits, and in 1938 on one to forbid the docking and nicking of horses.

From 1938 to 1956 there was no instance of cross-voting on any matter whatever, even in 'free votes', by ministers in the House of Lords. This development in the upper House corresponds with an almost similar development in the Commons.[2]

It is unusual for a minister or other office-holder to speak in a

[1] Lords Debs., 10th May 1934, vol. 92, col. 294.
[2] Cf. P. A. Bromhead, 'Free Votes in the House of Commons,' in *Durham University Journal*, 1953, pp. 105 ff.

personal capacity, and not as a government spokesman. Two exceptions may serve to illustrate the rule. In 1928 Lord Desborough, Captain of the Yeoman of the Guard, proposed the second reading of a private member's bill, which had already been passed by the Commons, to fix the date of Easter. Leave had been given to him to take charge of the bill in his personal capacity, 'owing to the interest which he had taken for some years' in this subject. He found it necessary, therefore, to begin by explaining his position.[1] In 1927 Lord Bledisloe, the Parliamentary Secretary to the Minister of Agriculture, gave his own private opinion on an amendment (dealing with farm cart lights), 'thanks to the dispensation which his noble colleague had permitted even to members of the Government'. On this occasion, however, Lord Bledisloe's views coincided with those of the official front bench.[2]

Similar considerations apply with regard to the Opposition Front Bench. In addition to the recognized Leader of the Opposition[3] (who still receives no salary for his office), a number of peers act as official Opposition spokesmen, and their position has tended to become more clearly defined in recent years. The division of functions among the Opposition Front Bench peers corresponds closely with that among the office-holders, except that with the Opposition spokesmen there tends to be less specialization than with the ministers. In the session of 1952–3 the Earl of Listowel, who had been Parliamentary Secretary for Agriculture when his Party was in power, looked after the Labour interest in agricultural debates, and Lord Henderson, a former Foreign Office spokesman, concentrated on foreign affairs. Lord Lucas of Chilworth took charge of a great many amendments to the Transport Bill, but also spoke on other matters quite unrelated to transport. On the Transport Bill itself, however, seven other members of the Opposition Front Bench made their contributions. Lord Jowitt's contributions as Leader of the Opposition were too varied for classification or analysis. He spoke on all the chief bills of the session, and also on an immense number of other subjects, large and small—many of them far too small to have demanded the attention of an Opposition leader of his standing in the Commons. Among these were two animal-protection bills, the problem of American competition in the export of motor-cars to Nigeria, and a bill to confirm the Colchester St. Mary Magdalene Hospital Charity Scheme.

[1] Lords Debs., 2nd July 1928, vol. 71, col. 794.
[2] Ibid., 20th December 1927, vol. 69, col. 1199.
[3] When the Labour Party is in opposition, the Labour peers elect their leader and deputy-leader. (Cf. Herbert Morrison, *Government and Parliament*, Oxford U.P., 1954, p. 134.)

THE REPRESENTATION OF THE GOVERNMENT

It is important to notice that peers on the Opposition Front Bench are even now much more inclined to ask questions, and so on, in their capacity as private members than are their colleagues in the House of Commons.[1]

In conclusion it may be said that, although membership of the House of Lords precludes a man from the highest offices in the state, a politician who is active and forward in the counsels of his Party has more scope for speaking on a wide variety of subjects if he is in the Lords than if he is in the Commons. As the House of Lords has come to interest itself in a greater variety of questions, so the work of the Party leaders in the House has become more varied, being always distributed among a relatively small number of peers.

[1] Cf. below, p. 226.

Chapter VII
PARTY ORGANIZATION AND DISCIPLINE IN THE HOUSE OF LORDS

ITS freedom from the domination of the two great rival party machines is often cited as one of the great virtues of the unreformed House of Lords. Since the disappearance of the last of the small tribe of Independent Members in 1950 the House of Commons has consisted almost entirely of loyal supporters of the two major Parties; even the Liberals in the Commons have dwindled until they are a tiny minority. A peer, on the other hand, can sit as an Independent without danger of losing his seat, and if he belongs to a party he can disobey the Whips with impunity.

In *Vacher's Parliamentary Companion* for August 1955, 496 peers are described as Conservatives or Unionists, 11 as National Liberals,[1] 42 as Liberals, 55 as Labour, and 6 as 'Independent'. But apart from these there are 236 non-party peers,[2] including the two Archbishops and 24 bishops, the Law Lords and the Royal dukes (whom convention prevents from participating in ordinary debates). Many of the non-party peers are peers of first creation. Most ennobled public servants, military or civil, think it fitting that they should not identify themselves with any political Party, and rather similar considerations apply to the industrialists and other men of distinction outside the field of politics—though this was less true thirty years ago than now. It is probably safe to assume that the inclinations of most of these 'non-party' peers are much nearer to the Conservative than to the

---

[1] For the purpose of this study Unionists, National Liberals, etc., are counted as Conservatives.

[2] The term 'non-party' should be applied to these peers with appropriate reservations. It would strictly be more accurate to call them 'peers about whose party allegiance no information is given in the reference books'.

Labour Party. The Liberal Party, with a total of about 40 peers, has a much bigger representation in the Lords than in the Commons. Of the peers who attend fairly regularly (the first two classes of Chapter III, above), one-eighth are Liberals or members of no Party.

Thus while the House of Commons consists almost entirely of members of two large rival armies, the House of Lords has a substantial element of non-party peers. Although it is possible to complain against the House of Lords on the ground that it is dominated by a Conservative majority, its membership is far more diversified than is that of the House of Commons. Furthermore, there are grounds for arguing that the dominant position of the Conservative Party in the House encourages an attitude of independence among the peers.[1] It is usually possible for a group of Conservative peers to oppose their own front bench without thereby helping the Labour Party.

Each of the two main Parties in the House has its Chief Whip and Assistant Whips. They send out party notices (or 'whips') about forthcoming business to those peers who have indicated that they wish to receive them. The Whips try to ensure a reasonable turnout of members of their Parties when divisions take place, but they can apply no sanctions; their only weapon is persuasion.

One part of the work of the Whips as party organizers is their task of encouraging peers of their own Parties to speak in forthcoming debates. The Opposition Whips, in particular, have to try to ensure that their Party's point of view is adequately represented in debate; when the Conservative Whips were careless in this regard at the second reading debate on the Plural Voting Bill of 1906, and the debate was over in an hour and a half, much public resentment was caused by the summary rejection of this important measure.[2]

During the present century, whenever Labour or Liberal governments have been in power, Conservative peers have tended to decide in concert, together with the Conservative leadership in the Commons, on the extent to which they will use their powers. Little formal machinery has, however, been established for the sake of securing united action. As long ago as 5th April 1906, when the new Liberal Government was bringing its first controversial measures before

---

[1] In the late 1920s, when Lord Inchcape was asked if he would like to receive the Conservative Whip, he replied that he would, provided that he could be left free to vote for his free trade principles. Lord Plymouth told him: 'There are several other peers who sit on our side who are in exactly the same position, and I am sure no one would consider this a bar to receiving our Whip' (Hector Bolitho, *Lord Inchcape* (John Murray, 1936), p. 223).

[2] Cf. Lord Newton, *Lord Lansdowne* (Macmillan, 1929), p. 358. In the conditions of more recent years the habit of prior discussion in party groups and committees has helped to secure adequate participation in debate.

Parliament, Lord Lansdowne wrote a memorandum suggesting that 'an endeavour should be made to set up some machinery for establishing closer contact between the Opposition Front Benches in the two Houses of Parliament'. He suggested that a committee of four or five of the leading Conservatives in each House should meet once a week. Even in the conditions of 1906 Lord Lansdowne's suggestion was not adopted; Mr. Balfour thought that a meeting of this kind would duplicate the work of the Shadow Cabinet. In 1929 Lord Newton wrote, 'It is a singular fact that such co-operation, though manifestly essential, is still lamentably lacking.'[1]

Inevitably the life of the Parties within the House has tended to become more closely organized in recent years. Before a debate the peers of a particular Party who are interested in its subject-matter will probably wish to hold a preliminary discussion among themselves, in order to make plans in concert beforehand about their approach to the subject. Among the Conservatives the organization known as the Independent Unionist Peers corresponds with the 1922 Committee in the House of Commons. It does some of its work through committees, each of which has its own chairman. The proceedings of these groups of peers, whether formally constituted or not, in relation to forthcoming debates, are private and cannot here be discussed or evaluated in detail, but it must be assumed that they have some importance. If there are disagreements within a Party, they may sometimes be settled by private deliberation, rather than on the floor of the House. It would be rash to generalize too far about the rôle of committees and groups, but it would probably be fair to say that they have not developed enough power or influence to decrease the effectiveness of open debate. On balance, their effect on the debates in the House, by cutting out duplication of arguments and settling minor points through informal discussion, is probably constructive and useful rather than otherwise.

The Conservative peers, as a body, have some part to play in the affairs of the national organization of their Party. Together with the Conservative members of the House of Commons, the prospective parliamentary candidates and the members of the Executive Committee of the National Union they share in the 'election' of a new Leader of the Party. The Conservative peers select two of the fourteen members of the Party's Advisory Committee on Policy and one member of the Consultative Committee on Party Finance.[2]

In 1906–9 the Conservative and Unionist peers generally followed their leaders in deciding whether or not to defeat the Government.

[1] Lord Newton, *Lord Lansdowne*, op cit., p. 353.
[2] Cf. R. T. Mackenzie, *British Political Parties* (Heinemann, 1955), pp. 22, 211 and 213.

PARTY ORGANIZATION AND DISCIPLINE

When Lord Lansdowne (acting in close liaison with Mr. Balfour) advised discretion, his advice was, for the most part, followed. In 1906 the Conservative peers were convinced by his argument that the highly controversial Trade Disputes Bill was not a favourable ground for conflict between the two Houses; the Bill was allowed to pass, unamended, without a division. On the Education Bill, on the other hand, the Conservative peers voted faithfully for the destructive amendments which their leaders supported, though two Conservatives voted with the Government against insisting on the Lords' amendments.

The story of the struggles among the Conservative peers over the Parliament Bill in 1911 has often been told; in this case the diehards, who would not accept Lord Lansdowne's advice to allow the Bill to pass, and so to save the House from being flooded with Liberal creations, were led by peers of very high standing in the Party. In the final division the 114 'Halsburyites' vastly outnumbered the 37 Conservatives who followed the advice of Lord Lansdowne.[1]

In 1945–51 the Conservative peers, with hardly ever an exception, followed the advice of their leaders, among whom the Marquess of Salisbury was very prominent.

Two instances are sometimes cited in which votes on important questions were influenced by speeches made in open debate, rather than by the advice or instructions of party leaders. It is said that in 1945 many Conservative peers came down to the House prepared to vote against the Labour Government's financial arrangements with the United States, but that they were dissuaded from doing so by the speech of Lord Keynes; in fact only three Conservatives went into the lobby against the Government, and 23 in support. Many Conservatives abstained. Again, a speech by Lord Halifax in 1947 is said to have influenced some peers who had intended to vote against the Government's decision to withdraw British Forces from India by a certain date; in the event no division was called.[2]

We can learn much about the pattern of party behaviour in the House of Lords from a detailed study of the divisions which have been held in the House over the past generation or so (cf. Figure 2). There might be some value in drawing up some kind of index of cohesion of the members of each of the parties by taking the figures of voting on both sides in all divisions over a period of say forty years, and finding out how many divisions during each period produced cross-voting among the members of each Party, and how great was the extent of the cross-voting. Such figures must be treated with

---

[1] Cf. Roy Jenkins, *Mr. Balfour's Poodle* (Heinemann, 1954), p. 183, etc.

[2] Cf. Lord Pethick-Lawrence in *The Future of the House of Lords* (Hansard Society, 1954), p. 74.

PARTY ORGANIZATION AND DISCIPLINE

great caution, however; the character of the divisions in the House of Lords is rather different today from what it was in the 1920s and 1930s. The number of divisions has become smaller; nowadays divisions rarely take place except on questions which involve cleavages of opinion between the two major Parties.

Discipline among Conservative peers has been incomparably

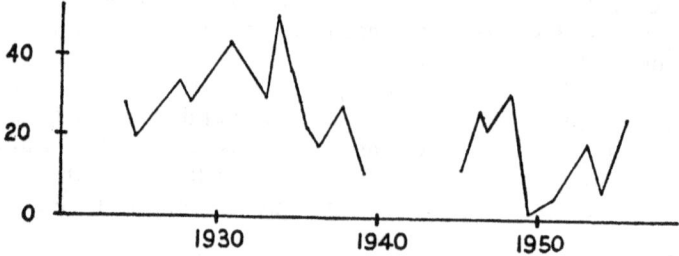

Figure 1.—Number of divisions per session, 1924–56.

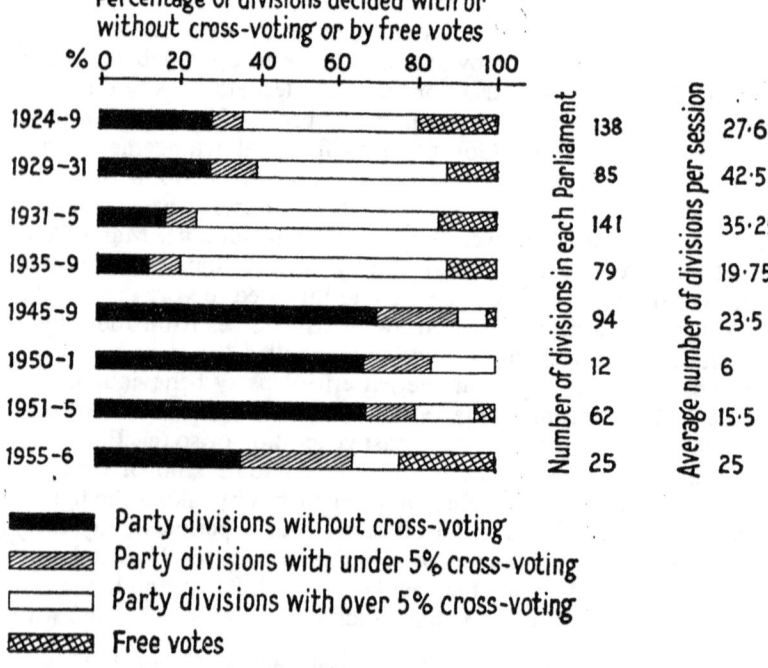

Figure 2.—Party solidarity and cross-voting in peacetime divisions in each Parliament, 1924–56 (Conservative and Labour peers only).

better observed in recent years than it was twenty or thirty years ago. In the 1920s and 1930s there were few divisions in which all the Conservative peers voted together; in recent years cross-voting has been as rare as it was usual before 1939.

It is not only that the number of Conservative peers voting against their leaders has declined. Thirty years ago many divisions took place at the instigation of Conservative rebels, who were often numerous enough to put Conservative governments in danger of defeat. When Conservative governments did in fact suffer defeat, it was usually at the hands of their own right wing. Sir Ivor Jennings wrote in 1939, on the basis of the experience of the previous twenty years, 'the House of Lords is always a little more to the right than a Conservative government'.[1] Mr. Baldwin's second administration was defeated eight times in the Lords in 1925-9, and the National Government seventeen times in 1931-9.

Whenever a Conservative government has been faced with a dangerously large number of rebels on its own back benches it has, naturally enough, worked hard to ensure the largest possible attendance of loyal supporters, and it can be assumed that the total numbers voting on such occasions have been swollen by the activities of the Government Whips. Examples are provided by the votes on India in 1934 and 1935, on the coal industry in 1938 and on independent television in 1954.

A detailed study of the voting in the House of Lords in the 1920s and 1930s suggests that in this period the Conservative peers had so little to fear from the small and divided Opposition that the distinction between party votes and free votes was not always clear. Complete observance of party discipline was very rare.

During the session of 1924-5, the first session of Mr. Baldwin's second Government, out of 18 divisions there was only one, on a Labour amendment to the Rating and Valuation Bill, in which there was no cross-voting among the Conservative peers. In each of two other divisions there was only one Conservative rebel, but in all the rest several Conservative peers voted against the main body of the Party. On an amendment to the Government of India (Civil Services) Bill 18 Conservative peers voted against the Government, as compared with 45 with it. Among the Liberal peers, too, cross-voting was very usual.

The session of 1926 produced rather more divisions on party lines. In some of these, notably two on the Coal Mines Bill, Conservatives voted solidly with the Government. On the Government's Electricity Supply Bill, however, there were four divisions which produced large hostile Conservative votes, though not large enough to defeat the

[1] Sir W. Ivor Jennings, *Parliament*, op. cit., p. 378.

Government. Much the same thing happened on the Mining Industry Bill, on which a former Government Chief Whip twice voted with the Conservative rebels, together with the Labour and Liberal peers. On the Lead Paint (Protection against Poisoning) Bill, several Conservative peers voted in favour of a Labour new clause which proposed to strengthen the Bill by forbidding the use of lead paint in painting the inside of buildings.

The Government suffered two defeats at the hands of disaffected Conservative peers in the session of 1926. When Lord Oranmore and Browne proposed that a select committee should be set up to enquire into Irish land purchase, his motion was carried, against the Government's wishes, by 35 votes to 33. In the next session the Government suffered another defeat on the same subject at the hands of a group of Conservative dissentients, this time by 54 votes to 36. The Government was again defeated over a clause in its Landlord and Tenant Bill, on which a majority of 35 peers, mainly Conservative rebels, outnumbered the 29 who followed the Whips. On an amendment to the same Bill there was a tie, and the Government was saved from defeat only by the Lord Chancellor's casting vote.

The intensely controversial Trade Disputes Bill of 1927 produced solid party votes, on both sides of the House, on the modern pattern, not only on the second and third readings, but also on seven amendments in committee and on report. Party discipline was also solid in the 1927 session on two matters of detail in the Aliens Restriction Bill, on an agricultural question and on a Liberal motion condemning the Government for extravagant military expenditure. Many Conservative peers voted against their Whips, however, on a matter of detail in a Nursing Homes (Registration) Bill.

In 1928 the Government was actually defeated (by 63 votes to 55) on the second reading of its own Rabbits Bill, which had already passed the House of Commons.[1] When the Government brought to a conclusion a century of evolution of the franchise, by bringing in its bill to give the vote to women of over 21 years of age, 21 Conservatives voted in the minority against the second reading. Lord Newton's amendment, proposing that the right to vote should be given to both men and women at the age of 25 only, was defeated

---

[1] Lords Debs., 10th July 1928, vol. 71, col. 900. The Rabbits Bill sought to revive the right which was enjoyed by an occupier of land (under cancelled enactments) to be protected from the depredations of his neighbour's rabbits. The Bill had passed its second and third reading stages in the Commons without a division. The Government, in response to many demands from private members, had already brought the Bill forward, in a different form, in the previous session. On that occasion it was introduced as a Lords Bill, and the Lords sent it to a select committee, which reported adversely. The Government had made changes in the meantime, but the majority in the Lords was still not satisfied.

by the moderately large majority of 87 to 41, the 41 being mainly Conservatives.[1]

During Mr. Ramsay MacDonald's two Labour administrations the voting in the Lords was without any regular pattern. The official Conservative Opposition, though it was clearly strong enough to defeat the Government at every turn, preferred, for obvious reasons, not to use its numerical superiority too destructively. There were 53 Government defeats (out of 86 divisions), but few solid votes of Conservative peers.

After 1931 some elements among the Conservative peers felt justified in voting against the National Government's more 'progressive' proposals. On many topics a fairly regular pattern of voting emerged, with the Government opposed in the division lobbies by right-wing Conservative peers rather than by the official Opposition. On the Children and Young Persons Bills of 1932 it was the right-wing Conservatives who contrived to defeat the Government on three important committee points. In a division on Indian policy the Government was victorious by 106 votes to 58, with the large anti-Government minority consisting almost entirely of Conservative peers. On the second reading of the Government of India Bill in 1935, 55 peers, nearly all Conservatives, voted for Lord Lloyd's amendment, but 236 supported the Government. Six of the eight divisions in committee took place at the instigation of dissatisfied right-wing Conservatives. On the Town and Country Planning Bill there were many instances of substantial revolts by Conservatives against the Government's proposals. In 1938 the Government suffered defeats, all on amendments concerning quotas, on the Cinematograph Films Bill. Each time the hostile majority, in a rather thinly-attended House, consisted mainly of Government supporters, together with a few Liberal and Labour peers. In the Commons the Government secured the rejection of the disputed amendments, and at the next stage in the Lords contrived to bring along enough tame Government supporters to produce a Government majority of 95 to 21 against insisting on the Lords amendments. Even at this stage, however, 16 of the 21 votes against the Government were cast by Government supporters. Seven of these had not voted in the earlier divisions.

The most important breaches of Conservative discipline in this period were on the Coal Industry Bill of 1938. On a series of right-wing amendments, almost all of them concerned with the protection of property-owning interests, the Government was opposed by large but varying numbers of Conservative peers, and although it secured the rejection of some amendments, it also suffered defeat on several

[1] Lords Debs., 12th June 1928, vol. 71, col. 444.

important points. Throughout these transactions, there was a fairly substantial floating vote of Conservative peers who voted sometimes with the Government and sometimes against it. The greatly varying size of the vote on both sides illustrates the high degree of personal independence with which the individual members of the upper House were approaching their function of voting on this matter.

The Government made no secret of its annoyance at being treated in this way by a large body of its own supporters in the Lords. Back in the House of Commons, Mr. Stanley, President of the Board of Trade, in introducing the Lords' amendments, put it in this way: 'I regret to say, strange as it may seem, that during the passage of the Bill in another place, through what could have been nothing but a series of mischances, the Government were, on several occasions, defeated in the Lobby.'[1]

The Government acquiesced in some of the Lords' amendments, but secured the reversal or modification of others in the Commons. For the final stage in the Lords, the consideration of the Commons' amendments to the Lords' amendments, the Government succeeded in packing the House with peers ready to support it on the points on which it would not give way, though even at this stage nearly 30 Conservatives voted against the Government's modified proposals as finally approved by the Commons.[2]

In the whole session of 1937–8 there was only one division (out of a total of 27 for which the Whips were put on) in which the Government's ranks were unbroken; this was on a Labour proposal for the nationalization of the coal-mining industry.

During the war of 1939–45, only six divisions took place in the Lords on points to do with bills, and in all of these the Government was victorious. The party truce was fully observed in the Lords; the divisions did not touch party politics. The Labour peers were themselves divided in two of these cases and the Conservatives in all of them.

Since 1945 party discipline has been almost as complete in the House of Lords as in the House of Commons. There have been few free votes, and in party divisions there has been very little cross-voting indeed. Under the Labour Government the Conservative peers were numerous enough to be able to defeat the Government whenever they chose to do so. But the peers on the back benches quickly recognized that the decision just when to use the strength of superior numbers, and when to allow the Government to have its way, could best be left to the Conservative leaders. The Opposition Front Bench

[1] Commons Debs., 6th July 1938, vol. 338, col. 415.
[2] Lords Debs., 14th July 1938, vol. 110, cols. 872 and 888.

was loyally supported by the Conservative peers whenever it divided the House against the Government and also when it did not divide.

Now and again one or two individual Conservative peers voted against the main body of their Party. In 1948 five Conservative peers supported the Labour Government, against the main body of their own Party, on the proposal, in the National Health Service Bill, to pay small fixed salaries to general practitioners; the same thing happened in a vote in committee on the British Nationality Bill. Five Conservative peers voted with the Labour Government on the Parliament Bill the first time it came up for second reading,[1] but none the second or third time.[2] The only government bill to produce any substantial cross-voting during the whole period of 1945-51 was the Justices of the Peace Bill, on which there were three amendments over which party solidarity was broken on both sides. There was one Labour peer against the Government in each of the three divisions; the Conservatives divided 15 to 7 on the first amendment, 11 to 12 on the second and 16 to 4 on the third. But these were not in any sense Party questions.

On the Criminal Justice Bill the Conservative peers divided 16 to 14 in favour of Lord Simon's amendment proposing that the Court of Appeal should be able, like the French *Cour de Cassation*, to order a new trial by the lower court. Only two Labour peers voted against the Government, and the amendment was defeated. Both Parties allowed free votes on the amendments proposing to cancel the abolition of (*a*) the death penalty and (*b*) corporal punishment, but there was little cross-voting. Only three Conservative peers voted against each amendment. Later, on the Government's compromise clause on the death penalty, the voting was on party lines, with only one Conservative and one Liberal peer voting for the Government's proposal.

On a more specifically political question, there was cross-voting in 1951 on Lord Stansgate's motion implying a condemnation of the Government's action in banishing Seretse Khama. In a way, the Government suffered a moral defeat more telling than the ordinary defeats in party divisions, to which it had become accustomed. Only nine peers voted against the Government, but the nine included Lord Chorley, who had held office until shortly before, and three other prominent Labour peers, besides the Liberal leader Lord

[1] Lords Debs., 9th June 1948, vol. 156, col. 600.
[2] Ibid., 23rd September 1948, vol. 158, col. 238; 29th Nov. 1949, vol. 165, col. 1039. On the first division (9th June 1948) 15 non-party peers voted with the Government, and 25 against it; on the second, two with the Government and 38 against it. A similar change of allegiance among Liberal peers reflected dissatisfaction with the Government's intransigence. In the first division the Liberal peers divided 23 to 3 for the Government; in the second 11 Liberals voted against the Government and none with it.

Samuel and Whip Lord Rea. Of the 23 peers voting against the motion, 14 were office-holders and two Conservatives. The main body of Conservative peers abstained. Shortly afterwards, however, there was a normal party vote, and a Government defeat, on Lord Salisbury's motion that the banishment of Tshekedi Khama should be rescinded. One Conservative, the Marquess of Ailesbury, voted with the Government; he had also done so in the first division.

For the rest, except that occasionally one Conservative peer, usually Lord Merthyr, voted with the Government, the voting of the peers of the two main parties in 1945–51 was always on party lines. Even a free vote, on Lord Reading's Rights of the Subject Bill in 1947, failed to produce any breach in the ranks on either side. There was from time to time division among the few Liberal peers who voted, and most (but rarely all) of the non-party peers' votes were generally cast against the Labour Government.

Whenever there was a division, then, the Labour Government was almost automatically defeated by a ratio of at least two or three to one. It is worth mentioning, though, that by 1949, after four years of new Labour creations, the representation of the Labour Party in the House had reached respectable proportions. In one division, on a Conservative motion demanding an increase of war pensions, the Labour Party mustered 29 peers to the Conservatives' 31.

The return to power of the Conservatives in 1951 did not lead to a reversion to old voting habits in the House of Lords. The total number of divisions called in 1951–5 was the lowest in recent times over a comparable period. In the normal non-free votes party discipline has been well observed by both Conservative and Labour peers, though on a few occasions, as in 1945–51, one or two Conservatives have voted against their own front bench. Though time for private members' bill has been provided in the Commons since 1949, such bills have produced very few divisions in the Lords, and other subjects for free votes have been rare. Even the occasional free votes have tended to produce voting mainly on party lines.

The first session of the Conservative Government, that of 1951–2, produced only 12 divisions. On the only free vote (on a proposal to limit the killing of rabbits with cruel traps), only nine Conservatives opposed the 46 who followed the advice of the Minister; otherwise the Conservative ranks were broken on only three occasions, each time by only one or two peers. In the session of 1952–3, there were 13 divisions on the Transport Bill, three on the Iron and Steel Bill, and three on other matters. Three peers, all Conservatives, voted alone against the Government's Prevention of Crime Bill; they disliked the idea of forbidding people to carry weapons for their own defence. There was perhaps a faint echo of the 1930s here, but the heirs of the right-wing rebels of those days made an unimpressive showing. On the highly controversial Rhodesia and Nyasaland Federation Bill the division of opinion in the country was not by any means entirely on party lines, but when a Labour peer proposed to insert a guarantee against the colour bar, no Conservative voted against the Government. On the denationalization bills there was only one instance of cross-voting; Lord Sandhurst spoke and voted against the Government on the proposed transport levy.

The session of 1953-4 produced the first substantial breach of party solidarity since the war. The Conservative Government's proposal to allow independent or commercial television aroused deep hostility in the country, not only among Socialists but also among some elements normally supporting the Conservative Party. When it became known that the Government was resolved to insist on strict observance of party discipline on the question in the Commons, the opponents of commercial television had some hope that the Lords would offer effective resistance. Before the Bill came forward Lord Hailsham, a Conservative, moved a motion expressing disapproval of the Government's general intentions, and it seemed as if the Government was in some danger of being put in a minority. When the division was taken, however, the Government had used its weapons of persuasion to such effect that it had a big majority in a vote of 157 to 87. Nineteen Conservative peers voted among the large minority of 87 condemning the Government's policy.[1] The minority also included four bishops and 15 other non-party peers, as well as the Liberals and Socialists. Six months later, when the Independent Television Bill came up for second reading, 11 Conservative peers were among the minority of 64 against the Bill. (The strength of the majority was 130.) When the Bill came to the committee stage, however, the number of Conservatives voting against the Government fell to between three and five in each of the six divisions.

The rest of the 16 divisions of the session of 1953-4, which were on a wide variety of subjects, produced party votes with scarcely any exceptions. The main exception was on the National Art Collections Bill, on an amendment proposing that the Lane pictures should all be sent to Dublin. There was cross-voting on both sides, but the amendment was defeated by 51 votes to 10. On the Pests Bill a free vote was allowed on the old question of rabbit-traps, but only seven Conservatives voted against the main body of their Party. The Government Whips were put on against a private member's bill to improve the position of certain conscientious objectors, and no Conservative peer disobeyed them. Two Labour peers voted with the Government, against the majority of their colleagues. For the rest, the only

[1] Lords Debs., 26th November 1953, vol. 184, col. 748.

Conservative peer to vote against the Government in any division was the Earl of Glasgow, who voted with the Opposition on an amendment to the Landlord and Tenant Bill.

Since 1954 there have been some indications of a return to the more independent voting habits of the years between the wars, though now the Conservative dissidents have sometimes been to the left of the Government. Three divisions on committee points in the Road Traffic Bill of 1955 produced substantial Conservative revolts. Sixteen Conservative peers voted for a Labour amendment to provide that traffic inspectors should be appointed by the Minister; the Government was supported by only seventeen Conservative back-benchers, and suffered defeat. There was another large breach in the Conservative ranks over a Labour amendment regarding the application of the speed limit to station wagons, and the Government was again defeated. In the third division there were only ten Conservative rebels, and the Government obtained its majority.

Ten Conservatives voted against the Government in favour of an increase in officers' retired pay, but the Labour peers abstained, and the thirteen office-holders who voted were just able to tilt the balance in the Government's favour in a vote of 21 to 18. On a government bill on requisitioned houses one Conservative peer voted for a Labour amendment. The only division of the session in which the voting was solid was on a Liberal attack on the potato marketing scheme. There were only seven divisions in the whole session; in the seventh there was a free vote.

The session of 1955–6 produced more divisions than the preceding sessions, and there was rather more cross-voting. Of the 25 divisions of the session, six were on private members' proposals, and were decided by free votes. There was a revolt by some Conservative back-benchers, rather reminiscent of the revolts of the years between the wars, when nine of them voted against the third reading of the Kent Water Bill. Although this was a private Bill, for which the Government had no responsibility, the Government apparently considered that it had a duty to secure the passage of a Bill which had already been approved by a Private Bills Committee. If the Bill had been rejected, a dangerous precedent would have been established. The other Parties took the side of the Government in this, and the third reading was passed by 73 votes to 9.[1] Another Conservative revolt took place on the second reading of the Government's Pensions

---

[1] Lords Debs., 14th July 1955, vol. 193, cols. 75–480. It was pointed out during the debate that the Bill was the outcome of four years of negotiations between local authorities, and that it had been considered at 45 sittings of the Select Committees of Commons and Lords; it seemed inappropriate for peers to destroy the Bill on its third reading.

(Increase) Bill. The Earl of Cork and Orrery moved a reasoned amendment, 'That this House declines to give a second reading to a Bill concerned with Civil pensions only, until further detailed information is available about the detailed application of the proposed pension increase to Service pensions.' Six Conservative peers, together with five Liberals and three others, voted against the Government, but the second reading was carried, with the support of the Labour peers and 21 Conservative back-benchers, by a comfortable margin. On the Road Traffic Bill five Conservative peers voted for an unsuccessful Labour amendment aimed at increasing the power of the police to control pedestrians; in each of the three other divisions two or three Conservatives voted with the Labour peers. Four Conservatives voted for a Labour amendment to the Transport (Disposal of Road Haulage Property) Bill. In all the four divisions on the Restrictive Trade Practices Bill the voting was wholly on party lines, with both Liberal and Labour peers opposing the Government, which was consistently supported by the three non-party peers who voted.

There was only one instance of cross-voting among Labour or Liberal peers in the session; Lord Winster voted for Lord Cork's amendment to the Pensions Bill.

The slight increase in cross-voting among Conservative peers in 1955–6 was accompanied by a continuing decline in the Labour voting strength in the House. Five years earlier the usual number of Labour peers voting in normal party divisions was around 20; by now it had fallen below 15, and in the divisions on the Road Traffic Bill was under ten. The slight sign of independent voting behaviour among Conservative peers on committee points in bills is of only small significance in comparison with their solidarity in the votes on the British attack on Egypt on 1st November and 12th December 1956. On 1st November 69 Conservative back-bench peers voted with the Government, and only one against it. This was a rather special case; while it could well be argued on the one hand that peers ought to obey their consciences when fundamental national interests are at stake, it could also be said on the other hand that, as irrevocable action had already been taken, a show of disunity ought to be avoided. Sixty-seven peers in all attended but did not vote.

These considerations did not apply, however, to the division on the Government's policy six weeks later, when only two Conservative peers voted for the Labour amendment and none against the Government's own motion. Both on 1st November and 12th December some peers who had spoken against the Government abstained in the divisions. On both occasions the Labour peers voted solidly against the Government. Although, as Marshal of the Royal Air Force Lord

Tedder pointed out during the debate, the division of opinion in the country cut right across Parties, the Lords voted on party lines no less than the Commons.[1]

This examination of the development of the practice of the House of Lords with regard to party discipline suggests that a very great change has taken place since the war. It seems true to say that nowadays the distinction between free votes and votes controlled by the Whips is almost as clear in the Lords as it is in the Commons, and that in party votes cross-voting on any substantial scale is almost unknown. This fact corresponds with the parallel development in the House of Commons, but many of the reasons generally advanced for that development in the Commons are absent in the Lords. It must be remembered, on the other hand, that the conditions of membership of the House of Lords put no pressure on peers to attach themselves to parties; peers who wish to feel free to vote against the party which they normally prefer, may prefer not to be members of any party. The number of non-party peers has in fact doubled during the past twenty years.

The presence in the House of a coherent group of Labour peers may possibly have contributed to the strengthening of party discipline. In local councils, particularly where the Labour Party has been strong, there has been a tendency towards a two-party system, and a decline of the true independence of members even of groups describing themselves as 'Independents'. The recent developments in the House of Lords seem to agree with these trends in local government, but they may also be said to reflect the ever-increasing scope of the responsibility of the Government of the day, which becomes more and more nearly all-embracing. As it comes to be felt that most decisions ought to be made by the Government which will then take responsibility for putting them into effect, so it seems inappropriate for individual members to presume to set their own private views against those upon which the Government, after hearing all sides of the question, has finally decided. Similar considerations probably encourage unity even among Opposition peers. Finally, the desire not to help the other side through a show of disunity seems to be an ever-stronger binding force in British Parties, effective without any need for electoral sanctions.

[1] A more recent instance of the disinclination of Conservative peers to oppose their front bench in the division lobbies is provided by the proceedings on the Shops Bill in 1957. Cf. below, p. 184 n.

PART III
THE LORDS AT WORK

Chapter VIII

LEGISLATIVE PROCEDURE IN THE LORDS

THE work of the Lords in relation to legislation demands special and detailed study. This field of their activity covers three of the four functions which the Bryce Conference, with fairly general acceptance, considered appropriate to the second Chamber.[1] The first two functions differ profoundly from one another. That of delaying controversial proposals, once approved by the Commons, until public opinion has had a chance to express itself, postulates a power and a right to thwart altogether the wishes of the Government, even if only for a short time. The very essence of this power is conflict—conflict at least with the majority of the popularly elected Assembly, and conflict almost certainly with the Government as well. The function of revising bills sent up by the Commons, by amending them and by making up for the imperfection of the discussions in the lower House, may also involve conflict, but generally on a far lower plane and often not at all. The function of dealing in the first instance with bills of the sort that do not produce party strife is really little different in essence from that of revising bills sent up from the Commons.

The present detailed study of the work of the Lords in relation to legislation will be based mainly on the classification suggested by the Bryce report. It will begin with a discussion of the way the interposition of delay has worked out in practice (Chapter IX); it will then examine the revising function (Chapters X–XIII); and finally it will be concerned with the bills first introduced in the Lords (Chapter XIV). The discussion of the revising function will necessarily be much

[1] Cd. 9038 of 1918, para. 6.

the longest, and it will distinguish the periods in which the Government had the support of a majority of the peers from those periods when it was in a minority. The present political conditions with regard to private members' bills are such that bills of this type can most conveniently be dealt with separately from Government bills (Chapters XV–XVI).

A little must be said about the formal procedure with bills in the House of Lords. All public bills, whether proposed by the Government or not, and whether first introduced in the Lords or brought up from the Commons, have to go through the same main stages as in the Commons, with a few minor variations. The first reading is normally formal, and is a means whereby the House is acquainted of the bill's existence.[1] The main debate on the principles takes place at the second reading stage. Opposition may be expressed, as in the Commons, by an amendment to put off the second reading for six (or three) months or by a reasoned amendment. The acceptance of such an amendment is equivalent to the rejection of the bill.[2]

The form of debate at the second reading in the House of Lords is much the same as in the Commons. A minister or other office-holder proposes the bill on behalf of the Government. If the appropriate minister or a representative of the department concerned sits in the House of Lords it will be his duty to make an opening speech. If the department responsible for a bill has no representative sitting in the House of Lords, the bill will be introduced on its behalf by a peer who holds some ministerial office—usually the peer who regularly speaks for the department concerned or, if the bill is very important, one of the leading ministers. The peer in charge of a bill will, if he is not the minister or junior minister directly concerned, have to be coached by the department before he brings the bill forward in the House.

---

[1] It is very rarely found convenient to hold a preliminary debate on the first reading. Such a debate is really related to the question whether or not it is desirable that the bill should be brought in at all.

The practice of having a first, second and third reading on a bill was known in the fifteenth century, and was the rule by 1509, when the Lords Journals begin.

[2] It is also possible to vote against the motion for the second reading even when no amendment to that motion has been moved. This practice is rare, and would normally be followed only in a case in which objection to the measure had arisen during the debate. (Cf. Erskine May, p. 475.) If the motion for second reading is negatived the second reading can theoretically be proposed again on another day, but, in the words of Erskine May, it is usual to treat it as a rejection of the bill, which is thenceforward removed from the order paper. There is here a small technical difference between Lords and Commons; in the lower House the practice of voting against the motion for second reading appears to have become altogether obsolete. Erskine May's latest example from the Commons (op. cit., p. 506) is from the year 1886; for the Lords he gives an instance from the session of 1937–8.

LEGISLATIVE PROCEDURE IN THE LORDS

Normally the minister's speech is followed by a speech from a member of the Opposition, who has been appointed by his Leader to present the Party's case. The debate then proceeds as in the House of Commons, though with no time limit, until all the peers who wish to speak have done so. For a bill of any substance the front benches will put up closing speakers to wind up the debate.

Perhaps the main difference between second reading debates in the Lords and those in the Commons lies in the greater readiness of the Lords to let the second reading stage pass without very lengthy discussion. Some bills in recent years have been debated for two or three days in the Lords on second reading, but even in these cases the debates have generally been shorter than the corresponding debates in the lower House. In the Lords, on all but the most important bills, a second reading debate usually draws only two or three speeches from back-benchers. As in the Commons, there is a tendency for peers who participate in second reading debates to refer to particular points, in the hope that the minister's mind may be prepared for possible concessions at the committee stage.

The bill is discussed in detail, clause by clause, in committee, when amendments may be proposed, debated and decided upon. The report stage (technically, consideration of the committee's report) allows for a further detailed discussion which follows the same pattern, and at the third reading the House finally decides on the bill as it emerges from the detailed examination in committee and on report.

In its broad outlines, then, the Lords' procedure on bills is similar to that of the Commons. Some differences from the Commons must be noticed, however. The chief of these are the following:

(1) As the Lords are not concerned with the provision of money from public funds,[1] there is no need for any money resolution there

---

[1] It is not proposed to discuss here in any detail the special situation of the House of Lords with regard to measures imposing charges on the public funds. In the words of Erskine May (p. 779), 'the financial powers of the House of Lords are limited, first by the ancient "rights and privileges" of the House of Commons, and secondly by the terms of the Parliament Act, 1911'. The first limitation is expressed in the terms of the resolutions of 1671 and 1678, 'that in all aids given to the King by the Commons, the rate of tax ought not to be altered by the Lords', and 'that all aids and supplies, and aids to His Majesty in Parliament, are the sole gift of the Commons; and all bills for the granting of any such aids and supplies ought to begin with the Commons; and that it is the undoubted and sole right of the Commons to direct, limit and appoint in such bills the ends, purposes, considerations, conditions, limitations and qualifications of such grants, which ought not to be changed or altered by the House of Lords'. (Cf. above, p. 10.)

According to these rules, if the Lords make any amendment which affects public funds they infringe the privileges of the Commons. It must be remembered, however, that in modern conditions the dominant position of the Government influences the operation of the rules regarding the relationship between the two

with bills involving expenditure, such as has to be passed in the Commons before the clauses involving expenditure can be discussed in committee.

(2) As it would be a breach of the privileges of the Commons for the Lords to amend a Supply bill, it would be useless for the Lords to discuss a Supply bill in committee, and there is therefore normally no committee stage for such bills. (Cf. Erskine May, p. 786.)

(3) With the committee stage, the important difference between Lords and Commons is that, while the Commons send most bills to standing committees, the Lords do not, and indeed have no standing committees. With all bills (except those sent to select committees or joint committees),[1] the committee stage in the Lords is taken on the floor of the House, with the whole House resolved into committee for

Houses. On occasion, the Commons agree to waive their privileges, and to accept amendments made by the Lords which technically affect the Commons' privileges. (Cf. Erskine May, p. 788.)

The Parliament Act of 1911 made special provisions with regard to 'money bills', whose character it defined. A 'money bill' is a bill which the Speaker of the House of Commons, acting according to the definitions laid down by the Act, has certified to be a money bill. It must deal only with taxation, the Consolidated Fund, public money, the raising or repayment of loans by the state, or matters incidental to these subjects.

In defining 'money bills' thus narrowly the Act upholds the principles of the Lords' Order of 1702, which condemned the practice of 'tacking'. The Speaker has interpreted the rules so strictly that in most sessions since 1911 he has not certified the Finance Bill as a 'money bill'. (Paradoxically, it seems that according to the practice followed by successive Speakers since 1911, the 1909 Finance Bill itself would not have qualified for a certificate as a money bill.) Even so, it is not unknown for peers to be surprised at a particular decision of the Speaker. In December 1956 the Government brought in a bill to provide for an increase in petrol duty. If the bill was to be of any use it had to be passed at once. But two of its clauses were concerned with making it easy for bus and taxi operators to increase their fares. It was indisputable, in a way, that the provisions of these clauses were 'subordinate matters incidental to' the taxation proposals, but there was nevertheless some expression of disappointment in the Lords when the bill came up certified as a money bill, so that it became impossible for the upper House to make amendments. (Cf. Lords Debs., 18th December 1956, vol. 200, cols. 1181–1208.)

[1] In practice a bill is only sent to a select committee, consisting of a small number of peers, or to a joint committee, consisting of a few members from each House, if it seems desirable to hold an enquiry into the effects that the bill will have on existing interests. In addition, 'consolidation' bills, which bring together into one measure all existing legislation on a particular topic, without changing the law, are considered by a Joint Committee on Consolidation Bills. A select committee normally hears outside witnesses, in much the same way as an American standing committee or sub-committee holds 'hearings' before going into 'executive session'. Although the device of the select committee has a very long and unbroken history, it is now rarely used in relation to ordinary legislation. (Cf. Jennings, *Parliament*, Cambridge U.P., 1939, p. 265; Eric Taylor, *The House of Commons at Work*, Penguin, 2nd ed., 1955, p. 179.)

the purpose. In having no standing committees the House of Lords differs greatly from most other European legislative assemblies. It has not found the creation of such bodies necessary for the sake of enabling it to cope with its business. It was mainly considerations of time that first led the Commons to introduce standing committees, though it has also been argued that such committees are good in themselves, even if not necessary, on the ground that they are better adapted than the committee of the whole House for the detailed discussion of bills. Proposals for the introduction of a system of standing committees in the Lords have been made, but they have not found favour with the majority of the peers.[1] It is probably fair to say that the relatively co-operative and non-partisan atmosphere of the Commons standing committees is present in a committee of the whole House in the Lords.

(4) A very minor point is that the motion to go into committee on a bill is still occasionally debated in the Lords. In this matter the Lords still keep a practice which the Commons long ago discarded, for the reason that a debate on this motion tends merely to duplicate the second reading debate.

(5) There is a fairly substantial procedural difference from the Commons with regard to the third reading stage. In the Commons only verbal amendments are allowed at this stage; in the Lords there is no such limitation, though S.O. No. 30 does require previous notice to be given of amendments. In practice, the right to propose amendments at this stage is used not infrequently, but the amendments are by custom generally restricted to the final settlement of questions left open on committee and report, or to minor changes whose desirability had not been noticed earlier. The introduction of new subjects is discouraged. This must not be taken to imply that only agreed amendments are proposed on third reading. Even at this late stage, amendments are sometimes withdrawn, and it has been known for divisions to take place.[2] Over 70 amendments were put down for the third reading of the Copyright Bill in 1956.

---

[1] A select committee was set up to examine the desirability of the introduction of standing committees as long ago as 1848, but nothing came of the proposal at that time. In 1890, however, two standing committees were set up, with the intention that they should only deal with the drafting of bills. Complaints were soon made that they had introduced amendments of substance, and they were abolished in 1910. In 1927 Lord Burnham proposed that they should be set up again, but his proposal was not accepted. (Lords Debs., 1st March 1927, vol. 66, col. 261).

[2] E.g., on a Conservative amendment to the River Boards Bill in 1947. (Lords Debs., 18th December 1947, vol. 153, col. 364.) On this occasion the Government was defeated, but the amendment was reversed in the Commons, and the Lords did not insist on it.

One source of third reading amendments appears to have been removed by a

(6) S.O. No. 41 of the House of Lords provides that no two stages of a bill are to be taken on any one day. This prevents the Lords from taking the third reading immediately after the report stage, as is often done in the Commons. But the Lords can, and often do, suspend their own Standing Order on this matter. Indeed, just before the summer recess the Government sometimes asks the Lords to pass a bill through all its stages on the same day; they did this in August 1956.[1]

A bill may begin its parliamentary career in either House. If it has been first introduced in the Lords it is known as a 'Lords Bill'. If the House which has been the second to consider the bill inserts amendments, the text must go back to the other House for consideration of these amendments, which may be accepted there or rejected or further amended. If they are accepted, the bill goes for the Royal Assent; otherwise, it goes backwards and forwards between the two Houses until agreement is reached.

Thus with a bill originating in the Commons, if the Lords introduce amendments, the next stage after the third reading in the Lords is the consideration of the Lords' amendments in the Commons. Each of the Lords' amendments may then be debated and made the subject of a vote. If any of the Lords' amendments is rejected or further amended by the Commons, the Commons appoint a committee (of members from both sides of the House) to draw up reasons for their disagreement. The reasons are generally stated in a single short sentence with respect to each amendment which is the subject of disagreement. The bill then goes back to the Lords, with certain amendments disagreed to, and the Lords have before them the reasons for disagreement assigned.

On each of these amendments the Lords have then to decide whether to 'insist' or not to insist on their former opinion. If the Lords insist on any amendment they appoint a committee to draw up reasons for that insistence, and the Commons in their turn debate the Lords' reasons. At this point, the Commons may either give way or insist on their disagreement. In the former case, the matter is settled

---

change in practice introduced early in 1957. Previously, if a bill had not been amended in committee of the whole House, the report stage was taken immediately, without amendment, so that proposals for amendment which had been held over at the committee stage had to be dealt with finally (if at all) on third reading. On 5th February 1957 the House agreed with a report from the Select Committee on Procedure to the effect that even if a bill had not been amended in committee, the report stage would be taken after an interval, and that amendments might then be proposed. (Lords Debs., vol. 201, cols. 418–22.)

[1] Cf. Lords Debs., 1st August 1956, vol. 199, col. 525. On this occasion the Opposition spokesman objected, not to the general principle of the suspension of the standing order, but to its suspension with regard to this particular bill, which was in effect deprived of any committee stage.

and the bill can go for the Royal Assent; in the latter case the bill is normally lost, as a result of the deadlock between the two Houses.

The matter is further complicated by the fact that at any stage either House, on receiving notice of the disagreement of the other House, may, instead of 'insisting' on its disagreement, produce a new amendment in place of the old one. There is, in theory, no limit to this process, but in practice one House, usually the Lords, soon agrees to a form insisted upon by the other.

Until the middle of the nineteenth century the Houses communicated with each other by means of 'conferences', which were in fact usually formal meetings at which the managers handed over communications in writing and then dispersed without further ado.[1] In 1851, both Houses agreed to send written messages to each other; the change made no real difference. Before 1740 real conferences were sometimes held, at which managers appointed by the two Houses tried to reach agreement in the same way as the managers do in the American congressional conference committees today. In 1703, for example, a free conference tried, without success, to reach agreement after the Lords had introduced unacceptable amendments into the bill for the suppression of occasional conformity.[2] The old type of free conference was revived once, but unsuccessfully, in 1836, on the Municipal Corporations Bill. In 1906 an informal committee of party leaders was set up, as a result of 'a private arrangement between Lord Lansdowne and Lord Crewe', to try to reach agreement on the disputed Lords' amendments to the Education Bill, but this was really a conference between spokesmen of the Parties, not of the two Houses of Parliament.[3]

Completely informal and private discussions between Party leaders may take place even now with regard to Lords' amendments, but these are merely part of the process of private discussion which goes on constantly with relation to points of detail in legislation. The Bryce Conference did suggest in 1918 that there might be a regular conference committee for settling differences between the Houses, but such machinery would scarcely be suitable to the conditions of British politics, and the suggestion has not been followed up.

[1] Cf. Erskine May, p. 809.
[2] Cf. Turberville, *The House of Lords in the XVIIIth Century*, p. 53.
[3] Cf. Asquith, *Fifty Years of Parliament*, vol. ii, p. 44; Newton, *Lord Lansdowne*, p. 356; J. Pope-Hennessy, *Lord Crewe* (Constable, 1955), p. 109. The Government representatives were the Prime Minister, the Minister of Education and Lord Crewe; Balfour, Lord Lansdowne and Lord Cawdor represented the Opposition, and the Archbishop of Canterbury was added at the suggestion of the King.

Chapter IX

THE PARLIAMENT ACT OF 1911 AND ITS EFFECTS

1. THE ACT AND ITS BACKGROUND

UNTIL 1911 there were no statutory rules governing the relations between the two Houses of Parliament with regard to legislation. The Commons had declared that the Lords should not interfere with the details of Supply, and the Lords had acted within the spirit of that declaration for so long that something like a rule appeared to exist. It was apparently still possible for the Lords to reject outright a bill concerned with finance without breaking the rule—as they had done in the case of the Paper Duty Repeal Bill in 1860—but opinions differed about the propriety of such an action. Their right to amend or reject ordinary bills still remained complete and had been freely exercised.

From the Reform Act of 1832 to that of 1867 they had used their powers with great moderation, but since 1867 they had become readier to destroy progressive measures of Liberal governments. There were good grounds for arguing that the changed conditions of political life had made it necessary that their powers with regard to ordinary legislation should be clearly defined and restricted. On the one hand the extension of the franchise had sharpened the distinction between the two Houses, by making the House of Commons more nearly representative of the whole people, while the House of Lords remained as unrepresentative as before; on the other hand, the constant extension of ministerial responsibility for legislation was making unsatisfactory any situation in which a government's bill, passed by the Commons, might be blocked by the Lords.

After the split in the Liberal Party in 1886, the House of Lords contained an overwhelming Conservative and Unionist majority, which thwarted the legislative intentions of Liberal governments, however strong their majorities in the Commons. Many Conservative peers had not yet come to accept the implications for their House of the changes in the electorate; they found it quite right and natural that they should turn out in enormous numbers to defeat the Government's measures. In these circumstances, the conflict of 1909-11 was inevitable; its outcome produced a new situation to which the mass of Conservative peers acclimatized themselves gradually, but in the long run successfully.

Already before 1886 the Lords had obstructed several important government measures sent up from the Commons—the Ballot Bill and the proposal to abolish the purchase of army commissions in 1871, and the franchise extension of 1884. All these measures were, however, enacted with little delay. In 1892-5 the actions of the Lords were more serious, with the defeat of the Irish Home Rule Bill, the Scottish Local Government Bill and the Succession to Real Property Bill, and the effective destruction, through amendment, of the Employers' Liability Bill. These experiences had led the Liberal Party to believe that some limitation of the power of the Lords was necessary. In 1906, soon after the return to power, this time in great strength, of the Liberals, the Lords made and insisted on unacceptable amendments to the Education Bill,[1] and the Bill was dropped. In 1907 the House of Commons approved a pugnacious resolution: 'in order to give effect to the will of the people as expressed by their elected representatives, it is necessary that the power of the other House to alter or reject bills should be so restrained by law as to ensure that within the limits of a single Parliament the final decision of the Commons shall prevail'.

During the first three years of Liberal rule the Lords rejected or mutilated several important government bills, but for a time no action was taken to put the 1907 resolution into effect. It was only after the Lords, by rejecting the Finance Bill of 1909, had challenged the financial privileges of the Commons,[2] that the Government brought

[1] The Lords devoted sixteen afternoons to the committee stage of this Bill.

[2] As the Lords did not amend the Finance Bill, but rejected it, their action was not in direct contravention of the terms of the Commons resolutions of 1671 and 1678. On the other hand, there was no precedent for the outright rejection of a comprehensive bill of this sort, and in view of the generally vague character of British constitutional rules it could be argued that the Lords' action was unconstitutional.

In reply to this charge it could be claimed that the practice, introduced by Gladstone nearly fifty years before, of bringing in comprehensive annual finance bills, had itself been a constitutional innovation. Furthermore, it was believed in some quarters that the provision for a land tax in the Finance Bill of 1909 had been included with the deliberate intention of provoking the Lords to an action which

in the Parliament Bill, to define and restrict the powers of the Lords with regard to legislation. That Bill was finally passed, against bitter opposition, in 1911, after two general elections and with the aid of the Government's threat, if necessary, to advise the King to create enough new peers to give the Government a majority in the House of Lords.

Under the Parliament Act of 1911 the Lords could do no more than prevent a bill from passing for three sessions (or two years approximately). They could hold up a 'money bill' for only one month. That at least was the intention; three years later, however, Speaker Lowther discerned an obscurity in the wording of the Act. Sub-section (3) of Section (2) provided: 'A Bill shall be deemed to be rejected by the House of Lords if it is not passed by the House of Lords either without amendment or with such amendments only as may be agreed to by both Houses.' The Act did not make clear what the position was to be if, after a bill had been passed by the Commons in a third session, the Lords indefinitely postponed coming to a decision on it. Apparently it would be impossible for the bill to go for the Royal Assent until the very end of the session, because until that moment the Lords were still in a position to pass the bill, if they were to feel so inclined. The Royal Assent could thus, it appeared, not be given until the moment of prorogation, by which time it would be too late. Speaker Lowther concluded that in such a case 'the only way of putting the Act into force was to wait until the fourth session, when the bill, not passed by the Lords in the third session, could be introduced into the House of Commons, endorsed with the Speaker's certificate and submitted to the Crown direct, without being sent to the Lords'.[1] But this was certainly not the intention of the Parliament Act.

The Act was an important constitutional innovation, for it introduced a new element of statutory definition of the relationships between the two Houses, in addition to the conventions which had until then been found enough. But more interesting than the form of the Act, as modified in 1949, has been the process whereby the House of Lords has adapted itself, in dealing with bills, to its formally restricted powers.

2. THE IMMEDIATE SEQUEL

The passing of the 1911 Parliament Act, with the fierce opposition and the bitterness which it engendered, left the Conservative Party in general, and the Conservatives in the House of Lords in particular,

would give the Government an excuse for making a direct attack against the power of the Lords. For a new examination of the evidence, cf. Roy Jenkins, *Mr. Balfour's Poodle* (Heinemann, 1954).

[1] Viscount Ullswater, *A Speaker's Commentaries* (Arnold, 1925), vol. ii, p. 113.

little disposed, for the time being, to accept the situation with good grace. During the next three years, up to the beginning of the war in 1914, the Lords still felt quite justified in using to the full the powers that were left to them, and they had no hesitation about rejecting the main controversial bills sent up from the Commons, in order at least to delay their enactment until the provisions of the Parliament Act could be invoked.

The most important of these bills was that by which the Liberal Government in 1912 proposed to give home rule to the whole of Ireland. The circumstances in which the Lords rejected this measure, and indeed the whole atmosphere surrounding the bill, were quite without parallel in recent times. No other bill since the Reform Bill of 1832 has aroused such furious or such dangerous controversy. It was indeed partly because of their fear of an Irish home rule bill that the Conservatives, inside the House of Lords and outside it, had fought so hard against the imposition of a limit to the delaying power of the Lords. Bonar Law and other responsible Conservatives now argued that, with the Lords shorn of their power to block legislation, the King ought to reinterpret his constitutional duty to follow the advice of his Ministers. Bonar Law submitted a memorandum to the King, in which he said: 'If the Home Rule Bill passes through all its stages under the Parliament Act and requires only the Royal Assent, the position will be a very serious and almost impossible one for the Crown. . . . In such circumstances, Unionists would certainly believe that the King not only had the constitutional right, but that it was his duty, before acting on the advice of his Ministers, to ascertain whether it would not be possible to appoint other Ministers who would advise him differently and allow the question to be decided by the Country at a General Election.'[1] Not content with pressing such novel advice on the King, the Party's leaders gave countenance to preparations for armed resistance in Ulster.

As the Conservative leaders were moved to such extremities as these by their dislike of the Government's policy, it is hardly surprising that they thought it proper for the House of Lords to use the delaying power that was still left to it after the passing of the Parliament Act. Party leaders, backwoodsmen and all, turned out in great force to vote against the Bill each time it came up to the Lords for second reading. Their action, as it turned out, was of more practical effect than they had expected. The Bill finally passed, under the Parliament Act, in 1914.[2] But by this time war had

[1] The memorandum is quoted in Harold Nicolson, *George V* (Constable, 1952), p. 201.
[2] The technical circumstances of its passing were rather confused, because of the difficulties mentioned above (p. 136).

begun, and the Government had in any case decided to modify its intentions by introducing a separate bill temporarily excluding Ulster from the operation of the Act. The coming of the war obliged the Government to suspend entirely, for the time being, the operation of the Act, and it was not until 1922 that home rule was actually achieved—in an unforeseen form and with Ulster excluded.

The action of the Lords in rejecting the Bill in 1912 and 1913 had, therefore, the indirect effect of putting off the achievement of home rule for some ten years. It also had, indirectly, the effect of preventing entirely the inclusion of Ulster within the Irish Free State, which was later to become the Irish Republic. But for the action of the Lords in 1912, home rule for the whole of Ireland would presumably have become effective forthwith. It was only in 1913 that the Government became converted to the opinion that Ulster would have to receive special treatment. The very fact that the Government itself did become so converted is perhaps a partial justification of the Lords' first rejection of the Bill in 1912.

The Lords themselves did not assist the Government to make its own conversion effective. The most satisfactory way of providing for the exclusion of Ulster would probably have been by the introduction of amending clauses in the original Government of Ireland Bill. But if the Bill had been presented in this amended form in 1913 it would have counted, under the Parliament Act, as a new bill, and would in its turn have had to pass both Houses of Parliament in three sessions before it could become law. If the Government had used this device for giving way in part to their opponents, they would therefore have had to face a further year's delay before the Bill could become law, and this they naturally did not wish to do. They therefore presented the Bill again in its original form, together with an amending Bill which proposed that there should be a plebiscite and that those parts of Ireland which were found to desire special treatment should be excluded for six years from the operation of home rule. But the Lords introduced unacceptable amendments even into this measure, and if it had not been for the outbreak of the war the Government would have been forced, either to bring the Bill into operation for the whole of Ireland at once (which it did not wish to do), or to attempt to find some compromise, or to accept further delay until the new bill had also gone through the procedure of the Parliament Act.

The second of the great contested measures of 1911–14 was the Welsh Church Disestablishment Bill, which was three times rejected by the Lords, but finally enacted under the provisions of the Parliament Act. It did not receive the Royal Assent, however, until 18th September 1914, after the beginning of the war, and its operation was suspended until after the end of the war.

THE IMMEDIATE SEQUEL

A third bill of the Asquith Government went half-way to being passed under the Parliament Act procedure. The Temperance (Scotland) Bill of 1912 was passed by the Lords, but with such extensive amendments that the Government decided to hold it over and treat it as though it had been rejected. It seemed to the Government better to face a two-years' delay in order to get the Bill they wanted, than to bring into force the emasculated measure which the Lords were then prepared to pass. In 1913 the Bill was passed by the Commons once again, but this time, faced with the apparent certainty that if they held their ground the Bill would be passed, in a form mainly objectionable to them, in the next year, the Lords decided to be much more accommodating, and the Bill was allowed through, with some concessions to the Opposition but without sacrifice of principle.

The fourth important bill to be rejected was that for the abolition of plural voting. It was first passed by the Commons only in 1913, so it had not yet been passed three times by the Commons when the war began, and was therefore finally lost. The Lords delayed this reform for thirty years.

The beginning of the war in 1914 put an end to all legislative activity of the kind which might have produced conflicts of principle between the two Houses. From 1919 until the end of the second war in 1945 the Conservative Party was, with two brief intervals, itself the dominant element in the Government. True to its past, and to the allegations that it was never prepared to oppose the Conservative Party, the House of Lords did not reject any of the important measures of the successive Conservative or Coalition Governments;[1] there was thus never any question of the Parliament Act being put into effect. The Lords did, indeed, on occasion make things difficult for these Governments by their amendments in committee, but for the present we are concerned only with the outright rejection of bills, or with the mutilation of bills on such a scale as to make the Government prefer to resort to the procedure of the Parliament Act rather than to accept the Lords' amendments.

It was only during the brief periods of Labour rule in 1924 and 1929–31 that the Lords might have been expected to use their delaying power. In 1924 the Government, lacking experience and quite at the mercy of the Liberals, did not introduce any measures to which the Lords objected at all seriously, and there was no important conflict. The Labour Government of 1929–31, although it too was in a minority in the Commons, ran into more serious difficulties, and the

[1] The Lords did indeed reject the Rabbits Bill of 1928, but the Government did not consider its responsibility to be deeply engaged over this former private member's bill. Some opposition members in the Commons complained.

Lords did actually reject one government bill outright. The Government's Education (School Attendance) Bill, whose purpose was to raise the school-leaving age, was rejected in the Upper House on second reading by the large majority of 168 votes to 22.[1] There was no hesitation about this rejection; the number of peers voting was larger than in any other division in the session, and the majority was not composed entirely of Conservatives, but included some Liberals as well as a few non-party men. The minority voting with the Government, on the other hand, included a few Conservatives. If the Government had remained in office it might have been inclined to use the procedure of the Parliament Act to secure the passage of the Bill in the next two sessions over the Lords' veto, but the matter was never put to the test. The subject of disagreement was of a milder and less explosive character than the rejected bills of 1912–14 or earlier, but the Bill did have some implications for the policy of dealing with unemployment, such as the Government, if it had remained in office and been steadfast in its policies, might have considered to merit the use of the Parliament Act procedure.

3. THE LORDS AND LEGISLATION TODAY

The real test of the adaptation of the House of Lords to its new and restricted functions came in 1945–50, when for the first time since the days of Asquith there was a reforming and anti-Conservative administration in power backed by a good majority in the Commons.

The five-years' period of strong Labour government produced a new Parliament Act, still further limiting the delaying power of the Lords, so that after 1949 a bill could go for the Royal Assent, in spite of rejection by the Lords, after being passed through the Commons in two, instead of three, successive sessions. But on the other side, although there were many measures thoroughly unpalatable to Conservatives, the behaviour of the Lords in 1945–50 had little in common with that of 1906–14, or even of 1911–14, after the passing of the first Parliament Act. In 1911–14 the Lords, not yet adapted to their new rôle, three times rejected two of the main controversial measures of the Government, and twice rejected another measure which aroused nearly as much feeling; in 1945–51 the only bill which the Lords rejected was the Parliament Bill, which did, after all, concern exclusively the Lords' own powers. Faced with a reforming administration no less vigorous than that of 1906–14, the Conservative peers showed that they had learned the lesson of 1909–11, and conducted themselves with great moderation. The Conservative peers of our own time have approached their functions in a quite different way from

[1] Lords Debs., 18th February 1931, vol. 79, col. 1161.

THE LORDS AND LEGISLATION TODAY

their predecessors of before 1914, and if we wish to assess the legislative rôle of the modern House of Lords we soon find that the subject can no longer be treated mainly in terms of conflict. There is, of course, still conflict—if there were not, the House would indeed be moribund—but both parties conduct the conflict with a realistic readiness to search for acceptable solutions.

It would perhaps be rash to assert that the new spirit is permanent, or that it is part of a single continuous trend; we must remember that the Lords behaved with moderation for thirty years after 1832, and that a single individual, the fifth Marquess of Salisbury, has had a remarkable influence over the Conservative peers during the past fifteen years. Nevertheless, the recent moderation of the Lords fits in, not only with a new and inevitable interpretation of the rôle of a non-elected assembly in modern Britain, but also with a trend in political affairs which affects far more than the House of Lords.

This trend is so well recognized today that reference to it is a commonplace. It was already to be discerned well before 1910. Sir John Marriott, in the 1910 edition of his book *Second Chambers*, wrote that although the House of Lords had suffered a decline of power, it had lost power, not to the lower House as such, but rather to the Cabinet, in relation to which the House of Commons as a body had in its turn suffered a great decline.[1] In 1904 Sir Sidney Low called the House of Commons 'a machine for discussing the legislative projects of ministers'; ten years later the same author wrote: 'The power to shape legislation is in practice confined to those members of the House who form the inner ring of the Cabinet for the time being.'[2]

The strife of the early years of the twentieth century was caused, not only by differences between Liberals and Conservatives, but also by the failure of the House of Lords to accept the implications for itself of the changes in the character of political power. As the House of Commons became more representative of the whole people, so it became more dominated by the Parties. So long as the Conservative peers believed that they should counteract the power of Liberal governments in the Commons, serious friction was bound to ensue.

The tendencies so well observed by Low have continued, and during the past half century the House of Lords, like the House of Commons, has continuously been adapting itself to the new situation; in the process of adaptation it has greatly changed its activity even since the time when Low wrote, and has probably developed a far greater and more effective capacity for discussion of details—and even for influencing the course of events—than it could hope to have fifty years ago. As Parliament has been reduced more and more to

[1] Op. cit., p. 59.   [2] *The Governance of England*, p. 61.

the status of a body for the discussion of the projects of ministers, so it has become a more efficient machine for the purpose of that discussion, within the ever-greater limits imposed on it by the developing character of cabinet responsibility and its concomitant, the party system.

In the Commons the Government always has its own majority behind it, and a government bill will only be defeated if a substantial number of government supporters dislike it enough to vote against it or abstain. But if a government bill is opposed by enough government supporters for its second reading to be endangered in the Commons, the Government can these days be expected not to bring the bill forward there until the opponents on its own side of the House have been persuaded to withdraw their opposition. Thus, in the Commons, although the Opposition often divides against the second reading of a government bill, it can be assumed that the bill will not be defeated. In the Lords, on the other hand, the position is somewhat different; the Government of the day has not necessarily a majority behind it. A Conservative government probably has on its side a majority of at least two to one of the peers present at the debate, but a Labour government is inevitably in a minority, and could easily be defeated in the Lords on the second reading of any measure that it proposed. Just because of this the Conservative majority in the House of Lords has developed a policy of not voting against the second reading of bills brought in by Labour governments.

As the second reading debate in the Lords is not, as a rule, a preliminary to effective decision, the Committee and Report stages assume a special importance. Whatever the government in power, these stages produce numerous proposals for amendment and discussion about points of detail. Amendments are moved both by the Government itself and by back-benchers on both sides of the House, though usually, and particularly under a Labour government, there are more amendments from peers on the Opposition side than from peers on the Government side.

As in the Commons, the majority of private members' amendments proposed in Committee in the House of Lords are withdrawn after discussion. The proportion of amendments withdrawn is far greater nowadays than fifty or even thirty years ago. In recent years, because of the increasing domination of the Government, the House has come more and more to concede to the Government the right to have matters of detail decided in a way acceptable to itself. On committee points in government bills free votes are almost unknown. Nearly always the Government spokesman states his point of view, and the decision is made accordingly.

A few amendments moved from the floor of the House—not, in

THE LORDS AND LEGISLATION TODAY

general, very many—are accepted by the Government outright, and if this happens the House generally agrees. Others, again, the Government spokesman declares to be unacceptable. If this happens, the peers who favour the amendment must decide whether or not they feel strongly enough about the matter to press it to a division. Nowadays, however, whatever the government in power, divisions in committee are rather rare. On points of detail in government bills, it is generally felt that majority votes of the House are not the best way of arriving at final decisions.

A consideration of the rôle of the Lords with regard to legislation, even under a Labour government, would be thoroughly misleading if it concentrated entirely on amendments decided by divisions. In fact the most important part of the function of the Lords in relation to bills is to propose amendments for the Government's consideration. The government in power, whatever its complexion, will have its way in the long run. This is indeed one of the fundamental principles of the operation of the whole of contemporary British politics; it shapes the relations between the Government and the Opposition in both Houses of Parliament. On the other hand we must still remember that at every stage of the discussion of a bill, both inside Parliament and outside, both before the bill has been introduced into Parliament and afterwards, the Government is hearing arguments from all kinds of people, from interested bodies, from disinterested persons, and from members of the Commons and of the Lords on both sides, who may in some cases be speaking on behalf of interests outside. Sometimes the Government accepts the arguments which it hears, sometimes it rejects them, and very often it proposes some sort of compromise. Thus the contribution of the Lords on the committee stage must be regarded and judged as a part of a far-reaching process of discussion in Parliament and outside; it is complementary to, not distinct from, the other private and parliamentary discussions.

A little more must be said about the moving of amendments 'on behalf of' outside bodies. It is by no means unknown for a peer to say specifically that he is putting forward the views of some association or other. This practice has, however, incurred disapproval. As Lord Salisbury has put it, 'peers should not preface their speeches by saying that they are speaking as representatives of any association or body. . . . That is really quite wrong. Even if they are quite frank about it, it is not in keeping with the traditions or the character of this House. Noble Lords . . . sit here in their own personal capacity . . . and they cannot be a delegate for anybody else.' [1]

To say that a peer should not act as a representative or mouthpiece of an outside body does not imply that it is wrong or even undesirable

[1] Lords Debs., 14th November 1956, vol. 200, col. 321.

for him to put forward an amendment, or a point of view, that has been suggested to him, and that he has, through sympathy with it, made his own. Lord Chorley showed, in a rejoinder to Lord Salisbury, that he felt that this qualification should be made. Lord Salisbury's dictum should perhaps not be taken as implying a fundamental difference between peers and members of the House of Commons in this respect. It is true that M.P.s 'represent' their constituents, and that peers have no constituents to represent; but this does not imply that it is any less right for peers than for M.P.s to 'represent' particular associations. In the strict sense of the word 'represent', as has been often said in many places, members of the House of Commons ought not, any more than peers, to represent sectional groups, or to act as their 'delegates'; but this does not imply that no M.P. ought ever to state in the House of Commons the point of view of an association that has gained his sympathy, provided that he states that point of view as though it were his own, and takes personal responsibility for it. If this were seriously denied, the committee stage of bills would be deprived of much of its utility. The same general principle should surely apply, with little modification, to members of the House of Lords, particularly when they are dealing with the details of bills in committee.

Naturally there is a rigid convention, prescribed by ordinary rules of decent and responsible behaviour, with regard to peers' speeches on matters in which they are themselves materially interested. If a peer speaks on a subject in which he has an 'interest', he should declare the fact, and in general he should not initiate the discussion or move the amendment himself.

If a bill is not amended in the Lords, it does not necessarily follow that there has been no discussion of its details in committee or on report. Many amendments are moved more in order to ask for an explanation of how a bill will work out in practice than with the intention of introducing an actual change into the text. Others are abandoned after the Government has explained why it cannot accept them. In moving an amendment only to abandon it without asking the House to take a decision, a peer does at least oblige the Government to explain publicly the reasons underlying its policy on a particular matter, and in all probability to show how it intends its policy to work out in practice.

Very often amendments are withdrawn after discussion in committee, on the understanding that the Government will give consideration to the arguments which have been brought forward, and reserve its final decision for a later stage. Sometimes a minister expresses agreement with the objectives of an amendment and says he is ready to accept it in principle or in part, but is not ready to have it inserted in the bill until there has been opportunity for further consideration. In such a case he may invite the proposer of the amendment to hold it over for the time being, in order that the Government may give further thought to the matter and be ready with a final decision if the amendment is again proposed, with or without modification, at the report or (less frequently) the third reading stage.[1] An amendment withdrawn in this way is sometimes actually adopted by the Government and ultimately brought forward as a government amendment. In all cases, the essence of the transactions is the attempt to find a compromise, or at least a solution which can be made to appear defensible and moderate.

A special purpose often served by the proceedings in the Lords is the final settlement of matters which have been left undecided in the Commons. On a complicated bill first dealt with in the Commons, many amendments are withdrawn in committee and on report, against an undertaking by the Government to give further consideration. After further discussion in private, the Government may be ready to make its final decision by the committee or report stage in the Lords. On the Labour Government's Town and Country Planning Bill in 1947, for example, the Government accepted, or itself proposed, many amendments in the Lords in this way, and Mr. W. S. Morrison, on behalf of the Conservatives in the Commons, thanked the Minister 'and his advisers for the consideration they gave to arguments that were advanced in favour of amendments which were not made here, but were made later in another place'.[2]

It seems fair to say that the changes in the legislative work of the Lords over the past forty years have been changes for the better. They are not exclusively the result of the Parliament Act of 1911, but that Act, in a sense, showed the way. The Lords may feel impelled to

---

[1] The practice of holding over amendments to be settled on report was recently criticized by Lord Saltoun. He suggested that it was a misuse of the report stage, and that 'where new clauses, or important and controversial amendments, were introduced into a bill after the committee stage, the Government might take into consideration the practice of recommitting the bill, and then having—it would have to be by agreement on both sides—a formal and short report stage afterwards' (Lords Debs., 14th November 1956, vol. 200, col. 315). Lord Salisbury agreed that there was one fairly important objection to the use of the report stage for following up amendments; the discussion was indeed of a 'committee' type, and on report the rule that a peer should not speak twice to the same question might, if strictly applied, often prejudice the value of the discussion. On the other hand, to recommit bills in order to settle the amendments, instead of doing it on report, would be a time-consuming solution. On the whole, Lord Salisbury seemed to think the existing practice not unsatisfactory: 'Actually, we do not in practice have much difficulty about these things, which are usually discussed between the Parties and settled amicably on both sides' (Ibid., col. 322).

[2] Commons Debs., 1st August 1947, vol. 441, col. 799.

offer more positive resistance to future legislative proposals, and it is possible to envisage circumstances in which they would be right to do so, but it is to be hoped that the main lines of future development will be in the direction of extending the constructive capacity which the House has shown in recent years.

Chapter X

CONSERVATIVE AND NATIONAL GOVERNMENT BILLS, 1922–39

THE old opinion that the House of Lords goes to sleep during periods of Conservative rule, and wakes up in fury when leftish governments are in power, was perhaps well founded fifty years ago. The House of Lords of the early twentieth century probably deserved to be called 'Mr. Balfour's poodle'; its forwardness in rejecting or mutilating important Liberal Government bills in 1906–14 was matched by its compliance with the wishes of the Conservative Governments of 1895–1906. But its recent behaviour hardly justifies an assumption of such a simple distinction between its work under left and right governments.

Between the wars the House of Lords was by no means always subservient to the wishes of the Conservative or Conservative-dominated ministries which were in power throughout most of the period. Although no important government bills were rejected, many amendments were forced through against the Government's wishes. Indeed, the dominant feature of the work of the Lords with regard to legislation between the wars was the readiness of Conservative peers to create difficulties for Conservative-dominated governments. These governments were not prepared to enter into conflict with the House of Lords as such, and were often obliged to give way over points of detail in their legislation.

In 1929 the Government ran into some trouble over a Local Government (Scotland) Bill. Lord Lamington moved to delete a provision, which had been inserted in the Bill in the Commons in response to back-bench pressure, to allow payment to be made to councillors in respect of working time lost from their ordinary employment. There was a tie, and the provision was saved by the

Chairman's casting vote. On the report stage, however, in order to meet the objections of those peers who had voted against the Government, Lord Salisbury proposed a compromise by which maximum amounts of payment to councillors were laid down.

On the accession of Ramsay MacDonald's National Government in 1931 the Lords resumed essentially the same course which they had followed before 1929. The official Opposition in the upper House was now smaller than ever, but the Government was often opposed by large numbers of right-wing Conservatives. In the new Government's first session one action of the House of Lords brought it very serious unpopularity with the left. The Children and Young Persons Bill, as it came up from the Commons, included a provision for the abolition of the power of the courts to order corporal punishment for juvenile offenders. The Conservative peers voted almost solidly against this reform, which was rejected by 65 votes to 22, and although in the House of Commons the offending restoration of corporal punishment was promptly removed, the Lords insisted on their amendment, this time by a much narrower majority of 41 to 33. The Government gave way, and the Commons accepted the decision of the Lords, whose action delayed this particular reform for seventeen years.

On some parts of the Agricultural Marketing Bill of 1933 the Government received hardly any support at all in the Lords, and the Bill was enacted with some important amendments inserted against the Government's wishes. When the Earl of Radnor proposed to insert a proviso that regulations to be made under the Act must not be prejudicial to home products, the Government was defeated by 21 votes to 14. Of the peers who voted against the amendment, ten were office-holders and only four were back-bench peers. Later on, with regard to the composition of the marketing boards, the Government was even more severely defeated, this time by 28 votes to 13. The Government made no attempt to reverse these amendments in the Commons.

In June 1935, on its Housing Bill, the Government was again faced by many amendments concerned with the defence of property-owning interests. Of 35 amendments of substance which were moved during the committee and report stages, 32 were moved by Conservative peers, and the other three were moved by non-party peers who normally supported the Conservative Party. Of all these amendments eight were accepted, seven were negatived, four were rejected on division, and the remainder were withdrawn. One of the amendments accepted by the Government in the Lords was later modified in the Commons, which, at the request of the Minister, increased from five years to ten years the time-limit for public authorities' control over land.

CONSERVATIVE AND NATIONAL GOVERNMENT BILLS

In 1936, on the Government's Unemployment Insurance (Agriculture) Bill, Lord Phillimore proposed that in the country local post offices should deal with unemployment insurance business in order to save rural workers from having a long journey to the nearest Labour Exchange. The Government opposed this suggestion on the ground that village post offices would often be incapable of dealing with these complicated matters. Furthermore, the Ministry of Labour intended to set up sub-offices and to employ visiting officers in order to save rural workers from unsuitable journeys. It asked Lord Phillimore not to press this point, but to leave the Government to try out its own arrangements over a reasonable period. Several Conservative peers spoke for the amendment, however, and it was pressed to a division, in which the Government was defeated by 33 votes to 9. Shortly after this the Government was again defeated, this time on an amendment to halve the labourer's contribution in cases where he was paying through a friendly society. The majority of the peers were unimpressed by the Government's argument that, if the amendments were accepted, the industrial associations would at once complain that agricultural workers were being too well treated.

In these matters the majority of the peers did not insist on flouting the Government's will; at the third reading Lord Phillimore himself moved new compromise amendments, which were the result of discussions between him and his friends on the one hand and the Ministry's representatives on the other hand.

The National Government faced serious difficulties with its Coal Industry Bill of the session of 1937–8, which was concerned with the nationalization of mining royalties. It also proposed to create machinery for promotion of efficiency in the working of the industry, and it provided for compulsory amalgamation of collieries in certain cases. In the House of Lords there was a three-day debate on the second reading, in which most of the arguments brought forward were hostile, particularly to the parts of the Bill which dealt with the nationalization of royalties.

The Bill was given a second reading without a division, but on committee and report several important amendments were carried against the Government. The Lords made altogether 117 amendments, of which 109 were accepted by the House of Commons, and the remaining eight were dealt with by compromise proposals. The Lords devoted eight sittings to the committee and report stages (including the time spent on discussing proposed instructions to the committee)—fully two-thirds as long as the Commons had spent. No less than sixteen divisions were called. After clearing out of the way a Socialist proposal to convert the Commission into a national coal board (which was defeated by 108 votes to 5), the House passed on to the Conservative amendments. On the first of these, a proposal by Lord Balfour of Burleigh to postpone the vesting date of the Commission until the regional valuations were completed, the Government was badly defeated, by 55 votes to 34. A little later the Government was again defeated, this time by 59 to 58, on an amendment whose effect was to extend very considerably the range of compensation to royalty-owners. A third government defeat was on a proposal by Lord Hastings to make compulsory the publication of the total valuation for each region—an almost impossible condition. On report the Government suffered a further defeat over the question of the cost of surface damage claims. The other government defeats were on amendments linked with these points. On some amendments the Government succeeded in defeating the opposition by varying margins.

On the three most important matters of principle on which the Government had been defeated the House of Commons reversed the Lords' amendments, and in the upper House, when it came to the consideration of the Commons' reasons for disagreeing, the Government succeeded in getting its way by importing a very large number of tame supporters to vote for it. Lord Hastings moved not to insist upon his amendment which would have had the effect of postponing the vesting date, but he did propose an alternative amendment dealing with compensation, and this was accepted without a division. On the other two matters the rebel peers tried still to make their will prevail, either in the form of the original amendment or in some modified form, but the Government defeated them by large majorities.

The conduct of the Conservative peers in relation to this Bill brought upon them a good deal of opprobrium. Sir Stafford Cripps said that the insertion of many amendments designed to benefit royalty-owners or landowners was 'wholly consistent with the position of such an antiquated Chamber'.[1] The *Economist*'s opinion was that the three days of debate on second reading had done 'less damage to the Bill than to the Lords' own reputation for disinterestedness',[2] and the Lord Chancellor himself regretted that many peers who owned royalties were allowing their private interests to influence their judgment of the public interest.

Right down to 1939 the House of Lords was a place where even Conservative governments found themselves in difficulties with 'progressive' legislation. On uncontroversial matters the Lords made some contribution in the way of improvements to bills, and obliged the Government to explain its purposes or to accept modifications, but the positive contribution was less than in more recent years.

[1] Commons Debs., 7th July 1938, vol. 338, col. 418.
[2] *The Economist*, 7th May 1938, p. 290.

Chapter XI

LABOUR GOVERNMENT BILLS IN 1924 AND 1929-31

THE bills of 1924 produced a variety of divisions in committee and on report, with the majority of the peers sometimes supporting the Government and sometimes opposing it. The Government suffered defeats in committee or on report on the Prevention of Eviction Bill (twice), on the Legitimacy Bill, and twice on the London Traffic Bill, though on this Bill there were also two divisions in committee which went in the Government's favour. The Government was also defeated twice in committee on an Unemployment Insurance Bill, and likewise on a War Charges Validity Bill. On an Agricultural Wages Bill the Government was defeated twice and got its own way once.

Mr. Ramsay MacDonald's second ministry in 1929-31 produced some rather more substantial differences between Lords and Commons. The Lords actually rejected on second reading the bill to raise the school-leaving age to 15, and made controversial amendments to several other government bills.

The Unemployment Insurance Bill, which was brought up from the Commons in 1930, raised special questions with regard to the power of the Lords. The Bill needed to be brought into effect at once in order to be of any value, so with this measure the two-years' delaying power left to the Lords under the Parliament Act was in effect a power to destroy. The Bill proposed to improve the lot of the unemployed in various ways. The conditions for payment of 'transitional benefit' were to be made somewhat easier; training might be given to young persons receiving benefit; and an applicant for benefit was no longer to be obliged to prove that he was genuinely seeking work'.

151

The Conservatives criticized the Bill on the ground that it involved extravagant spending of public money. Nevertheless the Lords gave it a second reading without a division, and concentrated on trying to introduce amendments acceptable to themselves. In particular, they were adamant in insisting that the Bill should contain a provision limiting the period of its operation. Lord Salisbury's proposal, to make the Bill operative for one year only, was passed by 69 votes to 10, with some Liberals supporting the Government. The Commons defeated the amendment, and the Lords took the matter a step further by insisting on the one-year time limit, this time by 156 votes to 42. Seven Conservative peers voted with the Government on this occasion, as did a number of Liberals and non-party peers.

The action of the Lords in thus flouting the will of the Government produced a considerable storm in the country. There was talk of a constitutional crisis and the possibility of a dissolution, with the power of the Lords as the main issue. But when the Bill went back to the Commons for consideration of the Lords' reasons for insisting upon their amendment, the Government itself proposed a moderate compromise limiting the operation of the Bill to three years. The compromise was accepted in the Commons and eventually, without a division, by the Lords also, so all talk of constitutional crisis became irrelevant.

Although the compromise was forced on the Government against its will, it can well be argued that the Lords, in being content with a three-year time limit, were using their powers with a moderation that would hardly have been expected of them before 1914. The effect of the compromise was that there must be a review of the whole system of unemployment insurance after three years, and this was not necessarily a bad thing, even from the Government's point of view. Meanwhile, the Government set up a Royal Commission to look into the working of unemployment insurance.

In 1930 the Lords took the rather remarkable step of amending the Army and Air Force Bill, but the clause which they amended was one of a kind which could easily be regarded as suitable for such treatment in the upper House. In the Bill as introduced by the Government and passed by the Commons there was a clause abolishing the death penalty in the armed forces. In committee the Lords, by a vote of 45 to 12, deleted the clause abolishing the death penalty. The Commons promptly restored the clause, and the Lords gave way.

A little later in 1930 the Lords for a time insisted on serious modifications to the Government's Coal Mines Bill, which provided for a 7½-hour shift and set up machinery for consultation between mining undertakings. The Bill was nearly defeated in the Commons, where 40 Liberals voted against the second reading, leaving the

Government with a majority of only eight.[1] The Lords did not take advantage of this fact to vote against the second reading, however; once again they kept their opposition to committee points. The debates on the bill brought large numbers of peers down to the House, particularly on the day on which the Commons reasons for disagreeing were debated.

There was sharp disagreement over the Government's proposal to fix maximum output quotas. In committee the Government was defeated, by 136 votes to 38, on an amendment providing that the quota imposed for any particular district should not be less than the amount of coal consumed by industry and private users in that district in a given period. The minority included most of the Liberals who voted and some Conservatives. When the amendment was rejected by the Commons, however, the Lords gave way without any further division. On a rather similar question concerning the imposition of quotas for individual firms, however, the Lords eventually stood their ground, and insisted on their amendment by the very large majority of 208 votes to 16.

The most long-drawn-out conflict between the two Houses on this Bill was with reference to the length of the working week. One amendment, to the effect that miners were to be allowed to work for 90 hours during each period of two weeks, was rejected, in accordance with the Government's wishes. This did not mean, however, that the Lords were accepting the Government's policy in this matter in its entirety. As the Bill was drafted it did not allow a man who had once gone down the mine to begin his next period of work within 24 hours. An amendment whose effect was to allow a miner to go down again after 22 hours was carried by 123 votes to 16, with two Conservatives supporting the Government. A further modification was made to this amendment, and insisted upon by the Lords on consideration of the Commons amendments, by 162 votes to 16, in a division this time entirely on party lines. In its new form the amendment was again rejected by the Commons, but the Lords unrepentantly insisted on it, by 168 votes to 36.

Another Government defeat on this Bill took place over an attempt to reverse a defeat in the Commons. In its original form the Bill contained a provision for a central export levy, which the Commons deleted. In committee in the Lords, Lord Gainford, with the support of the Government, tried to reinstate the levy, but his amendment was defeated by 82 votes to 35. After this the Lords went further and deleted from the Bill also the provision for a district levy, which the Commons had allowed to remain in it.

On the Government's Housing Bill, which was largely concerned

[1] Cf. C. L. Mowat, *Britain Between the Wars* (Methuen, 1955), p. 364.

with slum clearance and the provision of subsidies, the Lords insisted upon an amendment protecting landlords against certain liabilities for decorations and repairs. Rather than accept the amendment the Government abandoned the whole clause. With regard to the compensation to owners, however, the Lords, after first making an amendment, did not insist upon it. The Lords passed and insisted upon an amendment whose intended effect was to give powers to Metropolitan boroughs instead of to the London County Council. This would seem inherently not to be a party matter, but it was treated as such on this occasion—not for the last time.[1]

With the Widows, Orphans and Old Age Pensions Bill the Lords succeeded in introducing two watering-down provisions, one of them to make the Bill apply only to necessitous widows (and not to all widows), and the other to limit the rather complicated provisions for participation in the scheme by self-employed persons in the event of their income rising above the maximum figure provided for by the Bill.

In the same session the Government introduced a Road Traffic Bill which was for the most part distinct from party controversy. There were several divisions in committee for which the Whips were not put on, though in each of these it was the side on which the ministers voted that won. There was, however, a difficulty over the power of local authorities to run motor coaches. In a thinly-attended House the Government suffered defeat in a division which was on party lines as far as Conservatives and Socialists were concerned, but in which the Liberals were divided. The total number voting was only 24 to 11.

In the session of 1930–1 most of the Government's difficulties in the Lords arose in connection with bills dealing with agriculture. Dr. Addison's Agricultural Land Utilization Bill, under which a new corporation was to run experimental farms, was opposed root and branch by a few Conservatives, but not by the Conservative Party as a whole. The differences of opinion within the House on this measure did not follow any regular pattern, and the Government found itself with a constantly shifting and changing set of allies, sometimes in a good majority and sometimes in a hopeless minority. Divisions were called on both the second and third reading, but in both cases it was only a few irreconcilable Conservatives who voted against the Government. The second reading was carried by 101 votes to 22, and the third reading by 62 votes to 6. In committee and on report, however, the Government was defeated in seven of the eleven divisions, and the Bill went for the Royal Assent much emasculated.

[1] Cf. below, p. 163.

LABOUR GOVERNMENT BILLS

The Agricultural Marketing Bill was debated by the Lords on committee and report at considerable length, but the attitude of the Opposition on this matter was extremely moderate, and only two divisions were called, in both of which the Government was victorious by a comfortable but not remarkable majority. Half a dozen amendments moved by Conservative peers were accepted by the Government, and some others were withdrawn. But it must be observed that the very small attendance of peers in the House during the later stages may have been partly responsible for the paucity of divisions. The Earl of Lauderdale did say that he would have liked to divide the House on one of his amendments, but that as he knew there was no quorum present he would let his amendment go, as he realized that if he called a division its only effect would be to draw attention to the lack of a quorum and to bring the day's business automatically to an end—and this he did not want to do.

Another agricultural bill, the Small Landholders (Scotland) Bill was also gently treated by the upper House. The Lords made some amendments against the Government's wishes, but did not insist on them when they were rejected by the Commons. One peer complained, however, that the proceedings of the lower House had not shown sufficient respect for the rights of the upper. He objected to the fact that the Lords' amendments had been 'cursorily dismissed' at four in the morning, and he suggested that such proceedings were bad for the prestige of Parliament. The Government spokesman, Earl De La Warr, gave a reply which a later generation of Labour Ministers was to reproduce, perhaps with greater complacency: 'The matter has been before His Majesty's ministers and the ministers' advisers, and the matter has had considerable discussion as a result of that consideration.'

The Government also introduced in the session of 1930–1 a highly controversial Representation of the People Bill, embodying many minor reforms in the electoral system, about which members of the Labour Party had for a long time been agitated. The proposal to abolish university representation had already been defeated in the Commons, because of the hostility of some Liberals. In the Lords the second reading was carried by 50 votes to 14, but in committee three important amendments, concerned with topics such as the use of motor-cars at elections, were carried against the Government, all by large majorities and with at least 100 peers voting in each division. In no case did the Conservatives vote solidly against the Government.

The Bill emerged from the Lords only a fortnight before the summer recess, and in the Commons the Government decided to defer the discussion of the Lords' amendments until the autumn. Mr. Snowden did say, however, in reply to a Question, that if there were a unanimous desire in the Commons for late sittings in order to discuss the Lords' amendments to this Bill the Government would not object.[1] The Government's slowness in this matter is one of the many things with which Ramsay MacDonald has been reproached by Socialist posterity, but it is hardly fair seriously to blame the Lords for thus delaying the reforms for nearly a generation—and this was indeed the effect of their actions, though they probably did not expect that such an effect would follow. As far as the Lords knew when they voted against the Government on these particular points, the House of Commons was going to reverse their amendments, and the Lords might finally have given way. In fact the Commons never considered the Lords' amendments and the Lords never had an opportunity for giving second thoughts to their decisions. Before the end of the summer recess the Government had been reconstructed and the new Baldwin–MacDonald coalition was in office.

[1] Commons Debs., 27th July 1931, vol. 255, col. 1941.

Chapter XII

LABOUR GOVERNMENT BILLS IN 1945-51

1. THE NATURE OF THE LORDS' CONTRIBUTION

THE General Election of 1945 returned to power a Labour Government with a majority in the Commons about as large as that possessed by the Liberals in 1906-10. Mr. Attlee's Government had a programme of legislative reforms even more far-reaching than that of its predecessors, and during the four full parliamentary sessions before the general election of 1950 it introduced a succession of important and complicated bills to which the Conservative Party was in general strongly opposed. In the Commons the guillotine procedure was freely used, and some of the Government's bills emerged from that House with many clauses and amendments undebated. In these circumstances the House of Lords, still with a big majority of Conservative peers, showed great capacity for adaptation of its methods and aims. All the bills which translated into legislative terms the main aspects of the Labour Party's policy were given a second reading without a division.[1] The Conservative peers, who acted under the guidance of their leader, the fifth Marquess of Salisbury,[2] had worked out their policy in the light of the

[1] It is tempting, though it would also be uncharitable and unfair, to compare the behaviour of the Conservative Party over these second readings with that of a dog who likes to chase a cat but not to catch one. In the House of Commons, where they well knew that they had no chance of success, the Conservatives divided against the second readings of the National Health Service, Civil Aviation, Bank of England, Town and Country Planning, Transport, Electricity, Gas, and Iron and Steel Bills. On some of these bills, they also divided against the motions to commit to standing committees and the money resolutions.

[2] He succeeded to the marquisate in 1947, but had himself been given a peerage in 1941.

circumstances. Until 1947 it was clear that a bill thrown out of the House of Lords would, in the long run, most probably be passed into law through the operation of the 1911 Parliament Act. When the Iron and Steel Nationalization Bill was to be brought forward in 1948-9, however, it was widely supposed that the Conservative peers would vote against the second reading because by then it would be too late for the Government to have the Bill passed in three consecutive sessions in the House of Commons before the end of the Parliament.[1] By passing the new Parliament Act, the Government deprived the Lords of the power effectively to reject the Iron and Steel Bill, which was in fact given a second reading without a division.

The work of the Lords on these bills was, then, mainly concerned with the discussion of points of detail. To the Government itself the committee stages were often of great value, in providing opportunities for dealing with amendments not finally decided in the Commons, and for bringing forward new amendments in fulfilment of agreements reached with outside bodies. Similarly, many government amendments were made in order to improve drafting, to remove possible obscurities or inconsistencies in the texts. With most of these amendments it would not really be fair to give credit to the House of Lords as such; the Government and its draftsmen had had to work in a great hurry, and they merely used the committee and report stages in the Lords for introducing improvements or changes which they had not had time to prepare earlier. But in addition the Government was forced to deal with great numbers of amendments proposed by peers, mostly of the Opposition. Some of these followed up the Commons proceedings, and some again were brought forward at the suggestion of outside bodies. Others were brought forward to deal with points which had passed unnoticed during the proceedings in the Commons. Several important bills had been hustled through the Commons under the guillotine, and some clauses were considered in detail for the first time in the Lords.

A few amendments were carried against the Government and later cancelled in the Commons; many were dropped when the Government refused to accept them, because it considered them undesirable or unnecessary; many others, after being discussed on the floor of the House and in private, led to action by the Government to attempt to satisfy the desires or misgivings of the peers responsible for bringing them in. In a single session, that of 1946-7, according to Lord

[1] Cf. C. R. Attlee, *As it Happened* (Windmill Press, 1954), p. 167. As Mr. Attlee puts it: 'For our first three years we experienced no trouble. The House of Lords fulfilled a useful rôle as a debating forum and a revising chamber. It was, however, clear that the Iron and Steel Bill would not get through the Lords without the use of the Parliament Bill.'

Jowitt, the Lords passed 1,222 amendments, of which 57 were rejected by the Commons.[1] In the session of 1948-9, according to the 1954 Fabian Society pamphlet, 619 amendments were made to Commons bills and 296 were proposed but withdrawn.[2]

Some light on the importance and extent of the private discussions which went on behind the scenes, and were an essential complement to the formal proceedings, is thrown by the speech of Lord Jowitt, the Lord Chancellor, at the beginning of the Committee stage of the Town and Country Planning Bill. 'I have been somewhat criticized', he said, 'for not being in my place on the Transport Bill yesterday. May I say I was not at the Lincolnshire or at Lords or Wimbledon. I was in fact working behind the scenes on this Bill, trying to make myself available to those of your Lordships who wished to come and see me on various difficulties.'[3]

In 1952, after the return to power of the Conservatives, Lord Jowitt summed up the situation of the Labour Government. In the conditions of 1945-51, he was 'forced to be reasonable'. 'As many of your lordships will remember,' he said, 'I used to get them round to my room and we would thresh out our problems frankly and in the most friendly way. Very often I used to be able to meet them on all sorts of topics. . . . If I could not, I explained why. . . . Sometimes I used to go round to ministers to try to get them to give way. The net result of all this was very satisfactory.'[4]

It has been said that 'the most notable and successful example' of the use of the technique of informal discussion was with the Companies Bill of 1947-8. Its whole structure was 'radically changed in respect of its accountancy provisions as a result of a series of informal conferences, attended by two peers representing each party, together with their technical advisers'.[5] This Bill, which, as enacted, occupies 350 pages of the statute book, was, however, in no sense a party measure, and was brought in as a Lords' bill.

2. THE GREAT SOCIALIST REFORMS

The Conservatives in general felt less hostile towards the Government's main reforms than the Conservatives of Balfour's day had felt towards the Liberal Government's policies. In Earl Attlee's words, 'There was not much real opposition to our nationalization policy.'

[1] Lords Debs., 25th November 1952, vol. 179, col. 530.
[2] Lord Chorley, B. Crick and D. Chapman, *Reform of the Lords*, op. cit., p. 16.
[3] Lords Debs., 26th June 1947, vol. 149, col. 458.
[4] Ibid., 25th November 1952, vol. 179, col. 531.
[5] Lord Chorley, B. Crick and D. Chapman, in *Reform of the Lords*, op. cit., p. 15.

The Conservatives were indeed strongly and fundamentally opposed to the nationalization of road haulage and of the iron and steel industry, and the Government had rather more opposition to face in the Lords over these two bills than over the others. The eight nationalization bills of 1945–9 produced between them 43 divisions in the committee and report stages in the House of Lords; 13 of these were on the Transport Bill and 13 on the Iron and Steel Bill. Again, these were the only two bills on which the Lords refused to accept the Commons' action in rejecting the controversial amendments; on the fiercely contested question of the date of the establishment of the Iron and Steel Corporation the Lords eventually got their way.

A study of the division lists shows that the House was not invaded by large cohorts of backwoodsmen at any time during the nationalization debates. The average number of peers voting was in the region of 80, and the largest number to vote in any of the divisions in committee or on report on these bills was 119. In the final vote on the postponement of the iron and steel vesting date the number voting was 132, as compared with 209 a year earlier on the proposal to abolish capital punishment.

Certain misgivings about the application of the principle of public ownership and control repeated themselves with respect to several of the bills. The Conservatives, both in the House of Lords and outside it, were anxious to circumscribe the powers of the ministers concerned with the various boards, to extend the scope of parliamentary control, to combat centralization, and to restrict the powers of the boards with regard to charges. Again, there were proposals for representation of interests on the boards, and proposals to define more explicitly the Ministers' duty to appoint men with appropriate experience to serve as members of the boards. Although the Parties as such differed on these matters, the differences involved were not in themselves fundamental differences of party principle.

The three chief bills of the session of 1945–6 were those dealing with the nationalization of the coal mines, with the establishment of the public corporations for civil aviation, and with the National Health Service.

Coal Nationalization

The Coal Nationalization Bill which the Labour Government introduced in its first session in office was much more far-reaching in its scope than the Bill of 1938,[1] but was treated far more gently by the Conservatives. The second reading debate lasted for two sitting

---

[1] Cf. above, pp. 119, 149 f.

days, and the speeches were mainly constructive rather than hostile. Even Lord Londonderry, who spoke as a coal-owner rather than as a spokesman of the official Opposition, said that it was better to seek to amend the Bill than to reject it.[1] In the whole of the committee and report stages there were only two divisions; both resulted in the defeat of the Government until the Commons restored the Bill to an acceptable shape. One of the divisions was on a proposal to insert into the Bill a clear and emphatic statement that no undue or unreasonable preference or advantages were to be given by the Coal Board in its sales of coal. The other was on a proposal at the report stage to insert a new provision with respect to the accounts of the Coal Board.

Civil Aviation

The Civil Aviation Bill aroused rather more hostility. In the committee stage the first battle was on a Conservative's proposal to set up a third Airways Corporation for Scotland. This idea had been put forward in the House of Commons, but, as the Earl of Selkirk claimed, was not treated as a Party matter until the Government made it so. After a fairly long debate at the committee stage, in which no less than eight Scottish Peers supported the Earl of Selkirk, in addition to two Party leaders, Lord Swinton and Lord Cranborne, the proposal was withdrawn for the time being. At the report stage, however, it was put forward again, and this time the Conservatives pressed it to a division and defeated the Government by 62 to 24.[2] In this division the voting was on party lines for the most part, although of the Liberals Lords Reading and Samuel supported the Government and Lord Beveridge the Opposition. The Lords' amendment duly went to the Commons, where it was thrown out. When the matter came back to the Lords again, the Lords accepted the verdict of the Commons.

Later on in the committee stage, Lord Swinton proposed to extend the right of private enterprise airways firms to run charter services. This time the Government went some of the way towards meeting the Conservatives, and at the report stage an amendment was made. The Government also inserted an amendment to reconstruct Clause 36 (dealing with the Air Transport Advisory Council), in order to meet the amendment which had been put down by Lord Swinton.

[1] This was the seventh Marquess, who had energetically opposed all trends towards public control over the coal industry before 1939.
[2] Lords Debs., 25th July 1946, vol. 142, col. 968. Here the Lords' action attracted considerable publicity; the *Glasgow Herald* gave it two columns on the centre page and also its first leading article.

LABOUR GOVERNMENT BILLS

National Health Service

The third major Bill of the first session of the Labour Government was that which established the National Health Service. It too had a second reading debate covering two sitting days, and the committee stage was spread over four days, representing a total time of over twelve hours. The Bill had not come up for second reading until after the summer recess, so the Lords had to deal with all the stages of the Bill during the short period between the reassembly of Parliament in October 1946 and prorogation. It should be added, however, that a preliminary debate had been held already in April 1946 on a motion moved by Lord Moran.

At the second reading debate the House of Lords had the benefit of speeches from two leaders of the medical profession. Lord Horder complained that there had not been enough consultation with the doctors during the framing of the Bill, and he referred to the Minister's claim that he had in fact had full consultations. 'I was myself present at two of these so-called consultations,' said Lord Horder. 'The Minister told us what he proposed to do; he answered a few of our questions, and the conference concluded with his telling us that what he had said was to be kept secret.'[1]

In committee and on report amendments were proposed by sixteen peers, other than government spokesmen, none of them on the Labour benches. Among the amendments accepted, in whole or in part, by the Government, were the following: the extension of the right of doctors to follow their own private patients into hospital; a provision that universities associated with hospitals should be given facilities for teaching and research; a proposal that medical practices committees should consult partners in an established practice before filling a vacancy; and a modification of the rules regarding the tribunal which was to deal with the disqualification of practitioners. The Government also abandoned its original intention that the Minister should make regulations covering the qualifications of local authority health officers.

On one matter concerning hospital endowments the Government, having remained adamant while the Bill was going through the Commons, was persuaded to accept a compromise in the Lords. The Commons had rejected an amendment to the effect that endowments should be kept by hospital management committees, instead of being vested in the Minister. In the Lords Lord Maugham proposed that those endowments which had originally been provided for a special purpose, such as the commemoration of some person, should be excepted from the general vesting in the Minister. After a debate of

[1] Lords Debs., 8th October 1946, vol. 143, col. 55.

THE GREAT SOCIALIST REFORMS

more than an hour the Lord Chancellor refused to accept the proposal at that stage. On report, however, he proposed a new sub-section (which was accepted) to secure the substance of Lord Maugham's proposal.

Of the three amendments carried against the Government on divisions, one (to give the management committees a clear legal status) was left undisturbed when the Bill returned to the Commons. The other two, however, were in due course cancelled. The first, already rejected in committee in the Commons, was a proposal that the London County Council should be empowered to delegate functions to metropolitan boroughs.[1] When the Bill returned to the Commons the Lords' amendment was rejected by a majority of 296 to 134. (Over 100 more Members voted in this division in the Commons than had voted in the original division on the recommittal stage.) The Lords then finally gave way, though Lord Balfour of Burleigh said that he was not convinced by the Minister's arguments. The Lord Chancellor insisted that the Government had not rejected the Lords' amendment out of hand, and that its mind had not been made up in advance: 'I was at pains, as I think the noble Lord knows, to get this matter reconsidered by the Minister and his officials.... I was concerned to put forward, so far as I could, the noble Lord's point of view, and to see that it was carefully considered.'

Town and Country Planning

The more controversial nationalization bills did not come up for discussion until the session 1946–7. The Conservatives greatly disliked some parts of the Town and Country Planning Bill, and divisions took place on several amendments concerned mainly with the protection of the rights of individuals against public authorities.

Altogether the Lords occupied 35 hours of sitting during the committee and report stages, as compared with the 82 hours in standing committee and on report in the Commons. The Lords made no less than 310 amendments to the Bill, of which 255 were 'in the nature of drafting amendments'. Of the 55 amendments of substance, 48 were either moved by the Opposition and accepted by the Government, or moved by the Government to meet points raised by Opposition or Labour members in Commons or Lords. Of all the amendments introduced in the House of Lords there were only four (with two others consequential on these) which the Government opposed in the Commons.

Perhaps the most interesting of these was Lord Samuel's proposal

[1] Cf. above, p. 154.

to exempt from development charge, subject to appropriate rules, lands owned by such bodies as universities, schools and the Salvation Army. The Lords also carried a proposal to extend the definition of 'dead ripe land', that is to say land which would be excluded from development charge because it was just about to be developed in 1939, but whose development was prevented by the war. The third division dealt with appeals against development charges, and the fourth concerned mineral rights. The last question was discussed at great length in both Houses; in the Commons the Minister appeared to doubt Lord Llewellin's contention that the matter had nothing to do with the landowning interest. On the contrary, Mr. Silkin thought that of all the amendments this was the one which had aroused the greatest interest in the Lords—apparently because the question of mining royalties affected the personal financial interests of many peers. All these amendments were rejected by the Commons, and the Lords acquiesced in their rejection.

Lord Ridley proposed that orders for joint planning committees should be laid before Parliament for 40 days, and that such orders might be annulled by Parliament during that period without prejudice to anything that had been done in the meantime. The Government accepted Lord Ridley's amendment in committee, but proposed a modification to it at the report stage. When the Bill went back to the Commons a Labour member, Mr. Medland, who had fought very hard but without success (and voted against the Government) on behalf of just this principle, rose to say that he would like to express appreciation on behalf of himself and some of his colleagues who worked in the committee upstairs. 'The point was resisted with some considerable force upstairs,' he said, 'but in another place better counsel prevailed.'

The Lords obtained a concession from the Government with regard to the power of public authorities to designate land for development. When the Bill came to the Lords it gave power to any minister or local authority to designate land before acquiring it, provided that it was to be taken over within ten years. During the committee stage in the Lords it was argued that this period was too long, and after a long debate the Lord Chancellor moved a compromise amendment to reduce the time limit to seven years for agricultural land. The Conservative peers agreed to this, but their colleagues in the House of Commons were not so easily satisfied. On the discussion of the Lords' amendments Mr. W. S. Morrison, who was leading for the Conservatives in the lower House, proposed further to reduce the period from seven years to four. When the Government refused this further concession, the Conservatives divided the House on behalf of the four-year period. But the Conservatives in the Commons were rather lukewarm in their enthusiasm. Only 46 of them—less than a quarter of their strength in the Commons at that time—went into the lobby in support of the amendment.

The Lords also obtained a concession from the Government on another matter of a rather similar type. The Lord Chancellor had moved a new clause in committee, providing that if land was not acquired within ten years the owner might serve notice requiring the planning authority to acquire it forthwith. Lord Llewellin first proposed that this period should be reduced to five years, and then, when this was not accepted, persuaded the Government to compromise at eight years. On this matter too the Conservatives in the Commons proposed a further modification, but this time they did not divide the House when the Government was adamant.

The potential scope for constructive work in the Lords is well illustrated by an amendment which was moved and withdrawn in committee, and then moved again in modified form on report. Its purport was that regulations ultimately to be made for fixing the amount of development charge should have regard to the terms and conditions on and subject to which planning permission had been granted, and should be determined without any undue or unreasonable preference or advantage to one applicant over another. The Lord Chancellor, having heard the Earl of Munster's argument, said: 'I have always been in complete sympathy with the broad general principle . . . but have found it exceedingly difficult to find a formula. With a sincere tribute to the noble Lord's ingenuity I have much pleasure in accepting the amendment.' In the Commons the Government introduced a further amendment, bringing the whole thing into the Bill instead of leaving it to regulations.

The Transport Bill

The next great measure of the session of 1946-7, the Transport Bill, was also examined with constructive intent, although there were more distinct issues of unresolved disagreement. When the Bill emerged from the Commons many parts of it had not been discussed there; *The Times* commented: 'If a revising chamber did not exist it would have to be invented.'[1] The Lords devoted nine days to the committee stage and two to the report. Altogether 240 amendments were made, of which some 200 were either drafting or made in order to give effect to understandings reached in discussions outside Parliament or in the committee and report stages in the House of Commons.

---

[1] Quoted in the Fabian Society pamphlet, *Reform of the Lords*, of 1954, p. 13.

Perhaps the most striking success of the Lords during the discussions of this Bill was with regard to the number of members which the Transport Commission was to have. In the original Bill it was to have only a chairman and four other members. The Commons standing committee had rejected Sir David Maxwell Fyfe's proposal that the number should be increased.[1] In the Lords, however, when Lord Beveridge proposed an increase to ten members, including the chairman, the Government accepted the amendment, or at any rate four-fifths of it, by agreeing to increase the number of members, apart from the chairman, to a permissible maximum of eight.[2]

Lord Teynham persuaded the Government to accept an amendment imposing upon the Minister the duty of informing Parliament, on appointment and annually thereafter, about the salaries, fees and allowances paid to members of the commission. Lord Addison, speaking for the Government, began by claiming that the amendment was unnecessary because this would be done in any case; later, however, he offered to think about the matter on report. But after the discussion had proceeded a little further he agreed to let the amendment be put in straight away in the form in which it then was. A further small change was proposed by the Government at the report stage, and accepted by the House. The Government accepted amendments forbidding the British Transport Commission to manufacture bodies for road vehicles, and obliging it always to give at least one month's notice before withdrawing any service.

There were ten major issues of disagreement, involving 42 separate amendments inserted against the Government's wishes. The Minister considered that all these amendments merely embodied Conservative Party policy,[3] and they were rejected with little ceremony when the Bill returned to the House of Commons.

The Government came in for some criticism for the way in which it had swept aside the controversial proposals of the Lords. *The Times* commented that many of the amendments introduced into the Bill by the Lords, and rejected in the Commons, would have improved the measure either by making for a more coherent administrative organization or by establishing better principles of democratic control. Lord Salisbury in due course complained of the Government's 'cavalier treatment'. 'One would have hoped that our amendments would at least have been given the sympathetic attention that was their due, even though all were not accepted; but it seems that the

---

[1] House of Commons Standing Committee, Official Report, 4th February 1947, cols. 1126–47.

[2] Lords Debs., 9th June 1947, vol. 148, cols. 391–9.

[3] Cf. Mr. Barnes's comment during the Lords' amendments debate (Commons Debs., 23rd July 1947, vol. 440, col. 1256).

THE GREAT SOCIALIST REFORMS

Government recommended that practically all of them should be rejected root and branch; and no discretion was in fact given to the Government majority in the other place to consider these amendments on their merits at all.'[1]

When the Bill returned from the Commons to the upper House, with all the controversial amendments rejected, the Conservative majority in the Lords showed their annoyance, not merely by words, but also by carrying against the Government three alternative amendments which the Government had to take the trouble to have rejected yet again in the Commons later on. One alternative amendment proposed in the Lords was, however, accepted by the Government at this stage.

Iron and Steel

The Iron and Steel Bill, which passed through Parliament during the session 1948–9, was more controversial than any of the Labour Government's other nationalization measures, and this fact was reflected in the proceedings in the House of Lords. Even this Bill was given a second reading without a division, but the committee stage produced a series of proposals for amendment to which the Government was not prepared to give any sympathy at all. With all of these the course of events was as might be expected; the Lords carried the amendments by divisions, and in due course the Commons reversed the decisions of the upper House. On every point but one the Lords gave way; they did insist, however, on their amendment postponing the date at which nationalization was to take effect, and in this matter the Government eventually conceded the principle. The 28 Lords' amendments made with the Government's agreement were almost entirely on points of drafting; none of them, in the Minister's words, made 'any material or significant change'. All the others were unacceptable to the Government because, as Mr. Strauss told the House of Commons, they either dealt with fundamental principles on which there was 'a gulf' between the parties, or made the task of the new Corporation impossible, or 'harmfully and unreasonably confined' its operations, or imposed absurd restrictions on it. The assumption underlying the proposed restrictions appeared to be, he said, that the Corporation would consist of 'a number of ignorant busybodies' and that the Minister was 'an irresponsible nitwit right outside the control of Parliament'.[2]

The first clause, dealing with the composition of the Iron and Steel

[1] Lords Debs., 29th July 1947, vol. 151, col. 672.
[2] Commons Debs., 25th July 1949, vol. 467, col. 1828.

Corporation, had already been debated at great length in the Standing Committee of the House of Commons, where several Opposition amendments were defeated. The Conservatives in the Commons had been concerned to incorporate into the Bill a clear definition of the qualifications required for membership of the Board; they had also wanted to see that certain interests would be represented. They had proposed, for example, that one additional member of the Board should be selected by the principal steel-using organizations. The Lords carried two amendments specifying that, out of the total of from six to ten members, at least three must have experience in the steel industry and at least one must have experience as a consumer of steel for industrial purposes. The Government, on the other hand, did not want to set rigid limits to the Minister's freedom of choice, and were not prepared to go beyond the formula that the Board's members must have capacity and experience in commerce, industry, administration or the organization of workers.

Lord Teynham withdrew an amendment (which had already been debated and withdrawn in the Commons Standing Committee), to the effect that, in so far as experience of administration was to be a qualification for membership, it must be 'industrial or commercial' administration.

After introducing two provisions circumscribing the activities of the Corporation the Lords turned to clause 3, on the 'general duties' of the Corporation. The Commons Standing Committee had been unable to discuss clause 3 because of the guillotine, but had discussed its principles later when Mr. Lyttleton moved and withdrew a new clause, and on report the Government made some concession to the Opposition's wishes by reconstructing the original clause 3, though without embodying the Opposition's amendments to it.[1] In the Lords some safeguards against discriminatory practices were inserted, against the wishes of the Government, which preferred that the Corporation should be left without such specific restrictions on its freedom.

The Lords showed themselves concerned with the danger of excessive centralization, and on report carried, against the Government, Lord Layton's proposal that the Corporation should be obliged to submit to the Minister a scheme for securing to the nationalized concerns the greatest possible autonomy.

Sharp controversy arose over the Conservatives' proposal to establish an Iron and Steel Prices Board. A new clause to effect this purpose was debated at some length in the Commons Standing Committee and very briefly on report, when the guillotine restricted

[1] House of Commons, Official Report, Standing Committee 'C', 15th March 1949, col. 1665; Commons Debs., 27th April 1949, vol. 464, cols. 187–238.

the debate to ten minutes. In the Lords the proposal was brought in again by Lord Swinton, and carried after being debated for nearly two hours. The final debate in the Commons on the Lords' amendments took the same length of time. So in this matter the Lords in effect compelled the Commons to give more time on the floor of the House to this question than had been given in the Standing Committee, though the final debate was between 7 and 9 in the morning, at the end of an all-night sitting.[1]

The Lords' amendments were dealt with in the House of Commons in two sittings, extending over 22 hours, of which only six hours were within the normal sitting time of the House. The first sitting began at 4 p.m. on 25th July 1939, and continued until noon on the following day. The Government was probably justified in regarding the controversial Lords' amendments as Conservative Party amendments. They were all moved, debated and voted on in the Lords as party questions, and on several of them the final debate in the Commons was considerably longer than the original committee debate in the Lords; the Conservatives were carrying on the struggle with all the means at their disposal. Eight of the ten main discussions were brought to an end by the moving of the closure. In one of the discussions, on the proposal that at least one member of the Corporation must have experience as a consumer of steel for industrial purposes, six Conservatives who were to hold ministerial office in the 1951 Government took part.

Although the Conservative majority in the Lords accepted the decisions of the Commons on all the amendments except that concerning the vesting date, Lord Salisbury made it plain that the acceptance was under protest: 'I sometimes wonder whether the Labour Party, in spite of all their protestations, really believe in the Second Chamber at all. That hardly seems credible, if they expect this House, with all its talent and experience, to sit long hours over bills with the object of making them more workable, and then, without even the façade of serious consideration, reject all the more important amendments that have been made, apparently just because they emanated from the House of Lords.'[2] He protested with especial vehemence at the rejection of the amendment instituting a price-fixing board.

The Lords' decision to insist on the amendment postponing the vesting date did lead the Government to propose a compromise, by which they really accepted the principle underlying the Opposition's

---

[1] House of Commons Official Report, Standing Committee 'C', 16th March 1949, cols. 1677–1708; Commons Debs., 27th April 1949, vol. 464, cols. 285–90; and 25th July 1949, vol. 467, cols. 2121–56; Lords Debs., vol. 163, cols. 446–80.

[2] Lords Debs., 28th July 1949, vol. 164, col. 626.

wishes. By inserting a new provision to the effect that no member of the Corporation was to be appointed before 1st October 1950, the Government conceded the substance of the Conservative demand that nationalization should not take effect until after the General Election.[1] There was indeed a certain irony about the business; the Government had at first cared so much about having the nationalization carried safely into effect before the forthcoming General Election, that they had (or so it seemed) brought in the Parliament Bill especially in order to achieve that purpose. They had laid themselves open to a charge of subordinating the constitution itself to a single political objective; yet in the long run, disturbed at the practical difficulties that might be caused through excessive haste, they abandoned the political objective at the behest of the House of Lords.

3. ORDINARY LEGISLATION

So far we have been concerning ourselves with measures of substantial importance, and with questions involving a certain amount of party controversy. We should, however, have a false picture of the work of the Lords in relation to bills in 1945–51 if we did not consider also the large numbers of less dramatic measures. A detailed examination of the proceedings in a single session shows that there was much unspectacular but constructive work to be done in the House of Lords.

During the Labour Government's first session in power, that of 1945–6, 63 Government bills came up to the House of Lords after passing through the Commons. One-third of these were amended in the Lords in committee or on report. Of those which the Lords did not amend some were bills of a formal or financial kind, scarcely susceptible of amendment, such as the Isle of Man (Customs) Bill and the annual Public Works Loans Bill. One or two, however, such as the Dock Workers (Regulation of Employment) Bill, were bills whose details had been discussed at some length in the Commons.

Of the 20 bills which were amended in the Lords in 1945–6 only one, the Coal Industry Nationalization Bill, produced substantial discussion in the House of Commons when it came to consider the Lords' amendments. This we have already considered. With the others the consideration of the Lords' amendments by the Commons was generally very brief. In most cases the Minister recommended the amendments to the House of Commons with the briefest explanation,

---

[1] Commons Debs., 16th November 1949, vol. 469, col. 2087. Mr. Herbert Morrison said that the substitution of a later vesting date was entirely due to 'the intolerable interference of their Lordships with the decision of the people'. (Cf. *Government and Parliament*, op. cit., p. 183.)

and the amendments were accepted without further ado. The proceedings were little more than a formality, because the Lords rarely introduced amendments which the Government was not prepared to accept. With most Lords' amendments what mattered was that the Government had accepted them; no further discussion was necessary.

There was a little difficulty over a point in the Furnished Houses (Rent Control) Bill. During the committee stage in the Lords four amendments, all from the Conservative side, were withdrawn for consideration by the Government. In due course the Government decided to accept them, and they were inserted in the Bill at the report stage. One of them empowered rent tribunals to increase rents of furnished accommodation when the landlord showed that the cost of services for which he had to pay had increased since the rent had originally been fixed. During the discussion of the Lords' amendments in the Commons a Labour member objected strongly, but his objections were overruled by the Minister.[1]

The most controversial amendment inserted by the Lords with the Government's acquiescence was on the National Service (Release of Conscientious Objectors) Bill. The main purpose of this Bill was to provide that men who had been registered as conscientious objectors, and directed to particular occupations other than the Forces, should be released from those occupations under the same time-table as members of the Forces. In the House of Lords it was pointed out that as the Bill stood some conscientious objectors might be placed in an advantageous position as compared with other men, their contemporaries, who had been directed to the mines or other industrial work. (At that time regulations were in force restricting the movement of labour out of certain essential industries. Some directed men were being prevented from returning to their normal avocations, or to occupations of their choice, beyond the date at which they would have been entitled to be released if they had in fact been sent into the Forces instead of being directed to civilian employment.)

Lord Llewellin put down an amendment with the intention of ensuring that conscientious objectors should not be advantageously placed as compared with the other directed men. The Conservative leaders interested themselves in the matter; Lord Swinton himself was the first speaker on behalf of the amendment.[2] After a discussion of about an hour at the committee stage, the amendment was withdrawn. It was discussed again and once more withdrawn on report. Finally, as a result of considerable private discussion, the Lord Chancellor agreed to accept the amendment, and it was inserted in the

[1] Commons Debs., 11th March 1946, vol. 420, cols. 892 ff.
[2] Lords Debs., 5th February 1946, vol. 139, cols. 216 ff.

Bill at the end of the third reading stage.[1] Even in the Lords the Government received some criticism for giving way. Bishop Barnes of Birmingham said that the acceptance of this watering-down amendment would be received with great regret by all pacifists; Archbishop Garbett of York, however, made it clear that Bishop Barnes was not speaking for the whole body of the Church.

In the Commons the Government had to cope not only with the serious objections of some of its own supporters, but also with a jibe from Mr. Butler, who said that by accepting the amendment the Government had really thrown the whole Bill away. Nevertheless the Government in the Commons stood firmly by the concession which it had made in the Lords.[2]

On the National Insurance (Industrial Injuries) Bill the Government made a number of concessions in the Lords. The most important was one whose effect was to give the Friendly Societies direct representation in the membership of local advisory committees.[3] Back in the Commons there was little discussion, but Mr. Butler had the opportunity of saying that the Government was doing this in order to appease the consciences of the 200 Labour Members of Parliament who at the time of the election had signed a pledge that the Societies would be made an integral part of the National Insurance scheme.[4]

On the Borrowing (Control and Guarantees) Bill a sharp conflict developed over a Conservative proposal to set a time limit of five years to the operation of the Bill. A similar amendment had been discussed in committee in the House of Commons, when a division had taken place and the will of the Government had naturally enough prevailed. In the Lords, however, the Conservative peers inserted the time limit into the Bill against the Government's wishes. Back in the Commons Mr. Dalton moved the rejection of the amendment, and in doing so unequivocally rejected any claim by the Lords to have a right to thwart the will of the Government on any point. 'If there were to develop a conflict between the two Houses on this subject, His Majesty's Government would regard it as a serious matter of principle, and at the right moment we should regard it as our duty to make further recommendations to the House. . . .' This was 'an endeavour on the part of non-elected persons . . . to frustrate the clear intentions of the elected majority of this House'. The Lords' amendment was duly thrown out one morning at 3.15 a.m.[5] Back in

---

[1] Lords Debs., 26th February 1946, vol. 139, cols. 880 f.
[2] Commons Debs., 20th March 1946, vol. 420, cols. 1922–49.
[3] Lords Debs., 15th July 1946, vol. 142, cols. 405–8.
[4] Commons Debs., 30th July 1946, vol. 426, col. 913.
[5] Commons Debs., 25th June 1946, vol. 424, col. 1274.

the Lords again, however, the Government agreed to limit the control to amounts of over £10,000.

None of the other Lords' amendments of this session were controversial. Several of them were made because the Government had decided to defer the solution of many points of detail until after the last stages in the Commons. On the Building Restrictions (Wartime Contraventions) Bill the Government moved many technical amendments in the House of Lords, because the House of Commons committee stage had already begun before representations were received from a number of important local authorities. The results of the Government's discussion in private with the representatives of the local authorities were embodied in the amendments which the Government itself proposed in the Lords; the Commons accepted them without a word.[1]

On the Acquisition of Land (Authorization Procedure) Bill, over 20 amendments with which the Government was sympathetic had been proposed in the House of Commons but allowed to stand over until the Lords committee stage, in order that the Government might have more time finally to make up its mind on details. In due course the Government itself brought forward the amendments in the House of Lords, where they were accepted.

On the Cinematograph Films Bill the Government, in fulfilment of a pledge given in the House of Commons, proposed an amendment to the effect that one of the representatives of the film producers on the Films Council should be a representative of makers of specialized films, not intended for use as first features. On the Local Government Bill the Government accepted a Lords' amendment to the effect that three copies of draft valuation lists for rating purposes should be provided. This too had originally been proposed in the Commons, and when the Lords' amendment came up in the Commons Colonel Wheatley, who had originally interested himself in the matter, complained that he had had to wait so long in order to have his point dealt with.

On the report stage of the National Assistance Bill the Government accepted a Conservative peer's amendment, whose effect was to make more explicit the provision that full use should be made of local knowledge. An amendment had already been made in the Commons, but some Conservative peers had argued, both on second reading and in committee, that the amendment had not gone far enough.

On the Motor Spirit Bill, whose chief objective was to protect the petrol rationing system against possible abuses, such as the use for private purposes of petrol supplied for commercial use, most of the

[1] Commons Debs., 11th March 1946, vol. 420, cols. 900-3.

amendments made in the House of Lords were brought in in order to implement undertakings given in the House of Commons. Many of these, according to the Attorney-General when he presented the Lords' amendments to the Commons, would have been made in the Commons at the report stage if there had been time.[1] Many interesting changes were introduced in the Lords. The original Bill had provided that an owner of a petrol pump who put commercial spirit into a private pump might be disqualified for a time from selling petrol. It was pointed out in both Houses that this provision might drive out of business owners of petrol pumps in isolated areas and thus deprive local residents of essential services. An amendment was therefore made in the Lords providing for alternative severe penalties instead of disqualification in appropriate cases. The Lords also persuaded the Government to accept a provision that proceedings were not to be instituted under the Act except with the consent of the Minister of Fuel and Power or the Director of Public Prosecutions.

This brief survey of the Lords' amendments to bills in 1945–6 gives some idea of the scope and character of the less spectacular contributions of the House of Lords to legislation under a Labour Government. A study of one of the other sessions of 1945–51 would produce broadly similar results.

Although many Lords' amendments were introduced in order to tidy up questions left undecided in the Commons, many others, even under the Labour Government, introduced new matter. On the National Assistance Bill of 1947–8 there was originally a provision that the registration authority might refuse to register a Home if any person was employed there who in the authority's opinion was unfit to be so employed. During the committee stage in the Lords the Earl of Iddesleigh, on behalf of the Salvation Army, suggested that it would be enough if the registration authority were to be concerned only with the fitness of persons engaged in the management of Homes, and not with that of all persons working at such Homes. Eventually the final form of the amendment was agreed upon at a meeting between the Earl of Iddesleigh, Lord Henderson, who was in charge on behalf of the Government, and a representative of the Salvation Army.[2] On the same Bill at the committee stage the Government introduced some amendments as a result of discussions which it had had with representatives of the London County Council.

The fact that an amendment has been inserted by the House of Lords with the agreement of the whole House does not necessarily satisfy the Commons that the amendment should be accepted with-

---

[1] Commons Debs., 27th May 1948, vol. 451, cols. 481 ff.
[2] Lords Debs., 26th April 1948, vol. 155, col. 360.

ORDINARY LEGISLATION

out explanation. Usually in commending a Lords' amendment to the Commons the Minister in charge of a bill gives a brief explanation of its purport. It is not unknown for him to use the very same words as have been used in the Lords at the original introduction of the amendment.[1] Even under the Labour Government, however, the Opposition in the Commons was prepared to be restive if important new material first appeared in the Lords. In 1950, on the Diplomatic Privileges Bill, when the Government recommended a highly technical Lords' amendment to the lower House, a Conservative complained that this intricate matter had been introduced at so late a stage in the Bill, when it was no longer convenient for the Commons to do very much more than accept it.

One of the most controversial actions of the Lords under the Labour Government was the deletion of the death penalty abolition clause from the Criminal Justice Bill in 1948. So many special problems were involved in this affair that discussion of it will be deferred to a separate chapter. Mention must be made here, however, of another controversial amendment to the same Bill. After the death penalty clause had been disposed of in committee, Lord Goddard, the Lord Chief Justice, proposed an amendment to remove the Government's clause abolishing corporal punishment.[2] On this matter too, the general opinion of the Lords was against the liberal reform of the criminal law and Lord Goddard's amendment was carried by 29 votes to 17. The 'anti-liberal' vote on this question was less than a sixth of the vote for keeping the death penalty, but the division was taken at 11.15 p.m., when all but the most enthusiastic peers would have gone home.

The position with regard to this matter was quite different from that with regard to the death penalty. The Government had been quite firm all along about its intention to abolish corporal punishment. When the Bill returned to the Commons, the Government had no hesitation about advising the House to reject the Lords' amendment by reinserting the clause in its original form, and the Government got its way by 232 votes to 62. Some (not many) Conservatives voted with the Government in this division; they included some members of the Conservative front bench. On this matter the Conservative peers were more 'reactionary' than the Conservative leaders in the Commons. In due course the Bill went back to the Lords for reconsideration of the Commons' rejection of Lord Goddard's amendment, and this time the Lords accepted the verdict of the Commons.

[1] Cf. Lords Debs., 20th April 1948, vol. 155, col. 199, and Commons Debs., 12th May 1948, vol. 450, col. 2138.
[2] Cf. above, p. 71.

4. CONCLUSION

The work of the House of Lords during 1945–51 has often been praised, both by Conservatives and by Socialists. The results of the present examination and analysis of its contribution suggest that the praise was well earned. The House showed both assiduity and adaptability in dealing with a situation quite unlike any with which it had ever been confronted before. Above all, though it almost never coerced the Government, it persistently obliged the Government to justify its decisions, and it sometimes persuaded the Government to be accommodating on matters with regard to which it had been adamant in the Commons. Several points were indeed keenly disputed, but on these the Lords did no more, in the long run, than oblige the Government to keep its supporters in the Commons sitting up late on a few nights, cancelling Lords' amendments.

A rather regrettable feature of the Lords' debates on the committee stage of bills between 1945 and 1950 was the small part played by back-bench Labour peers. It is often complained that back-bench members on the Government side of the House of Commons contribute little beyond their votes, particularly during committee stages of bills. This complaint was heard in 1945–51 more often than usual. It could have been made even more forcibly with regard to the Labour peers. On most of the nationalization bills and other important bills hardly any amendments were proposed by Labour peers, who were for the most part silent and rarely spoke except in order to support their own Front Bench.

Chapter XIII

CONSERVATIVE GOVERNMENT BILLS OF 1951-6

AFTER the General Election of 1951 there was once more a Government majority in the House of Lords, but now the Government was safer and stronger than its predecessors between the wars, and able to carry its measures through the Lords, in principle and in detail, with very little opposition from its own right wing. The Labour Opposition, usually numbering between 15 and 30 peers present in the House, was never likely to outvote the Government, but was more stable and coherent and better organized than any Opposition of the period between the wars. Under the Labour Government of 1945-51, a serious party difference on a committee point would be settled by a division, in which the Government was defeated, but whose effect was reversed in due course by the Commons. Under the Conservative Government, controversial points have again been decided by divisions, but as the Opposition has regularly been defeated, the Government has not had to find time in the Commons for the business of reversing controversial Lords' amendments. On the other hand, the Government has introduced or accepted some important amendments in the Lords, and the Opposition has debated them indefatigably in the Commons.

As in 1945-51, the divisions on amendments to bills have since 1951 been mainly on party lines. The Labour peers have divided against the Government rather less frequently than did the Conservative peers when they were in opposition; this is perhaps partly because the Labour peers had no hope of winning, though it may also be because the Government has had less controversial legislation to bring forward. The principal difference between 1945-51 and 1951-6 has been that the Lords' activities in the earlier period necessitated a few extra late sittings for Mr. Attlee's supporters in the House of Commons, while the Conservatives have not had this inconvenience imposed upon them. Late sittings on Lords' amendments have been made necessary, not by hostile decisions of the upper House, but by the Government's willing acceptance in the Lords of changes which the Labour Party in the Commons has found objectionable.

In general, under the Conservatives as under the Labour Government, the proceedings on government bills in the Lords have been useful mainly as occasions for the discussion of amendments which were eventually dropped, or accepted, with or without modification, in accordance with the Government's wishes, without any vote being taken.

On the whole, the period 1951–6 differed less from 1945–51 than from 1919–39. During the 1920s and 1930s there were many divisions on bills in committee, and the voting was hardly ever entirely on party lines. Conservative governments had nothing to fear from the Opposition, whose size was negligible, but plenty to fear from right-wing Conservative peers. Since 1951 the main opposition, as in the Commons, has come from the Left, and the Government has regularly been victorious in divisions by a margin of two or three to one. At the same time, with the increase in party discipline has gone a decline in readiness to call divisions at all. As in the House of Commons, the progressively greater acceptance of the dominating position of the Government has been matched by a growing flexibility in the actual process whereby the Government decides just what it shall recommend to be done. The Government of the day is not nowadays afraid of being defeated in either House by weight of numbers in the division lobbies, but from its position of security and strength it is often amenable to reason and argument. When arguments have failed to persuade a minister, it is only if they are exceedingly dissatisfied that Opposition peers think it is worth while to register their protest by dividing the House.

The change that has taken place in the past twenty or thirty years can best be illustrated by an examination of the proceedings on a few bills of the earlier and more recent periods.[1]

With the Opposition powerless and the Government back-benchers no longer rebellious, it might have been expected that the Lords would not have much to contribute to legislation. In fact, however, the Lords have continued on the course on which they embarked in 1945. On some bills the proposals for amendment and the speeches in committee have come more or less equally from back-benchers on both sides of the House. Any government is rather more inclined to make

---

[1] Some of the divisions on bills in 1920–39 have already been referred to above, in chap. VII, in the course of the discussion of party discipline.

concessions to its own parliamentary supporters than to members on the other side of the House. Thus the committee stage of a bill in the Lords under a Conservative government may in many cases produce not less but more changes than when a Labour government is in power.

With some bills, however, the Lords' proceedings have been less productive than under the Labour Government. Many of the Conservative Government bills have been allowed to go through committee with very little reaction from the Conservative back-bench peers. The Government's Housing Subsidies Bill of 1956, for example, had occupied the Commons on the floor at the committee stage for forty hours. When the Lords' committee stage was taken, however, the whole proceedings occupied no more than 46 minutes.[1] No back-bench Conservative spoke. Only two amendments were proposed, both of them by Lord Silkin, who was the natural leader for the Labour Party in this matter, being a former Minister of Town and Country Planning. Each of these amendments produced a fairly short speech from Lord Silkin and a reply of little greater length from the Earl of Munster, who was acting as the Government's spokesman. On one of the amendments, on which Lord Silkin found the reply 'entirely unsatisfactory', the Opposition showed its 'displeasure at the reply in the usual way'; on the other Lord Silkin said he did not think it was really worth bothering to waste time on a fruitless division.

In one important respect the strength of the Government's majority in the Lords has indirectly diminished the capacity of the upper House to make useful contributions to legislation since 1951. We have seen how usefully and successfully the habit of informal discussion was developed in 1945–9, and how valuable a complement this system was to the actual process of debate on the floor of the House. After the change of government in 1951 things became different. In 1952 Lord Jowitt compared the situation under the Conservative Government with that of the earlier period, when he was 'forced to be reasonable'. 'Today the position is altered. They (Ministers) can bludgeon their bills through. . . . With regard to one bill recently I did feel that we were not consulted at all . . . we were not summoned to any sort of conference.' He hoped to see 'some improvement, and some development, perhaps, of the system of consultation and the like, which we had in the old days'.[2]

The bills for the denationalization of road haulage and iron and steel each produced several controversial Opposition amendments, which were easily defeated in divisions which followed party lines.

---
[1] Lords Debs., 20th March 1956, vol. 196, cols. 579–91.
[2] Ibid., 25th November 1952, vol. 179, col. 531.

On the Transport Bill of 1952–3 the main interest was in the reception given to the Lords' amendments in the House of Commons. The Lords made 71 amendments, of which, according to Mr. Crookshank, 24 were consequential or drafting, seven were put forward as a result of representations by the British Transport Commission, five were put forward to meet Opposition criticism, three more went some way to meet the Opposition point of view, and the rest were either uncontroversial or made in order to clarify the existing provisions of the Bill.[1]

The Government at first decided to give two days in the Commons to the consideration of the Lords' amendments, but the Opposition fought hard and long. On the first day, 21st April 1953, the proceedings continued for fifteen hours, until 7.30 a.m.; on the second day for nine hours, until 1.15 a.m. They then continued for a third day until 3 a.m., and on the fourth day the Government moved an allocation of time motion, by means of which the proceedings were finally concluded at 10.30 p.m. on 27th April, having by then occupied almost 40 hours. On one amendment alone, which in the Lords had been 'produced only at the end of the debate, with no comment of any kind', there was a debate of over five hours in the Commons, half of it devoted to an Opposition amendment to the Lords' amendment.[2] On the next amendment, of which the Opposition spokesman in the Lords had said 'This has met us completely', there was a further debate of over an hour, and a division. During the proceedings in the Commons there were no less than 34 divisions in the four days, including ten on closure motions and four on motions to suspend the Ten O'Clock Rule. (In the Lords there were 13 divisions on this Bill, and seven on all the other controversial questions of the whole session put together.)

Although the Lords' amendments had been debated at such length, the Opposition in the Commons were still violently dissatisfied at the limitation of the debate, and put down a motion of censure (which was debated on May 5th) to the effect that the proceedings had been 'detrimental to the privileges of the Commons and derogatory to the legislative status of this House'. Mr. Herbert Morrison, in moving the censure motion, complained that 'another place was used as a legislative stooge by Her Majesty's Government to evade the House of Commons and to prevent us from discharging our duties properly'.

The Conservative Government's first serious difficulties in the House of Lords arose over the Bill of 1953–4 for the establishment of the Independent Television Authority. The Bill was very unpopular with some important sections of public opinion, usually friendly to

[1] Commons Debs., 27th April 1953, vol. 514, col. 1807.
[2] Ibid., 21st April 1953, cols. 871–976; cf. col. 950.

the Government, and strong opposition to it was expected in the Lords, from Labour and Liberal peers, from many Independents, and from some Conservatives. As the Bill began its parliamentary career it seemed to face greater dangers in the House of Lords than in the Commons, where the Government's majority, though small, was solid and well-disciplined.

In the Lords, the first discussion of the Government's proposals was on a preliminary motion moved by Lord Hailsham.[1] For this debate the Government, full of apprehension lest the voting should go against its policy, took great pains to ensure that there would be a big attendance of amenable peers. These precautions were clearly necessary. Lord Hailsham pressed his motion to a division, and got no fewer than 87 peers to support him in the lobby, 37 Labour, 19 Conservatives and 31 others. In any ordinary division, such a number would be a large majority of the peers voting. The Government's appeal for support was so effective, however, that it collected 157 peers to vote against the motion. Meanwhile the Bill was prepared and carried through the House of Commons, against vigorous opposition and with the help of the guillotine. On the second reading in the Lords, which did not take place until 30th June and 1st July 1954, the Government again got a big majority, though this time the numbers voting on both sides (130 to 64) were considerably less than at the preliminary debate. The Government insisted that it was justified by public opinion in pressing on with the Bill. Many people, according to Lord Salisbury, wanted an independent television programme. 'If we refuse these people what they want, on the grounds that we, superior people, know better than they what is good for them, then it will be a bad day both for this House and for the country.'

At the committee stage the pattern of debate tended to revert to party lines; Lord Hailsham was the only Conservative peer to propose any amendment. He kept up his opposition to the end, but in committee he found relatively few supporters for his crusade on the Conservative benches. The Opposition amendments were put forward mostly by front-bench peers, Lords Jowitt, Listowel and Silkin. Six amendments were pressed to divisions, and in each case the Government obtained its usual majority of two or three to one.

There has been one recent instance of the withdrawal of a government bill in the House of Lords as a result of opposition expressed during a second reading debate. Soon after the beginning of the session of 1953–4, Lord Mancroft, Under-Secretary of State at the Home Office, brought forward the Inventions and Designs (Crown Use) (Lords) Bill. At the second reading debate[2] Lord Wilmot, who

---

[1] Lords Debs., 26th November 1953, vol. 184, col. 747.
[2] Lords Debs., 1st December 1953, vol. 184, cols. 768–98.

spoke for the Opposition, delivered a vigorous attack upon the Bill. 'This is a revolutionary Bill,' he said; 'it takes some sweeping powers and embodies them in the law of the land . . . strikes at the very root of private property in industrial patents and processes . . . there has been no consideration for industry up to now. . . . It seems to me remarkable to introduce a bill of this magnitude without a prior consultation with the interests and persons affected.' Several other peers, on both sides of the House, made similar objections. Lord Balfour of Inchrye, a Conservative, complained in particular about the failure of the Government to consult the Federation of British Industries.

After the debate had run its course, occupying some two hours, Lord Woolton rose to wind up the debate on behalf of the Government. 'I have noted,' he said, 'the general feeling in the House, and there is another factor in my mind, which is that the consultations with industry, which have in fact begun, undoubtedly had not finished when the Bill was drafted.' Because of the reception given to the Bill in the House he felt that it should not be proceeded with for the time being. He accordingly moved that the debate should be adjourned, and his motion was accepted. No further progress was made with the Bill during that session.

The Iron and Steel Bill, by which the iron and steel industry was to be returned to private ownership, was a party measure of first-class political importance. The Labour Party opposed it no less enthusiastically than the Conservatives had opposed the Nationalization Bill three years earlier. In the House of Lords the proceedings followed party lines. Only four amendments were moved at the committee and report stages by private member peers other than Labour peers. Three of these were accepted (one on its second appearance at the report stage) and a fourth was withdrawn after the Government had given assurances that it was not necessary. The rest of the amendments, apart from a few proposed by the Government, were brought forward by Labour peers, most of them by Lords Silkin and Wilmot. The number even of these was remarkably small. Four were eventually accepted by the Government and thirteen rejected, three of them by divisions. Ten others were withdrawn and abandoned. Of the Labour amendments accepted by the Government, one provided that any producer who intended to close a works should inform the Board of his intention 'as soon as possible', instead of merely 'as soon as practicable'. Another strengthened the Board by allowing it to ask for information from the Iron and Steel Trades Federation.

The amendments moved from behind the Government were not of very great importance. Lord Hawke persuaded the Government to accept an amendment whose effect was to enlarge the Minister's field of choice in making his appointments to the Board. Lord Wolverton was successful with an amendment whose effect was to ensure that the Minister would not have power to operate ships.

On the Agricultural Land (Removal of Surface Soil) Bill, the only amendments made in the House of Lords, apart from government amendments, were two proposed by Lord Jowitt. One of these provided that there were to be no prosecutions under the Act save with the consent of the Attorney-General. The other, which Lord Jowitt moved after taking advice from a fellow-peer with great knowledge of the preparation of asparagus beds, reduced the rigidity of some of the controls to be established.

On the Education Bill of 1952–3, the only amendment made was an anti-municipal-trading one proposed by Lord Jessel from the Conservative benches. The Bill as introduced in the House of Lords allowed a local authority to provide school transport over and above that which it was obliged to provide free of charge, and to charge fares for this additional transport. Lord Jessel proposed that the power of a local authority to provide such additional transport should be allowed to operate only on condition that the vehicle-licensing authority considered the existing transport facilities inadequate. The Government accepted this, with a small modification proposed by itself.

In the session of 1953–4, an important amendment was made in the House of Lords to the Atomic Energy Authority Bill. In the Commons there had been a good deal of discussion about the definition of the grounds upon which a member of the staff of an atomic energy establishment might be sent to a tribunal in order to have his reliability on security grounds examined. In the Commons it had been found impossible to find a satisfactory definition in this matter. In the Lords, after more discussion, a new form was found, the essence of which was to provide that security grounds meant 'grounds which would be grounds for dismissal from the civil service under arrangements in force at the relevant time'. As so much discussion had taken place both in the Commons and in private before the Lords' committee stage, this Lords' amendment can hardly be attributed solely to the activities of members of the House of Lords.

The Government's Housing (Repairs and Rents) Bill of the session 1953–4 had been guillotined in the House of Commons, and a number of important sections of it had not been discussed there. The committee and report stages of this Bill in the Lords therefore provided the first opportunity for discussion of amendments to these clauses. The Government gave way, in part at least, to several of the arguments of the Labour peers. It accepted a Labour amendment which limited the amount of back rent that a landlord could be entitled to collect in certain circumstances. When this amendment went back to the Commons several Labour members observed that it had not been discussed during the Bill's first passage through the Commons, and expressed regret that the Government's concession had not gone further. As originally introduced the Bill provided that a landlord might obtain a grant towards the cost of repair of a house whose expectation of useful life would in normal circumstances appear to be at least ten years. Labour members thought that this treated landlords too favourably, and wanted the minimum expectation of life to be increased to twenty years. In the Commons the Government had made no concession on this point, but in the Lords the ten years of the Bill was raised, as a compromise, to fifteen years. Several other minor amendments, slightly unfavourable to landlords, were introduced in the House of Lords in order to satisfy the wishes of Labour members in both Houses. When the Bill went back to the Commons for discussion of the Lords amendments Mr. De Freitas, who was representing the Opposition, went out of his way to give his thanks to Lord Silkin for his 'vigilance' in looking after the interests of the Labour Party while the Bill was going through the Lords.

A few amendments brought in in the Lords, both to this Bill and to the parallel Bill dealing with Scotland, aroused annoyance among Labour members of the House of Commons. The most interesting of these "landlords' amendments" gave a Scottish landlord (or his agent) the right to enter his property, for the purpose of taking measurements and so on, provided that he gave the tenant 24 hours' notice in writing.

On the whole rather fewer amendments have been proposed, and fewer made, to bills under the Conservative Government than during the reign of the Labour Government. Committee stages of bills have been less protracted. Most of the work on bills in committee in the Lords since 1951 has consisted of the discussion of amendments put forward by a very small number of Labour front-bench peers. Labour peers on the back benches have moved far fewer amendments than did Conservative back-bench peers between 1945 and 1950. At the same time the Government's own supporters have, on most bills, had very little to say. It would not be entirely fair to suggest that this necessarily proves correct the popular argument that the Lords have less to do under a Conservative Government.[1] It is partly true that the Labour Government, between 1945 and 1950 at any rate, imposed

---

[1] The rôle of the House of Lords in relation to the Shops Bill of 1956–7 is hard to assess. The Bill was brought in as a Lords bill, and had a leisurely passage through the House. In Committee and on recommittal it took 22 hours, spread over six sittings between February and May 1957. The Labour peers proposed many technical amendments, and divided on one which was designed to strengthen

special legislative burdens on the House of Lords by the speed with which they carried their vast programme of legislation through the Commons. The Government relied heavily on the House of Lords, both for the examination of clauses which were never discussed in the Commons because of the guillotine procedure, and for the final settlement of amendments left undecided in the Commons. As the volume of controversial legislation has been considerably less since 1951 than it was during the reign of the Labour Government, it could be expected that the quantity of amendment of the Lords would be less in any case.

the Bill. The Liberals strongly attacked the Bill's main provision, which was to impose new restrictions on shop opening hours. They moved a wrecking amendment (to delete Clause 1), and divided the House on it. A few Conservative peers supported the Liberals' objections by speeches but not by votes. There was no division on second or third reading. In one of the Committee divisions the Government was opposed only by the Labour peers, in the other only by the Liberals, so in the matter of voting the Bill could be said to have had a smooth passage through the House of Lords. But all through the five months from second reading the proposal to restrict opening hours was made the object of continual and vigorous attacks in almost every respectable non-socialist newspaper and journal, both in letters to editors (mainly, it would seem, from Conservative voters) and in editorial comment.

On 30th May, a fortnight after the third reading in the Lords, Mr. Butler announced in the Commons that the Bill would be dropped for the current session; though pressed by Labour Members he would give no undertaking for the future. The reason Mr. Butler gave for the abandonment of the Bill was lack of time, but this explanation does not appear to have been altogether genuine; had the Government really wanted to fit the Bill in to the parliamentary timetable it could well have done so. It seems fair to assume that the Government dropped the Bill, for the time being at any rate, because of its bad reception. The strictures and the adverse votes of the Liberal peers cannot alone have induced the Government to change its course, but the speeches in the House of Lords of some prominent and recently-ennobled Conservative former M.P.s and ministers may have had some effect. It can probably be assumed that the most potent factor was the Government's appreciation of the Bill's unpopularity, as shown by the reactions of the Press and by words spoken privately to ministers and Whips by Conservatives in both Houses of Parliament. The adverse Conservative speeches in the Lords were the part of the iceberg that showed above the water. The whole business is an excellent illustration of the process (cf. above, pp. 141–3) whereby major legislative decisions are made by the Government, reacting to opinions conveyed to it by various means, rather than in the division lobbies of either House of Parliament.

Chapter XIV

BILLS FIRST INTRODUCED IN THE LORDS

ONE of the four functions which the Bryce Conference Report considered to be appropriate to a Second Chamber was 'The initiation of bills dealing with subjects of a comparatively non-controversial character which may have an easier passage through the House of Commons if they have been fully discussed and put into a well considered shape before being submitted to it'. The Bryce report was not proposing an innovation; it was merely referring to a practice of long standing, to which objection had never been made. There are only two restrictions on the power of the Government to bring in bills for consideration by the Lords before they have been through the Commons. In the first place there is the formal rule that Supply bills must originate in the Commons; in the second place there is the unwritten rule that all the important bills should start their parliamentary career in the popular House.

If this discussion were concerned mainly with a formal description of the powers of the two Houses it would need to include a full disquisition on the implications of the privileges of the Commons over the granting of Supply. Our present purpose, however, is to attempt to analyse current political realities, so the rules regarding Supply will be described as briefly as possible. The only rule that really matters is the provision that only the Government may propose legislation involving expenditure. The rule that if a bill involves expenditure of public money it must include a statement of the means whereby the money is to be provided, and that that statement must be brought in in a Committee of the whole House in the Commons, would at first sight appear to make impossible the introduction in the Lords of bills entailing expenditure or affecting taxation. In practice, however, this rule, in its operation, is nowadays little more than an archaic for-

BILLS FIRST INTRODUCED IN THE LORDS

mality, and where the rule is inconvenient it is circumvented with ease. Bills entailing substantial expenditure, or imposing taxes, are indeed never introduced in the Lords, but it would be unsuitable in any case to introduce them there.

The Government often finds it convenient to introduce bills entailing slight expenditure in the Lords, and not in the Commons. In the session of 1948–9, for example, eight of the bills introduced by the Government as Lords' bills entailed expenditure. When this happens, the House of Lords is asked, on the third reading, to make the 'privilege amendments', by which the House 'omits' the sentences in the bill which deal with the provision of money, so that the bill may go to the Commons without the provisions which would infringe the Commons' privileges. The offending words are not in fact omitted at all; they are underlined, and a note is inserted to say that, although they are still there, they must be deemed not to be there. They then remain 'omitted' in this way until they can be properly 'restored' on the basis of a resolution of a Committee of the whole House in the Commons. It is the task of the officers of the House to see that this solemn ritual is duly performed.

The citation of a concrete instance, where something went wrong, will serve to illustrate the working of the rules. In 1951 the Government brought in its Guardianship of Infants Bill as a Lords' bill, which the Lords duly passed. The third clause proposed to amend the Finance Act of 1949, and to affect the collection of taxes by raising the age and increasing the payments which were to be made without deduction of tax under certain maintenance orders. The Lords neglected to 'omit' this clause before sending the Bill to the Commons, and when the Bill was received in the lower House the Speaker announced that, because clause 3 infringed the privileges of the Commons the Bill must, in accordance with precedent, be laid aside.[1] The Government saw its own Bill spurned in the Commons after being passed by the Lords. The privileges of the House of Commons were upheld.

But in practice the course of legislation was not affected in the slightest degree. There was here no attempt by the Lords to infringe the Commons' privileges, but a trivial oversight by someone concerned in working the machinery. The oversight was quickly rectified. On the same day a new bill, the Guardianship and Maintenance of Infants (No. 2) Bill, identical with the first, was brought into the Lords. Standing Order No. 39 was suspended and the Bill was passed through all its stages at once. At the third reading the privilege amendments were made, i.e. the offending clause 3 was 'omitted' in the manner described above. The new Bill then went to the Commons,

[1] Commons Debs., 18th July 1951, vol. 490, col. 1246.

where it received its second reading six days later. Clause 3 was reinstated at the appropriate time, and the Bill went on peacefully to receive the Royal Assent.

As every bill must pass through both Houses of Parliament, it might be thought that it matters little whether a government bill comes first before the Lords or before the Commons. A convention seems to have developed, however, according to which it would be inappropriate for the Government to bring first into the Lords any bill involving serious controversy between the Parties, or any major questions of policy. The convention, if there is one, is of comparatively recent origin, and has never been explicitly defined. In 1716 there was some complaint in the Commons when the Septennial Bill was brought in as a Lords' bill; nevertheless, the Bill was passed.[1] Several important bills were introduced in the Lords under both Disraeli and Gladstone, but by 1910 Sir John Marriott could complain: 'With increasing uniformity, governments—of both parties—tend to introduce all their important measures in the House of Commons.' Marriott deplored this tendency, and recorded that leaders of the House of Lords found the procedure 'unintelligible', and had made formal protests against it.[2] Such complaints would sound rather strange and misplaced in contemporary conditions. It would by now probably be considered something of an affront to the Commons if the Government submitted one of its chief measures to the test of the upper House before it had been approved by the lower.

A distinction must be made between bills brought in by the Government and those brought in by peers not holding any office. Special conditions attach to bills of the second category, and it is proposed to defer the discussion of these bills to a separate chapter. For the present, then, we shall be concerned with bills brought in by the Government.

There is an important practical advantage in having a fair proportion of government bills introduced in the Lords in the first instance. If all bills went first through the Commons, the Lords would have no legislative work to do during the first part of the session, and they would be overburdened with work during the last part. A better distribution of the time of the two Houses can apparently be achieved if the Lords can spend some of their time during the first months of the session in considering bills which have been brought into their House in the first instance. Some governments have been blamed for introducing too few of their bills into the Lords, and for asking the Lords to deal with too many bills too quickly during the last part of the session. A mild complaint on these lines was made by

[1] Cf. Turberville, *The House of Lords in the XVIIIth Century*, op. cit., p. 165.
[2] J. A. R. Marriott, *Second Chambers* (1910 ed.), p. 57.

BILLS FIRST INTRODUCED IN THE LORDS

the leader of the Opposition just before the summer recess of 1956.

During the eight full sessions covering the period 1947–55, just over a quarter of all government bills were introduced in the first place in the House of Lords. The proportion was somewhat higher while the Labour Government was in power than after the Conservative victory of November 1951. Indeed, if credit is to be given for increasing the use of the House of Lords as a legislative chamber of first instance, it must apparently be given to the Labour Government which came into power in 1945. In each of the three full sessions of the period 1947–50, 20 or more government bills were first introduced into the upper House, and in the short session of 1950 the number of Lords' bills actually exceeded the number brought from the Commons.[1] Altogether in these four years the Labour Government introduced 78 bills into the Lords, as compared with 193 into the Commons. After November 1951, under the Conservative Government, the proportion of Lords' bills declined a little, and in the four years 1951–5 there were 45 Lords' bills as against 155 first introduced into the Commons.

In the years before the war, although not many government bills were first introduced into the Lords, some Lords' bills did, in fact, deal with controversial topics. In the session of 1933–4, the Government brought into the Lords a Betting and Lotteries Bill which was clearly bound to excite a good deal of opposition, and on which, in fact, there were four divisions on committee and report—two of them with over 100 peers voting. The Bill followed the lines suggested by the report of the Royal Commission of 1932, and was brought in in response to demands made over many years past by private members calling upon the Government to act in this field, which has often been regarded as a private members' preserve. One particular advantage obtained by the prior introduction in the Lords in this case was that it enabled several bishops to state their views, both on the second reading and at the committee stage, and to show by their votes that the Bill had, if not the support of the Church as a whole, at least the support of all the bishops who were inclined to speak in the debate.

In 1934–5 the Government made another response to strong pressure from private members in both Houses, by bringing in its Restriction of Ribbon Development Bill. This too was first debated in the Lords, though it was clearly a matter of great importance and likely to lead to long and complicated discussion. Parts of the Bill were highly controversial, although the controversy was not all on party

---

[1] Ten of the 22 government bills introduced in the Lords in this session were consolidation bills (cf. above, p. 130 n.), all of which were sent to the Joint Committee without being debated on the floor of the House.

lines. In the committee stage 50 amendments were moved, all by Conservative peers, and only ten of these were accepted by the Government or withdrawn against a promise of favourable consideration. Seven were defeated on division, and in each of these divisions a substantial minority of Conservative peers voted against the Government. The most important of the divisions was on one of the main clauses of the Bill, and the clause was only saved by 35 votes to 34, the 35 peers on the Government side including 10 office-holders. There was, indeed, something like an organized opposition to the Bill, with a leader in the person of Lord Hastings, who himself moved 16 of the amendments; the group voting against the Government was in each case composed mainly of the same peers, nearly all of them Conservatives.

In the Commons the Government accepted many important amendments, so that the Bill came back to the Lords almost completely reconstructed. The Commons' amendments were debated at great length, and further amendments to them were proposed, but in the long run the Bill was allowed to go forward for the Royal Assent in the form in which it had emerged from the Commons.

The 13 other government bills introduced first in the Lords in the session of 1934–5 occupied only an hour between them on committee and report. Even on second reading all but two went through without any real debate.

Although some credit has been assigned to the Labour Government of 1945–51 for its increased use of the Lords for the first discussion of bills, it must also be remembered that this policy was dictated not by any tenderness for the upper House, but, in the first place at any rate, by the vast extent of the Government's legislative programme. The Government had so many long and difficult bills to pass, that it put a considerable strain on the machinery of the House of Commons and made unprecedented use of standing committees. For some bills it imposed time tables whose effect was to prevent altogether the discussion of many important clauses at any stage in the proceedings in the Commons. The amount of work to be done by the Lords as a 'revising' chamber was much increased. If the Government had not made extensive use of the Lords for introducing its less important measures, the parliamentary machinery would have been even more strained.

In the session of 1947–8, 22 government bills were introduced in the House of Lords, and all of these except one—a very minor one—eventually received the Royal Assent. The total time spent on the second readings of these bills was rather over 20 hours (350 columns of *Hansard*), and about the same time was spent on the committee stages. The longest debates were on the Children Bill, which was debated for over four hours on second reading, and whose committee stage spread over two days, taking a total of over six hours. The report stage occupied a further two hours. The British Nationality Bill occupied almost as long, both on committee and on report, and the River Boards Bill, 'a simple measure of administrative reform', ran these two very close.

On the last-named Bill the Conservative peers carried their opposition to a division on an amendment whose aim was to give more scope for the representation of bodies interested in the drainage of the Welland and Great Ouse. Although the Government was defeated on this matter, the House of Commons in due course restored the form which the Government desired.[1]

The Companies Bill, with its 460 clauses, was one of the longest and most complicated measures of recent times, but nearly all the discussion took place outside the Chamber.[2] One speech of Lord Simonds in the House so impressed the Lord Chancellor that he persuaded his colleagues to withdraw a whole clause.[3]

The proceedings on the Water Bill produced an example of the difficulties in which the Government may find itself in the House of Lords owing to the absence of a minister directly responsible for a bill under discussion. The Bill was in the hands of the Earl of Listowel, who was at that time Secretary of State for Burma. During the second reading debate Lord Llewellin complained that he found the Bill difficult to understand, and observed that it made no less than 51 alterations of statutes by reference.[4] Lord Listowel answered that he could not deal with Lord Llewellin's points until he had consulted his advisers, but in the committee stage the Government introduced some new sub-sections whose purpose was to meet Lord Llewellin's wishes. In due course Lord Llewellin thanked 'the noble Earl and those who worked with him', both for taking him into consultation and for accepting his suggestions.

The House of Lords may be particularly well adapted for being the first House to deal with certain types of bills. Early in 1948 the Government brought in its Supreme Court of Judicature (Amendment) Bill, on which it was quickly able to have the benefit of the advice of the Law Lords. The advice was mainly given in private discussions outside; the committee stage lasted only for three minutes, during which Lord du Parcq thanked the Lord Chancellor 'for so readily accepting the suggestions which were made by some of his noble and learned friends and himself'.[5]

---

[1] Lords Debs., 18th December 1947, vol. 153, col. 364. [2] Cf. above, p. 159.
[3] Lords Debs., 11th May 1948, vol. 155, col. 739.
[4] Ibid., 27th November 1947, vol. 152, cols. 1006-11.
[5] Ibid., 29th January 1948, vol. 153, cols. 688 f.

BILLS FIRST INTRODUCED IN THE LORDS

The Lords' bills of the session 1948–9 have already been fully examined in the Fabian Society pamphlet of 1954, in Appendix II (pp. 38–41). The pamphlet gives a list of the bills, together with a statement of their objects and a summary of the proceedings on them. On the Coast Protection Bill, it refers to the expert contributions of Lord Stansgate, who 'had served on catchment boards and spoke for their interests'. Nevertheless the Commons devoted longer to the Bill than the Lords had done, and made 83 amendments, which the Lords eventually accepted *en bloc*. The Bill to reform the ancient administration of the New Forest produced a very expert discussion on second reading; Lord Robinson was Chairman of the Forestry Commission, Lords Radnor and Beaulieu were the two largest owners of 'common rights' in the forest, and two other peers who took part were local residents. On the Prevention of Damage by Pests Bill the Lords in committee cleared up 'much bad and ambiguous drafting'.

The House of Lords, so many of whose members have large agricultural interests and experience, is often particularly well adapted for the prior examination of non-political bills dealing with forestry, the affairs of the countryside, and the like. The Forestry Bill, which came forward for second reading on 20th February 1951, was another Lords' bill of some importance concerning agriculture and questions of local control. The committee stage, spread over three days, took nearly nine hours in all.

Perhaps the most important bill to have been introduced in the first place in the House of Lords in recent years was the Conservative Government's Road Traffic Bill of the session of 1954–5. There was ample precedent from before the war for road traffic bills being taken in the Lords first, though those earlier bills were in many cases private members' measures. Although by now governments have generally felt themselves obliged to take responsibility for legislation on this difficult question, private members in both Houses of Parliament feel that they have plenty to contribute, and road traffic bills often produce discussion of considerable length.

The most important and controversial proposal in this Bill was that all vehicles should be required to be periodically inspected, either by private agents or by officials appointed by the state for the purpose. The second reading debate took four hours,[1] and the committee stage took nearly 22 hours in all, spread over six days. The proceedings went on for so long that extra time had to be found by fitting in a Monday sitting (25th February). The report stage lasted for eight hours (on two sitting days), and the third reading for two

---

[1] Cf. above, chap. VI, p. 82, for a comparison of the length of speeches of peers and members of the House of Commons on the second reading of this Bill.

hours. There were no divisions on the second and third reading stages, although Lord Brabazon said that he had intended to move the rejection of the third reading. He had, however, been told that this was a Conservative measure, and that as he was a Conservative, he should not vote against his own government. He was not impressed by that argument at all. This was, he said, 'not a Conservative measure, not a Party measure, but nothing else but a departmental bill, and a very bad one at that'. It seemed 'to have no minister at the back of it, except perhaps the composite, mystical figure of "Mr. Lennox-Boyd-Carpenter" '.

Some 70 amendments were moved during the committee and report stages, half of them by Conservative peers, and the other half divided almost equally between Labour front-bench and back-bench peers. There were three divisions, all of them on Labour amendments, and almost all the other amendments were withdrawn, though half a dozen of them were eventually accepted at the report stage.

Although the Lords had devoted such a great length of time to the Bill, their labour was, in a sense, wasted, because the Bill was not enacted into law during that session. The Commons gave the Bill a second reading, but almost immediately afterwards the decision to hold a General Election in May brought the session to an end and the Bill had to be dropped until the new Parliament. It was then duly revived and passed into law, but this time the Government brought it in in the first instance in the Commons. Although the second reading had been allowed through without a division in the previous Parliament, the Opposition this time moved a reasoned amendment, condemning the Bill for not being comprehensive enough, and divided against it.

In the session of 1955–6 the Government introduced as a Lords' bill its complicated measure dealing with copyright law. The proceedings in the Lords occupied a great deal of time; although the second reading was taken on 15th November 1955, the Bill received its third reading only just before Easter 1956. The committee and report stage debates were spread over seven days, and occupied the House for 26 hours in all. There was here, then, an instance of the use of the House of Lords for the introduction of a bill of considerable scope, but of a technical and mainly non-controversial character. The proceedings were far more dominated by Party than might have been expected. Of 52 amendments (other than those moved by the Government) in committee, all but one were moved by Labour peers. Almost half were moved by Lord Lucas of Chilworth from the Opposition Front Bench, and almost all of the others were distributed among three other front-bench Labour peers. Only half a dozen Conservative peers spoke at all during the whole proceedings, which were largely dominated by four front-bench spokesmen, two on each side.[1] Nevertheless, the results of the Bill's passage certainly do not suggest that it had been put to the test of mere partisan strife. The Government accepted many of the Labour amendments, with or without modification, but three were decided by divisions, in which the voting was almost entirely on party lines although the subject-matter was by its nature nothing to do with party differences, but rather the concern of lawyers.

It is sometimes assumed that when a bill is introduced in the Lords in the first place, the burden on the Commons is reduced because most of the points of detail can be disposed of in the Lords, so that the Commons have nothing to do but make a final revision without spending much time. An examination of the parliamentary career of Lords' bills in recent times suggests that such an assumption is not altogether well-founded. Some Lords' bills are not debated at any stage on the floor of either House, but those which are debated generally take longer in the Commons than in the Lords.

In the session of 1948–9 thirteen government bills were enacted after being first introduced in the Lords and debated there.[2] On all but one of these the committee stage was longer in the Commons than in the Lords, although in each case the Lords had discussed the details first.[3] Altogether the time spent in standing committee or in committee of the whole House in the Commons on these bills (1300 columns of *Hansard*) was 50% longer than the time spent in committee in the Lords; approximately the same was true of the other stages. A study of the Lords' bills of the session of 1947–8 produces very similar results. Even the Forestry Bill of 1950–1, to which the Lords, with their great knowledge of the subject, devoted special attention, took a little longer on committee and report in the Commons than in the Lords.

These instances are taken from the period of the Labour Government, when the House of Lords was more active than usual in committee. Under the Conservative Government, in the session of 1951–2, in which the programme of legislation was much lighter, the Com-

[1] The two Labour protagonists of the Committee were replaced by two others for the Report.

[2] In addition, some other Lords bills were passed without debate on the floor of the House.

[3] The one exception was the Justices of the Peace Bill, whose committee stage in the Lords took four afternoons. The Fabian Society Pamphlet of 1954, at p. 41, observes: 'It is inconceivable that in mid-session the Commons could have spared four afternoons to the Justices of the Peace Bill.' This is true; nevertheless, it should be added the Commons did devote two afternoons to the committee stage, and that the time spent by the Commons on committee and report was three-quarters as long, even on this Bill, as the time spent on these stages in the Lords.

mons devoted eight times as much time (all of it on the floor of the House) to the committee and report stages of the Lords' bills as the Lords had done.

It may indeed be the case that the House of Commons spent rather less time on these bills than it would have done if it had been the first House to deal with them, but the reduction of the Commons' burden does not appear to have been particularly impressive.[1]

The citation of these facts does not imply an adverse reflection on the Lords, though it may at first sight seem surprising (and even disappointing) that the Commons find relatively so much to say about uncontroversial bills which have already passed the upper House. It is possible to suggest a threefold explanation. In the first place it seems that on any given matter more members have more to say in the Commons than in the Lords. Secondly, many of the amendments to bills proposed in Parliament are brought forward on behalf of interested bodies, and many interest groups, in their search for parliamentary spokesmen, are accustomed to having their opinions voiced by members of the House of Commons rather than by peers. Of the two Houses of Parliament, the House of Lords is the less favoured by lobbyists—and according to the thesis of Lord Salisbury (cf. above, p. 143) it is right that this should be so. Finally, members of the House of Commons—even Conservatives in opposition—have never acquired a habit of thinking that prior discussion of a bill in the Lords absolves them from the task of giving it full consideration when it comes down to their own House.

The fact that the Commons often find much to say on bills which have already been through the Lords does not detract from the value of the facility of introducing some bills in the Lords. Although the Lords' proceedings in matters of detail tend not to be very protracted, they are nevertheless usually of a very high quality. With bills dealing with intricate questions, such as the Companies Bill of 1948 and the Copyright Bill of 1956, the Lords have made immense improvements. Governments have derived inestimable advantages from being able to present such bills to the Commons in a form so greatly improved by the contributions of the Lords.[2]

[1] We should mention, for the sake of comparison, that on the five heaviest bills of the session of 1948-9, all of which were taken through the Commons first, the Commons standing committee took in all five times as long as the committee stage in the Lords.

[2] The story of the Shops Bill of 1956-7 has been told above (p. 184 n.). Apparently the Government brought it in as a Lords bill because, being approved in principle by organized shopkeepers and shopworkers, it seemed uncontroversial. It may be, however, that the Government was being very subtle. If it had introduced the Bill in the Commons it could not have dropped it without sad loss of face; as it was, a reasonably graceful pretext was at hand.

Chapter XV

THE LORDS AND PRIVATE MEMBERS' BILLS[1]

1. BILLS FIRST INTRODUCED IN THE LORDS

SUPERFICIALLY the House of Lords appears to enjoy substantial and valuable privileges in relation to private members' bills. In this matter peers enjoy the same rights as the elected members of the House of Commons. Any member of either House may introduce a legislative proposal for Parliament's consideration.[2] In one sense, however, a peer is better placed for proposing legislation than a member of the lower House; a peer has a better chance of having his bill debated. His chance of getting his bill enacted is, however, very small, unless the bill is entirely noncontroversial.

If a member of the House of Commons wishes to introduce a bill without having achieved complete agreement on the matter beforehand, he is virtually unable to get a full debate on the principles of his proposal unless he succeeds in winning a place in the ballot for private members' time.[3] In the Commons only six days each session are at present provided for the second readings of private members' bills. In each year, out of some 550 back-bench Members of Parliament none but the most fortunate among the twenty or so who have

---

[1] Bills dealing with the reform of the House of Lords are dealt with in Part IV.
[2] British peers are better placed in this respect than were the elected members of the French Council of the Republic under the original Fourth Republic Constitution; before it was amended bills introduced in the French second Chamber had to be transmitted to the National Assembly for prior consideration.
[3] A member of the Commons who has no place in the ballot may indeed make use of the Ten Minutes' Rule, but that merely allows him to make a short speech on behalf of his measure; only one opposing speech is allowed. (Cf. P. A. Bromhead, *Private Members' Bills*, Routledge, 1956, pp. 19, 155–61.)

won good places in the ballot succeed in getting legislative proposals actually debated.[1]

In the Lords on the other hand, if a peer introduces a bill he can be fairly sure that the second reading motion will at least be accorded the advantage of a debate. He has a right to put his bill down for second reading, but it is conceivable that his Party Whips may find that they would prefer to have something else debated at the time for which the bill has been put down. They may put pressure on him to postpone his bill, or to withdraw it altogether. It will then be for him to decide whether or not to be amenable to the demands made on him. If he chooses to insist on his second reading debate, he can, and he will get it. Moreover, because of the flexibility of the time-table in the Lords, there will be no fixed limit to the duration of the debate on his bill. It cannot be talked out, as so many bills are in the Commons, and as the quorum is only three, it can hardly be counted out. In the Commons a handful of hostile members may in many cases find it easy to defeat a bill by the employment of obstructive tactics; in the Lords, on the other hand, just because time is not subject to fixed limits, obstruction in the technical sense is almost impossible. Not only the second reading, but the later stages too, can be debated without having to be fitted in to a time-table.[2] The only procedural obstacle which a bill has to face is that produced by the quorum rule applied to divisions; if a question is pressed to a division the vote is not valid unless at least 30 peers take part.[3]

In relation to the objective of changing the law, however, the peers' privilege of initiating bills is really of little immediate value, except for agreed proposals. Any peer may indeed bring in a bill, and he may even succeed in passing it through all its stages in the Lords. But if the bill is to pass into law it must also pass through the Commons, and though it may be easy enough to find a member of the House of Commons who is prepared to take charge of the bill, there is virtually no chance that adequate time will be found in the lower House for debating the second reading in the current session.

It is this difficulty of finding time for a second reading debate in the Commons that constitutes the main obstacle in the way of an unofficial peer's bill. Since 1948, ten Fridays have been provided in each

[1] The action of the Government in providing time for the bill to abolish capital punishment in 1956 was quite exceptional.

[2] The debate on second reading or on committee may run on for two sittings, though this generally requires the co-operation of the Government Whips. In 1954, when much time was taken over the Protection of Birds Bill, Lord Salisbury said that 'the Government had afforded another day' to the Bill. His words implied perhaps more governmental control over time than there is formally (Lords Debs., 11th May 1954, vol. 187, col. 460).

[3] S.O. 50. For an example, cf. below, p. 203.

THE LORDS AND PRIVATE MEMBERS' BILLS

full-length session for private members' bills in the Commons.[1] Second reading motions have precedence on the first six of these, which are generally alternate Fridays between December and March. The order in which the bills are taken is decided by a ballot held near the beginning of the session. At least three balloted bills are down for each day. A bill brought down from the Lords, after passing through all its stages there, might have its second reading debated in the Commons on one of these six Fridays if all the Commons bills down for that day were disposed of very quickly. Such good fortune is almost unknown, however; no Lords' bill was debated on any of the 46 second-reading Fridays between 1948 and 1957. For practical purposes it must be assumed that the time available on the six second-reading Fridays of the session is already 'booked-up' for Commons' balloted bills before any Lords' bill has had a chance of reaching the House of Commons. A Lords' bill stands a slightly better chance of receiving a second reading debate on one of the last four private members' Fridays in the session. Even so, it will be preceded by the later stages of Commons' bills, and if there is any opposition it will probably be talked out. Even if a Lords' bill is debated on a Friday in the Commons, a vote on it can usually be prevented by a single hostile member.[2]

If a bill first passed by the Lords is so uncontroversial that the Commons will give it a second reading without debate, it can indeed be passed through that stage under the 'unopposed business' procedure, but this demands unanimous consent.

A bill which succeeds in getting a second reading in the Commons before Easter has a fair chance of passing through its other stages too. It goes almost automatically to one of the standing committees, which deals with the private members' bills in the order in which they have passed through the second reading stage. In the committee Lords' bills suffer no procedural disabilities as compared with Commons bills.

Four Fridays between Easter and the summer recess are provided in the Commons for the consideration of report and third reading stages. Bills are dealt with in the order in which they emerge from the standing committee. The four Fridays are generally found adequate for the report and third reading stages of all the bills which have been given a second reading. The Commons' procedure for private mem-

[1] In 1939–48 there was no private members' time at all in the House of Commons. In some sessions since then fewer than ten Fridays have been provided.

[2] If a member goes on speaking until the close of business at 4 o'clock, the debate is adjourned with no vote taken. Such obstruction can be overcome if the House agrees to a closure motion, but the Speaker usually refuses to put the question on the closure on a second reading unless the debate has lasted for the whole of the sitting. (Cf. P. A. Bromhead, op. cit., p. 29, and below, p. 210.)

bers' bills is thus reasonably favourable to bills which succeed in getting an unopposed second reading in that House. To get an unopposed second reading is, however, not at all easy. Any single member can prevent it by simply rising and saying 'Object'. If either the Government or the Opposition is at all hostile, the Whips will see to it that objection is made whenever the bill appears on the Order Paper; if any interest group outside the House dislikes the bill it will try to get a sympathetic member to obstruct progress and will probably be successful, provided the member is persistent enough. A bill will, then, be unlikely to be given an unopposed second reading unless all potentially hostile elements have been persuaded to accept it. In order to obtain universal agreement the promoters generally need to have extensive preliminary discussions outside Parliament, but the process of discussion in the Lords may conceivably help towards the creation of a situation in which an unopposed second reading may be obtained in the Commons.

On the other hand, so little use has been made in recent years of the right to introduce bills in the Lords, that it must apparently be assumed that in general those persons who wish to put private members' bills through Parliament have a rather low opinion of the value of the preliminary stages in the Lords as a means of promoting the necessary agreement in the Commons.

There is a second purpose which prior introduction in the Lords may achieve, even if it does not achieve the actual passing of the bill within a single session. If a project of legislation seems likely to arouse resistance it has little hope of passing straight through both Houses after being introduced in the Lords. But the promoters may very usefully bring it out and give it a trial run, as it were, in the Lords, in order to see just what objections are raised, and above all in order that the attitude of the Government to the measure may be discovered. (The Minister most nearly concerned is more or less obliged to arrange for the peer who represents his department to take part in the debate and to state the Government's general opinions about the matter.) Although the bill may have no hope of passing in the same session, the fact of its having been debated in the Lords may prepare the ground for some future introduction under the ballot in the Commons. Even a second reading debate, by itself, may be useful, and if the bill is allowed to go to committee, the discussion of the details and of proposed amendments may be of even greater value. Here too, however, little use has been made in recent years of the facilities provided by the House of Lords.

A third purpose which may be served by a discussion of a bill in the Lords is to persuade the Government to take the measure over and introduce it, either in the same session or in some later session, as a government bill. The debate in the Lords gives the advocates of the measure an opportunity of pointing to its advantages, and the possibility of persuading the Government of the value of bringing it in. This has been done on one or two occasions recently, but very rarely. Once again, little use is made of the potentialities of the House of Lords. It appears that, in the conditions of modern political life, the average group or association desiring to promote legislation prefers to exert direct pressure upon the Government, in the form of letters, memoranda and deputations to ministers and civil servants, rather than to have its case stated for it in the Lords by a friendly peer, and submitted to the opinion of the House.

These considerations suggest some interesting ideas with reference to the whole of the functions of Parliament. The main function of both Commons and Lords in present conditions is to discuss and criticize the Government's actions and intentions, rather than to be the really effective legislature in themselves. Some people may feel that bills proposed by private members are almost anachronistic in modern conditions. The Government does indeed accept responsibility for all its actions, and we have come to feel that it is therefore responsible for all legislation. It remains true, however, that although some of the bills introduced by governments are political measures, brought in in order to make operative the programme which the party put before the electors at the previous General Election, the great majority of bills are not party measures at all, but measures that have been made desirable by changes in the situation. With most of these measures bodies outside Parliament are directly concerned. In preparing its legislative programme for each session, therefore, the Government has to listen to arguments produced by different bodies, and to decide on the priorities. Its decisions are probably affected by the amount of influence that the different bodies have succeeded in bringing to bear. It might have been expected that in a healthy Parliament, parliamentary discussion, such as might take place in the House of Lords, would be one of the most potent influences in helping the Government to reach its decision on priorities between competing proposals. The paucity of private members' Lords' bills reflects the low prestige of the upper House as an initiator of changes in the law; on the other hand the number of general debates, as we shall see, has greatly increased.

The past generation has seen a big change in the habits of the Lords regarding the introduction of private members' bills. If we go back only a little way, to the years just before 1939, we find that unofficial peers' bills were fairly numerous—there were generally a dozen or more in each session—and occupied a fair amount of the House's time. Few of them passed into law as a direct and immediate result of their introduction into the upper House, but many interesting and constructive discussions were held. In the session of 1934–5, for example, although the Government took all the time in the Commons, twelve private members' bills were introduced in the Lords. All but one were debated. Five were rejected or withdrawn on second reading in the Lords; none of the others passed the Commons. The time spent in debating the private members' bills on second reading greatly exceeded the corresponding time spent on the Government's Lords' bills. Since 1945, however, bills of this type have almost entirely disappeared, and in the whole of the past ten years their total number has hardly exceeded a dozen.

It is proposed to suggest reasons for this change, and to discuss its implications with regard to a general assessment of the work of the House of Lords, later in this chapter. Before doing this, however, it will be useful to give an account of some of the bills actually introduced and debated, both before 1939 and after 1945. The bills introduced during the years between the wars were so numerous that it would be impracticable to attempt a full account of them here; it is proposed, however, to undertake a partial study.

Many bills of the 1920's were modest social reforms such as have recently taken most of the private members' time in the Commons. One was Lord Buckmaster's Bill to impose a minimum age for marriage. In his second reading speech he explained just why he brought this Bill forward. He was not, as some people seemed to think, acting merely as a conduit for other people's views. The fact of the matter was, he said, that after seeing a certain press report, he wrote to a welfare worker, from whom he learned that the League of Nations favoured the fixing of a minimum age of marriage everywhere; her organization had a bill already prepared and hoped that somebody would introduce it. Lord Buckmaster's sympathy was aroused, and he therefore introduced the Bill in the House of Lords, where he won the good will of the Government. Some peers were rather hesitant about giving their support, but they allowed the Bill to have a second reading. They then asked for a select committee, and their request was granted. The Bill survived the select committee and returned to the House, and after a short report stage was given a third reading without further discussion. It went through to the Commons, where it was dealt with expeditiously and obtained the Royal Assent.

In the same session a bill dealing with the registration of architects was passed through the House of Lords, though with some discussion at each stage. It also obtained the Royal Assent, as did Lord Darling's Bill for the preservation of infant life. It was indeed a measure of limited interest, as it dealt with a small and rather narrow category of infanticide, but its second reading debate lasted for nearly an hour, and the debate in committee for nearly two hours. It cannot be said therefore that it was a measure to which everybody simply gave immediate assent in every detail.

Lord Banbury brought in a bill whose object was to give magistrates the power to confiscate the animals of persons who had been convicted of cruelty, and to order that such people should not, at least for limited periods, own animals in the future. The Bill was given a second reading after a very short discussion, and then went to committee. The Government had shown its apparent hostility by taking no interest and putting down no amendments. It was suggested that, lacking the Government's support, the Bill would have little chance of eventually passing into law, and on this ground the adjournment was proposed. The general feeling was, however, that this was not adequate ground for abandoning the discussion, and the committee stage was allowed to proceed. In due course the Bill came up for third reading. This time, after a short debate, a division was called, and the Bill was narrowly defeated by 24 votes to 18. It is true that nothing positive was directly achieved by this debate, but an idea was canvassed which was later on to be adopted, in part, with regard to dogs.

During the 1930s several unofficial peers introduced bills dealing with road safety. Some of these went straight through to receive the Royal Assent; others were delayed for a session or more, either being taken up by the Government in later sessions or being allowed to pass all their stages as unofficial measures. There were from time to time suggestions that the Government itself ought to take responsibility in such a field as this, but on the whole the debates were valuable, if only in Bagehot's 'educative' sense.

In 1929 Lord Cecil of Chelwood brought in a bill which proposed that licences to drive vehicles should be given only to people who were physically fit, and that applicants for licences must pass some test of skill and of theoretical knowledge of the rules and principles of driving. At the second reading stage the Bill was debated for three hours. The Government spokesman, Lord Londonderry, refused to accept it, saying that though the idea was a good one its implementation would be better left to the Government, after it had had an opportunity of examining the report of the Royal Commission which was then sitting.

The Bill was given a second reading without a division, and sent to a select committee. Although the House eventually decided to proceed no further with the Bill, these discussions were useful in preparing the ground for legislation which was enacted not very long afterwards.

Another question raised by unofficial peers' bills during the 1930s was the matter of compensation for people injured in road accidents. In 1933 Lord Danesfort introduced his Road Traffic (Compensation for Accidents) Bill, which won general approval in the House, but was strongly opposed by a very tiny minority. It was granted a second reading, after a debate of about two hours, by a majority of 31 to 2, and then went to a select committee. At the report stage Lord Halsbury proposed a hostile amendment with regard to the definition of negligence, and pressed it to a division, in which he was able to find only one other peer to support him. There were, however, unfortunately for the Bill, only 25 peers against the amendment, so with a total of 27 peers taking part in the division the absence of a quorum was exposed, and the debate had to be adjourned.[1] The Bill made no further progress in that session. In the next session Lord Danesfort brought forward the Bill once again, and this time it passed its third reading but made no progress in the Commons.

In 1933 Lord Moynihan brought in a bill concerning the treatment of persons injured in road accidents and the remuneration of doctors called upon in such emergencies. This Bill went to a select committee, but made no further progress. Lord Halsbury's Bill on speedometers passed fairly quickly through all its stages in the Lords, but made no progress in the Commons.

In 1936 Lord Mottistone tried his hand with a Road Traffic (Safeguarding of the Public) Bill, which was negatived on second reading. His gracious acknowledgments to the Government ('Throughout my negotiations with regard to the Bill the Ministry of Transport have shown me every consideration and kindness, and have furnished me with every kind of statistic and advice') illustrate the sympathetic treatment which the Ministry gave during this period to independent proposals for the improvement of road safety.

In the same field Lord Newton brought forward a rather drastic proposal in 1938, to the effect that persons convicted of driving under the influence of drink were to forfeit their vehicles. The Government opposed this Bill, mainly on the ground that it would inevitably be very capricious in its operation. It would deprive one man of a car worth £5 and another of one worth £2,000, though both had committed the same offence. Nevertheless Lord Newton got no less than 17 peers in the lobby on his side on behalf of the second reading; there were 43 against.

In the same session the Lords rejected, by 27 votes to 10, Lord Elibank's Bill to stop the compulsory endorsement of licences of drivers who had been convicted of certain kinds of offences.

Leaving the subject of road traffic, we find that among bills originally proposed in the Lords during the 1930s and passed into law were:

Lord Asquith's Arbitration Bill (1933-4).

[1] A division is valid only if at least 30 peers vote.

Lord Eltisley's Marriage (Extension of Hours) Bill of the same session.

Lord Buckmaster's Protection of Birds Bill (1932–3). (This Bill passed through a select committee.)

Lord Iddesleigh's Shops Bill (1935–6).

Lord Wright's Solicitors Bill (1935–6).

Lord Rankeillour's Judiciary (Safeguarding) Bill (1936–7).

Lord Dawson of Penn's Infanticide Bill (1937–8).

Lord Alness's Divorce (Scotland) Bill (1937–8).

Lord Mersey's Quail Protection Bill (1937–8).

Lord Sempill's Prevention of Damage by Rabbits Bill (1938–9). (This Bill gave local authorities the power to oblige landowners to kill rabbits with gas.) In committee Lord Sempill himself proposed to insert an amendment to the effect that no person employed under any council under the relevant sub-section should use a spring trap to kill rabbits. The amendment was defeated by 49 votes to 9, with the Government itself leading the opposition to it.

From the autumn of 1939 to the end of 1948 the Government took all the time in the House of Commons. No unofficial peer's bill could therefore hope to be enacted unless it received a second reading in the Commons as an 'unopposed' measure, and in the Lords it seemed unnecessary and worthless to bring in private members' bills which had no chance of passing. The first to be introduced in the Lords after the war was a Liberal Party measure, the Preservation of the Rights of the Subject Bill. It was not expected to pass, but was brought in to afford an opportunity for a debate on the supposed restrictions on individual liberties which had been produced by the extension of the activities of the State, and by the extension of delegated legislation.[1]

The Bill contained a number of concrete propositions with reference to the limitation of the powers of the executive. It proposed that Parliament should have power to amend statutory instruments, and that no statute should be able to confer vague general powers on ministers in such a way as to protect them from *ultra vires* claims. There were also provisions against the so-called 'Henry VIII clause' in bills, by which ministers were given power to amend acts already passed. It proposed further to limit the powers of the executive by providing that there should be recourse to the courts against the quasi-judicial decisions of ministers, and it attempted to define and limit powers of entry of officials. Similarly the powers of marketing boards to impose fines were to be taken away from them and given to the ordinary courts. In the field of trade union law the Bill contained a clause against the 'closed shop', and it also proposed that certain

[1] Lords Debs., 15th May 1947, vol. 147, cols. 762–810.

BILLS FIRST INTRODUCED IN THE LORDS

unemployment benefit appeals should no longer need to be put forward through trade unions.

Although this Bill dealt with such important and fascinating questions of the functions of government, the debate did not attract a big attendance of peers; the main contributions to the debate were made by Liberals. Nevertheless, leading front-bench members of both Conservative and Labour Parties found it worth making contributions. Lord Swinton gave his general support to the objectives of the Bill in a short speech, but Lord Jowitt, in his final summing up on behalf of the Government, said he would, without hesitation, vote against the second reading. 'It is a thoroughly bad principle', he said, 'to dress up a manifesto as a Bill.' ('What have we been doing for the past months,' asked the Bill's proposer, Lord Reading, 'except translating manifestoes into bills?') The second reading was carried by 37 votes to 19. The division was on party lines, with Conservatives and Liberals voting together in favour of the Bill, and only Labour peers against it. Only two front-bench Conservative peers voted.

There was clearly no prospect whatever that the Bill would make any progress in the House of Commons, and in the Lords it did not go beyond second reading. The purpose of its introducers was not really to change the law, but to have a discussion on the matter. It was indeed, as the Government alleged, a manifesto dressed up as a bill, but, one may well ask, why should it not be? It was scarcely fair to blame the Liberal peers for introducing their ideas in the form of a bill; they had a number of specific proposals to make, and although they knew that these proposals could not at once be enacted into law, there was much to be said for introducing and debating them in the form of a bill, rather than in the form of a motion expressing general opinions. The debate provided the House of Lords with an excellent opportunity to perform its educative function. In Lord Reading's words, 'those who were responsible for the Bill naturally hoped that it would receive a sympathetic welcome, but I think that we were all profoundly surprised at the warmth and the width of the publicity accorded to it in the press. . . . Letters have been rained upon me.'

No other unofficial peers' bills were brought forward in the Lords in the session 1946–7. In the next session, however, which was the last in which no private members' time was provided in the Commons, Lord Normand put down a bill concerned with the regulation of solicitors. It made no progress even in the Lords, but in the following year it was brought in and passed as a government bill. The fact that it was first introduced by an unofficial peer may have expedited its final success.

In 1948–9 private members' time in the Commons was at last restored, but in that session it was wholly taken up by bills introduced in the Commons, mostly under the ballot. Two peers did, however, introduce bills, though one of them, which was concerned with the status of Newfoundland, made no progress. The other was Lord Mancroft's Bill, based on the recommendations of Lord Justice Denning's matrimonial causes committee, proposing that a man should be allowed to marry the sister of his divorced wife. Bills concerning prohibited degrees of relationship in marriage had been numerous in both Houses of Parliament during the previous half century. Successive modifications in the law had been made, nearly always against vigorous opposition, in which some peers had taken a prominent part. The debate on Lord Mancroft's Bill lasted two hours.[1] The Archbishop of Canterbury and the Bishop of London spoke against it, but Bishop Hunkin of Truro spoke in its favour, and Bishop Haigh of Winchester said that he would not oppose it. The Lord Chancellor said that the Government could not provide facilities in the House of Commons for the passing of the Bill, but would not positively oppose the second reading at this stage. If there were to be a division, there would be a free vote.

The Government had told Lord Mancroft privately that it would accept the Bill if it were unopposed in the Lords, but not otherwise. The objections of the Archbishop of Canterbury and the Bishop of London clearly put the Bill into the 'opposed' class. Lord Mancroft therefore decided that rather than allow the Bill to go for decision by vote on the second reading, he would withdraw it; the debate had shown that the Bill could not hope for a smooth passage.

The peculiar circumstances of the Parliament of 1950–1, in which the Labour Government had an infinitesimal majority in the House of Commons, produced one bill by means of which the Conservative Opposition in the Lords thought to irritate the Government. The Conservative Party was at this time vigorously opposing the operation of the existing Transport Act in so far as it concerned long distance road haulage. In the Commons the second Conservative member to win a place in the ballot introduced a bill to extend the permitted radius of operation of independent hauliers from 25 to 60 miles, and on 23rd February 1951 this bill received its second reading in the Commons, the Government being narrowly defeated. Meanwhile a parallel bill had already been introduced in the Lords by a Conservative peer and carried through all its stages there. The Transport (Amendment) Bill (Lords) had been given a second reading in the upper House on 21st November 1950. The debate was treated as a first-class Party occasion. Lord Rea for the Liberals followed Lord Teynham, and after him Lord Lucas of Chilworth, the Parliamentary Secretary to the Ministry of Transport, led the attack on behalf of

[1] Lords Debs., 24th March 1949, vol. 161, cols. 693–730.

the Government. After several other prominent peers had contributed, the Conservative case was closed by both Lord Swinton and the Marquess of Salisbury, and the Government's case by Lord Addison, Leader of the House. Like the debate the division was on party lines, and the motion for second reading was carried by 65 votes to 32—one of the largest numbers of peers to vote in a division during the last few years. The Government continued to oppose the Bill very vigorously, and Lord Addison even adopted the very unusual device of speaking against the motion to go into committee on the Bill.[1] At this stage also, Lord Salisbury spoke, as well as Lord Samuel and Lord Simon. The motion to go into committee was carried by a big majority, and the committee stage itself was disposed of in half an hour. The Government proposed no amendments, but three from Conservative peers went through without division. There was no discussion on report, and the Bill was in due course given a third reading (by 60 votes to 33) on 13th February 1951.[2] These proceedings in the Lords were a useful curtain-raiser for the second reading debate in the Commons ten days later on Mr. Bevins' Bill, but the Government succeeded in putting an end to the whole business by ensuring a full attendance of its own supporters in the Commons Standing Committee, where each clause of the Bill was thrown out. By this means the Bill was deprived of any chance of making any further progress.

The only other private member's bill first introduced in the Lords in that session was Lord Elton's proposal to make illegal the use of spring traps for killing rabbits. Its subject-matter was not the concern of the Parties as such, but it was a matter which had already aroused much public interest and strong feelings on both sides. This was by no means the only occasion on which this subject had been discussed in Parliament in recent years; it has always tended to be in difficulties because of hostility from whatever government is in power on administrative grounds.[3] The Ministry of Agriculture has for long been sceptical about the wisdom of forbidding spring traps. The Bill had much support among the unofficial Labour peers; ten of them voted in favour of the Bill, and only three against it. Most of the Conservatives supported the 'official' opinion, however, and the Bill was defeated by 49 votes to 22.

In 1951–2, the first session of the new Conservative Government, Lord Llewellin's Bill dealing with the removal of surface soil from agricultural land was passed through all its stages in the Lords, but made no progress in the Commons.

An excellent, but regrettably rare, illustration of the capacity of the

---

[1] Lords Debs., 12th December 1950, vol. 169, cols. 865–872.
[2] Lords Debs., vol. 170, cols. 274–96.   [3] Cf. above, p. 204.

House of Lords to help a bill on its way was provided by the Protection of Animals (Amendment) Bill of 1953 and 1954. The veterinary profession had 'felt for some time past that an amendment of the law relating to the use of anaesthetics for animals was long overdue'. As the Government remained inactive, a private member's bill was drafted, and brought in in the House of Lords by Lord Stamp. The second reading debate took place, in fact, at the very end of the session of 1952–3, so although the Bill was approved it clearly had no chance of making any progress. The date, 27th October 1953, was, however, also very shortly before the ballot for private members' bills for the next session in the Commons; the Lords' debate, which showed how useful the Bill was, was well timed from that point of view.

The outcome was very successful. Viscountess Davidson, who won the second place in the ballot in the Commons three weeks later, introduced the Bill, now under the title 'Protection of Animals (Anaesthetics) Bill'. It was given a second reading after a debate which lasted little more than an hour, and passed through its remaining stages in both Houses without trouble.

In the session of 1953–4 the weaknesses and the advantages of the device of introducing private members' bills in the House of Lords were illustrated by the proceedings on the Protection of Birds Bill brought forward by Viscount Templewood for second reading on 17th November 1953. As Lord Templewood pointed out, the arguments in favour of legislation in this field were very strong. The existing state of the law was in great confusion, and it was proposed to repeal no less than 26 Acts on the subject, some of them going back to the early days of the reign of George III. In addition, he said, there were no fewer than 250 regulations and orders, some of them contradictory, and many of them out of date. 'Home Secretary after Home Secretary for years past has wished to deal with the question, and during the last five years there has been a most exhaustive enquiry by the two advisory committees that advise the two Secretaries of State.' The proposals of the Bill followed the lines advocated by the advisory committees, which in their turn represented an impressive list of societies.

The Bill was well received during a long debate. Lord Jowitt argued that for a private member's bill it was drawn too widely, but Lord Lloyd promised the Government's full support and all possible help. The Bill had a remarkably long committee stage in the Lords, taking some five hours in all, spread over two days of sitting (1st and 10th December 1953).

In the ordinary way it would apparently have been of little use for the House of Lords to devote so much time to the discussion of a private member's bill which could hardly expect to receive an unopposed second reading in the Commons. On this occasion, however, it happened that Lady Tweedsmuir, M.P., who had won a good place in the ballot for private members' time in the House of Commons, had put down a parallel Bill, which came up for second reading in the Commons on 4th December. The House of Commons gave her Bill a second reading without a division, and its standing committee devoted four sittings to the consideration of the details. After the Commons' Bill had been through all its stages in the lower House, it was, in its turn, sent up to the Lords, and as the Lords' Bill which had already occupied so much time could not itself now hope to have time found for it in the Commons, it was dropped, and the Commons' Bill took its place. Very appropriately, the peer who took charge of Lady Tweedsmuir's Bill in the Upper House was Lord Tweedsmuir. It was given a rapid second reading (15th April 1954), and its committee stage took a further $3\frac{1}{2}$ hours. It finally passed the Lords after further discussion on 13th May. Some controversy between the two Houses arose over the question which particular birds were to be designated as harmful, and therefore excluded from the protection given by the Bill. These difficulties settled, the Bill received the Royal Assent.[1]

During the same session Lord Chorley, a Labour peer, brought in his National Service (Conscientious Objectors) Bill, whose purpose was to make provision for men who became conscientious objectors after completing their period of compulsory embodied National Service. The second reading motion was defeated by 39 votes to 12. Although this was a private member's bill, Government Whips acted as tellers in the division, and no Conservative peers voted in its favour, although two Labour peers voted against it.

In the session of 1955-6 three private members' bills were introduced in the first instance in the House of Lords. An uncontroversial Solicitors Bill was passed through all its stages without trouble. It received an unopposed second reading in the Commons, but was debated at some length on third reading there. On 20th December 1955 a second reading was given, after a debate lasting only 25 minutes and without a division, to Lord Merthyr's Bill whose purpose was to forbid attempts to build up the rabbit-population after the ravages of myxomatosis; soon afterwards, however, the Bill was withdrawn because the Government thought that its aims could be better achieved by a measure on different lines. The revised Bill was brought up just before Easter, and quickly passed by the Lords. It came up for second reading in the Commons at 1.14 p.m. on the penultimate private members' Friday. Although the Bill had been debated at some

[1] The will of the Commons, kinder to moorhen and little owl, prevailed.

length by 4 p.m., the Speaker refused to put the question on the closure, and the Bill was talked out.[1] It was lost for the session. Six months later, however, the Government took action on its own account.

On 24th January 1956 Lord Grantchester, on behalf of the Liberal peers, brought forward a Coercive Action (Relief) Bill, which dealt with one of the subjects covered by the Liberals' Rights of the Subject Bill of ten years earlier. Lord Grantchester's Bill had the purpose of protecting individuals or minorities among workers or traders from the oppressive action of majority groups in trade unions or traders' associations. The Bill was opposed from both Conservative and Labour front benches; the Government spokesman's complaint was that the objects of the Bill could not be achieved in practice through legislation. The Bill was defeated by 49 votes to 19. The Liberals, of whom a good number had come down to the House for this debate, were joined in the division only by two Conservatives and two non-party peers (of whom one had recently left the Labour Party); the majority was remarkable mainly for including no fewer than 15 office-holders, as compared with only nine Labour peers.

2. BILLS BROUGHT UP FROM THE COMMONS

The House of Lords has also to deal with private members' bills which have been brought up to it from the Commons, after having passed through all their stages there. The first point of interest in connection with these has to do with the Commons' time-table. There is no formal difficulty about finding time in the Lords; the position is the same as with Lords' bills. Bills which have not been able to pass their report and third reading stages as unopposed business cannot reach the Lords until after the first day allocated for the later stages of private members' bills in the Commons. This first day is normally after Easter. If the Lords amend a bill the Commons have still to find time for debating the Lords' amendments. Ideally this discussion should take place on one of the remaining private members' Fridays, rather than in time provided by the Government, but this ideal cannot be achieved unless the bill emerges from the Lords early enough. If the Lords amend a bill and do not send it back until after the last allotted day in the Commons, the final passage must be dependent

---

[1] This was the first private member's bill from the Lords to be actually debated on second reading on a private member's Friday since the war—and this was not one of the first six Fridays. For a discussion of the practice of the Chair in the Commons with regard to closure motions on Fridays, cf. P. A. Bromhead, *Private Members' Bills*, p. 28.

on the provision of time by the Government for the consideration of the Lords' amendments. Before 1927 the later stages of private members' bills had precedence on only two Fridays in each session, and Lords' amendments could usually only be taken in Government time. Since 1927, however, four days in each session have been given to the later stages, and the discussion of Lords' amendments has become correspondingly less dependent on the Government's good will. It has in recent years been the practice—so much so that it might almost be called the convention—that the Government should, if necessary, provide time for the consideration of Lords' amendments to private members' bills; but the Government is in no sense bound to do this.

Another point of interest is in connection with the responsibility in the Lords for private members' bills brought up from the Commons. Some unofficial peer must be found ready to take charge of the bill and pilot it through all its stages in the upper House, not only making an appropriate speech on behalf of its principles at the second reading debate, but also dealing with the amendments which may be proposed at the committee, report and third reading stages. If difficult amendments are proposed, the peer performing this task has a somewhat unenviable duty. The bill is not really his own, but in a sense the property of those who were responsible for it in the Commons, so he is bound to act to some extent under their instructions. Like an office-holder in charge of a government bill before the Lords, he will have to be coached beforehand, particularly before the committee stage, with reference to all the amendments that have been put down. But while a peer speaking on behalf of the Government in committee has had the benefit of detailed instructions from the civil servants of the department concerned, the unofficial peer has to be advised either by members of Parliament or by agents of the outside body or bodies who are primarily interested in the bill. These advisers, lacking the experience of civil servants in dealing with opposition, may find it difficult to forearm the peer against all the arguments which may be brought forward during the course of the discussions. He may have to decide quickly at what points he ought to make concessions, in order to avoid defeat in a division.

A third point of interest arises in relation to the question how far it is right for the Lords to set their opinion against that of the Commons on private members' bills which are not the concern of the Government. Normally, in discussions about the relations between the two Houses, it is assumed that the opinion of the House of Commons, against which the Lords may set themselves, is also the opinion of the Government. With private members' bills, however, the Government has normally no set opinion, at any rate when, as is usual, the decisions at the various stages are made in the Commons by free votes. The normal arguments about the position of the Lords in relation to governmental responsibility do not, therefore, arise. Rejection of a private member's bill sent up from the Commons does not involve a conflict between the two Houses in the sense in which we usually think of such conflicts. Furthermore, if the Lords should reject a private member's bill, it is not likely that the procedure of the Parliament Act would be able to ensure the passage of the bill in the next session unless it were taken over by the Government. The bill could be passed in the next session only in the event of a private member of the House of Commons using a good place in the ballot to bring it in, and even then it would have to be passed by the Commons once again in the same form. Thus, even under the Parliament Act of 1949, the House of Lords still has a real power, not merely to delay legislation, but, in effect, to prevent its enactment, in the case of private members' bills. Ministerial responsibility is not usually involved in such matters, and it might be argued that the Lords would be justified, if they felt so inclined, in using this power. In relation to the experience of recent years, however (with one important exception, the Death Penalty Bill of 1956) the question has been academic; the House of Lords has tended to treat with considerable respect all the private members' bills brought up from the Commons.

During the six sessions between 1948 and 1955 in which private members' time was allowed in the Commons, 54 of these bills came up from the Commons to the Lords, and of the 54 only one (the Cockfighting Bill of the session 1948–9) failed to pass into law—and it failed through lack of time.[1] With the others the House of Lords has generally managed to complete all the stages during the interval —often not a very long one—between the time when it has received the bills and the last of the days allocated for private members' bills in the lower House. An exception was the session of 1948–9, but the delay in this case was not the fault of the House of Lords. The trouble was that the last days in the House of Commons were so planned that the Lords could not help themselves. In this session only three, instead of four, days were provided for the later stages in the Commons, and these three days were on successive Fridays between the 24th June and the 8th July. Although the Lords received two bills immediately after the first of these days, it would have been necessary to complete all their stages within six sitting days of the House if they were to be sent back to the Commons in time to have the Lords' amendments dealt with by the last of the allotted days; to have done this would have been practically impossible, and the Lords did

[1] It was in fact passed into law in 1951.

not make the attempt.[1] The Adoption Bill and the Married Women (Maintenance) Bill both had their second reading stages taken in the Lords shortly after 8th July, which was the last of the days allotted in the Commons. These two were both amended in the Lords, and the discussion of the Lords amendments in the Commons was taken in Government time. The Law Reform (Miscellaneous Provisions) Bill was in an even worse case, because its last stages in the Commons were not taken until the last of the allotted days. In fact, however, the Government did provide time for the last stages of all these three Bills, and they were all passed into law.

In the five sessions of 1950–5, the Lords introduced amendments into nine of the private members' bills brought up to them from the Commons, but in six of these cases succeeded in returning the bills to the Commons in time for the Lords' amendments to be considered during the time allocated for private members' bills. The three bills which came back to the Commons with amendments after the end of private members' time were all in 1951–2, when the private members' time in the Commons had been much blocked by the important and complicated Defamation Bill. This was itself one of the three bills which had to depend on the provision of time by the Government for the examination of the Lords' amendments. It received its third reading in the Commons on the penultimate private members' Friday, 27th June, and as it required fairly prolonged debate at each of the three main stages, the Lords could not reasonably have been expected to try to return it to the Commons again by 11th July. The other two bills were both uncontroversial, and were disposed of with little trouble. It is fair to say, then, that the Lords have not been obstructive towards the private members' bills brought up to them in recent years.

The procedure of the House of Lords is perhaps superior to that of the Commons for the discussion of very uncontroversial private members' bills. Nearly half of the private members' bills enacted since 1948 have had their second reading stages taken in the Commons as unopposed business; the House has had to approve the principles without having heard a word of explanation about them, except in the few cases where the original introduction has been under the Ten Minute Rule. The greater flexibility of the time-table in the Lords has made it possible for all these bills to be briefly discussed, or at least explained, on second reading in that House.

Such few differences of opinion as there have been between the

---

[1] In 1954 it was the Labour leader Lord Jowitt who complained that the Protection of Birds Bill was 'rushed through' the House, because only a week elapsed between the committee and third reading stages (Lords Debs., 11th May 1954, vol. 187, cols. 456 f.).

two Houses with regard to private members' bills have arisen over individual amendments introduced in the House of Lords, generally on subjects with which the parties, as such, are not concerned. An example is provided by an amendment to the Married Women (Maintenance) Bill of 1949, whose main purpose was to empower the courts to take account of the fall of the value of money by increasing the allowance payable under a court order by a man to his wife from whom he was separated. Lord Crook persuaded the Lords to accept a new clause to the effect that when a man and his wife had made an agreement without a court order on the terms of a separation allowance, the wife might come to the court to get the amount increased.[1] Lord Crook's clause had been drawn up by co-operation between the promoters of the Bill and the Home Office. The Lord Chancellor repeated the lawyers' argument which had been successful in overriding the proposal for a similar clause in the Commons. In such a case, he said, there was after all an agreement, into which the parties had entered voluntarily; a provision for interference by the Courts with private contracts would introduce an unhealthy principle. In the Lords, the manifest justice of this clause was allowed to prevail over the lawyers' argument which had impressed the Commons, but when the Bill returned to the Commons the new clause was removed. In due course, Lord Crook himself moved not to insist on the new clause. It was clear, he said, both to him and to the original promoters of the Bill, that the question was a very controversial one, and on those grounds alone he thought that the upper House should not insist on its opinion. The Lords gave way.

In the session of 1955-6 a disagreement between the two Houses arose with regard to the Hotel Proprietors (Liabilities and Rights) Bill, which sought to redefine the liability of inn-keepers in respect to the loss or theft of guests' property. Under the Bill as brought up from the Commons, the maximum liability to any one person was to be £100. In committee Lord Faringdon, a Labour peer, proposed that the limit should be increased to £200. His amendment was narrowly defeated in a division which followed party lines. At the report stage, however, the amendment was moved again, and carried, against the Government's wishes and those of the Commons, by a group of peers mainly of the Left. Ten of the votes in the minority were cast by office-holders. On the other hand, eight Conservative peers joined the Labour and Liberal supporters of the amendment.

The Government was not, properly speaking, defeated, as the vote was a 'free' one, but the Commons threw out the amendment, and the Labour peers abandoned it. The manner of the rejection in the Commons drew from Lord Silkin a comment deploring the language used

[1] Lords Debs., 21st July, 1949, vol. 164, cols. 345-8.

in the Commons, which had implied an inferior capacity to make decisions on the part of the upper House. The opinion of the House of Lords, he said, was as good as that of the Commons.

The summer of 1956 saw the first attempt since the war to deny a second reading in the Lords to a bill brought up from the Commons. A division took place on the second reading of the Small Lotteries and Gaming Bill, but the Bill received a good majority of 70 votes to 7.

These differences between the Houses over private members' bills were unimportant compared with that over the death penalty; that is such a large subject, however, that it seems to merit special treatment in a separate chapter.

Chapter XVI

THE DEATH PENALTY QUESTION

IT is with regard to the proposal to abolish the death penalty that the House of Lords has made its most striking and effective (or destructive) contribution to the actual course of events in the past fifteen years. The proceedings on this matter in 1948 and 1956 raise many points of special interest, and need to be looked at in some detail.

Early in the session of 1947–8 the Government introduced its Criminal Justice Bill, which embodied far-reaching reforms in the penal law, in accordance with the movement of both ordinary and expert opinion in the past 30 years. The Bill was in no sense a party measure, and indeed embodied many of the proposals put forward just before the war by the National Government, but left in abeyance owing to the international situation. Earlier in 1947 Lord Templewood, who had been Home Secretary in 1938, had pressed the Government to delay no longer before bringing in the reforms which were generally considered to be overdue.

The Bill as originally introduced by the Government in the House of Commons said nothing at all about the death penalty. During the second reading debate in the Commons Mr. Ede, the Home Secretary, who was aware that many of his back-bench supporters were in favour of abolition, said that if any member should care to propose to insert into the Bill a provision for the abolition of the death penalty, the Government would leave the Labour members to vote freely, without guidance from the Whips.

Mr. Sydney Silverman duly put down a new clause, to which the Commons devoted a whole day's debate on the report stage. In many ways this clause was really analogous to a private member's bill; indeed both before and since 1948 there have been private members' bills for the abolition of capital punishment. During the debate Mr. Ede explained fully his reasons as Home Secretary for not wishing to have the death penalty abolished. His opinion as the responsible Minister was quite definite, and the advice which he gave to the House was quite clear. Although some ministers privately disagreed with him, the Government as a whole was behind him, and although the Government Whips were not put on for the Labour back-benchers, the ministers and junior office-holders were apparently instructed not to vote for abolition.[1]

In the division Mr. Ede and the Government had the support of the vast majority of Conservatives (only 13 of whom voted for abolition) and of a few Labour back-benchers, but the mass of Labour back-bench members was in favour of abolition, and Mr. Silverman's amendment was carried by the not too narrow majority of 245 votes to 222.

The Bill therefore went to the Lords with the abolition of the death penalty included among its provisions. Much interest was raised by the question of the attitude of the Government and of the Lords on this matter. It was well known that the vast majority of Conservative peers, like most Conservatives in the House of Commons, were against abolition. The debate raised the constitutional question how far it would be proper for the majority of the peers to give free rein to their opinions to the extent of overthrowing a decision reached in the Commons.

The case was not really parallel with the other occasions during the reign of the Labour Government when the Conservative majority in the Lords had thought it proper to vote against the Government's advice on specific points on the committee stage of government bills. In those matters the Lords did no more than make an ineffectual protest, in the expectation that their protest would be swept aside when the Bill returned to the Commons. On this question the majority in the Lords agreed with the Government, and the outcome of a negative decision by the peers was not yet plain, but in terms of the old language of conflict between the Houses there was clearly a chance that the Lords could really make their will prevail.

The second reading debate took two days, and much of the discussion was concerned with the proposal to abolish the death penalty. Lord Jowitt admitted that, as Lord Chancellor, as head of the judiciary, and as one concerned with the general protection of the public safety, he was not inclined to favour abolition. On the other hand, as a member of the Government he must also give the House

[1] Cf. Commons Debs., 15th April 1948, vol. 449, col. 1171, and P. A. Bromhead, 'Free Votes in the House of Commons', *Durham University Journal*, 1953, p. 105.

of Lords specific advice contrary to his own private and official opinion. This advice was that the Lords should not interfere with the decision of the popular House.[1] The Government had indeed given, at least by implication, some sort of pledge that it would accept the decision reached by the free vote of the Commons, and was to some extent bound by that pledge.

In committee the debate on the disputed clause covered eight hours, spread over two days of sitting. The debate was exceptionally well attended. The vote was taken at 7.45 p.m. on 2nd June, and in spite of the lateness of the hour the number voting exceeded 200. The idea that because a decision had been arrived at by free vote of the Commons the Lords ought not to interfere with it was not acceptable to the majority of the peers, and the new clause was rejected by a very large majority (181 votes to 28).[2]

The Bill therefore returned to the Commons without the death penalty abolition clause which the Commons had put in. It was evidently necessary for the Government to do something about it, as the Labour majority in the Commons could hardly be expected to accept the rejection of their clause by the non-elected assembly. The Government felt that its responsibility was in some sense engaged, and it therefore itself devised a compromise clause which would retain the death penalty only for some of the most obnoxious kinds of murder such as poisoning, murder committed in the course of a burglary, and murder of a policeman or of a prison officer. It can well be argued that with this compromise the Government were not really meeting their supporters at all, because in practice the Home Secretary could normally be expected to reprieve most murderers except those who committed murders of the more offensive kind. However, in the circumstances the Labour back-benchers had to be content with this rather unsatisfactory solution. The Government put the Whips on at the division, and the clause was carried by a large majority.

The new situation created further problems with regard to the proper rôle of the Lords. By this time the session was so far advanced that there was no time for the Bill to continue going backwards and forwards between the two Houses. It was clear that if the Lords rejected the Government's compromise clause the Government would have to choose between dropping the clause and losing the

---

[1] Lords Debs., 27th April 1948, vol. 155, cols. 396–9.
[2] Lords Debs., 2nd June 1948, vol. 156, col. 176. The 28 supporters of Mr. Silverman's clause included 22 Labour peers, 3 Conservatives and 3 others. Five Labour peers, none of them office-holders, voted with the majority. The total number voting was greater than on any other subject since 1945, except the Parliament Bill and the Independent Television Bill.

whole Bill for that session. It was in these circumstances that the compromise clause was heavily defeated in the Lords. Faced with the danger of losing their whole Bill, the Government advised the Commons not to insist on the compromise clause, and the Bill was passed, as it had been introduced, without any provision abolishing the death penalty at all.

It is hardly fair to describe these transactions as a conflict between Lords and Commons in the generally accepted sense; the House of Commons itself was not really in agreement with the Government. Although the Government took responsibility for the compromise clause it did so only to appease its own back-bench supporters. This fact no doubt weighed very heavily indeeed with the majority of the peers in deciding to vote against the Government's compromise clause when the matter came up for final review. The Lords had triumphed, but they had only restored the situation which the Government had originally desired.

In 1956 the House of Lords again stood in the way of a proposal to abolish the death penalty, already approved by the Commons. This time the measure had been passed through the Commons as a private member's bill, but in time provided by the Government. The circumstances closely resembled those of 1948. The Home Secretary had spoken against abolition, but a free vote had been allowed. The verdict of a House of Commons with a Conservative majority had been the same as that of a Labour-dominated House of Commons eight years before. There was perhaps some ground for arguing that the spirit of the Parliament Act demanded that the Lords should now acquiesce; the action of the Lords in 1948 had imposed a delay, not of one or two years, but of a much longer period, in which public opinion could be formulated—though it could hardly be said that any such formulation had really been made, or ever could be made, in a political sense, on such a question. Arguments of this sort failed to impress the Lords, and they rejected the Bill. The number voting was the largest in any division in recent times. The voting has already been analysed above, in Chapter III; for our present purpose it is interesting to observe that, while the number of peers opposed to abolition in 1956 (238) was barely 25% more than in 1948, the number who voted for abolition was now three times as great.

Once again the Government cast about for a compromise on the same lines as the spurned compromise of 1948; this time the compromise solution (which could be no compromise from the abolitionists' point of view) was introduced as a separate government bill in the following session of Parliament, and passed into law.

An interesting feature about these proceedings has to do with the question of public opinion. The Bryce Conference Report, in speaking of the power of the Lords to interpose delay so as to allow public opinion to be formulated and expressed, had in mind the power of delay from one session to the next or next but one; here, however, the delay was likely to be of longer duration. Mr. Silverman had put forward the Burkian thesis that a free vote of the House of Commons was the best available indication of the true state of public opinion, but several peers asserted their conviction that public opinion was really against abolition. The argument that peers should be much influenced, in formulating their decisions, by their personal or second-hand impressions about the trend of public opinion on a particular question, is an interesting one, and one which should not be followed up too far. Some peers may have good ground for thinking themselves peculiarly well able to judge the public interest, but their position in British society is not such as to entitle them to set themselves up against a majority of the House of Commons as interpreters of public opinion.

Chapter XVII
THE HOUSE OF LORDS AND GENERAL DEBATES

ONE of the functions which the Bryce Conference considered to be appropriate to a House of Lords was the discussion of general subjects connected with the Government's stewardship. As a check upon the executive, as a body which discusses what the Government is doing or is not doing, has done or has not done, ought to do or ought not to do, the House of Lords has functions closely parallel with those of the House of Commons. In this field the output of the Lords, in terms of time spent in debate, and of quantity and variety of subjects debated, has so greatly increased in the past half-century as to be almost entirely transformed in character.

There is theoretically one big constitutional difference between the debates of this type in the Lords and those in the Commons; the Government is not responsible to the House of Lords, not obliged to take notice of any motions which the Lords may pass expressing no confidence in the Government or censuring it or calling upon it to take specified administrative action. But as the passing of a vote of censure by the Commons, in the conditions of two-party government, is only a remote possibility, the Lords' constitutional inability to dismiss a government does not of itself place them at a serious disadvantage. Any government, Labour or Conservative, will be prepared to listen carefully and sympathetically to opinions expressed in the upper House. Debates in the Lords on administrative questions, in the words of Mr. Herbert Morrison, 'can, and at times do, stir public opinion, or they may ventilate real public grievances or have repercussions in the House of Commons; so they may make the Government conscious of some failure or shortcoming'. Mr.

THE HOUSE OF LORDS AND GENERAL DEBATES

Morrison continues: 'No Government therefore, whatever its political complexion, studiously and systematically ignores the opinion of the House of Lords. Indeed, it is the duty of the Leader of the House of Lords in the Cabinet to indicate to his colleagues the feelings of his House on subjects under consideration.'[1] There are two main devices by which members of the House may bring up for discussion, at length or shortly, the Government's executive policy. First they may ask parliamentary questions like members of the House of Commons; secondly they may initiate debates, generally on motions, but sometimes also on the basis of questions addressed to the Government. The longer types of debate may be brought up at any time, though only with notice. As we have seen above (Chapter V), there is no need for any elaborate machinery for allocating time among private members or for special adjournments to discuss matters of urgent public importance; when there is a demand that a subject should be debated, arrangements are made, and the debate eventually takes place.

1. PARLIAMENTARY QUESTIONS IN THE LORDS

In the early development of the device of the parliamentary Question—which has in recent times come to be perhaps the most characteristic British parliamentary institution—the House of Lords played a part equal with that of the House of Commons. Indeed it was in the Lords, and not in the Commons, that the first recorded Question was asked in 1721.[2] During the past hundred years, however, the device of the Question has not developed in the House of Lords in quite the same way as in the Commons. The essential principles, such as those governing the admissibility of particular types of questions, and the right to ask supplementaries, are the same in the Lords as in the Commons, but there is some divergence in practice, corresponding with the differences in character between the two Houses.

The Lords' procedure, like that of the Commons, recognizes three distinct types of question: starred questions (for oral reply) (S.O. 39); questions for written answer (to be published in *Hansard*); and private notice questions (S.O. 31). In addition, the House of Lords also allows unstarred questions, which require notice and may lead to debate; these have no exact equivalent in the Commons, but resemble the half-hour debates on the adjournment with which the lower House ends each day's business.

As in the Commons, question time in the Lords now comes at the

---
[1] Herbert Morrison, *Government and Parliament*, op. cit., p. 176.
[2] Cf. Patrick Howarth, *Questions in the House* (The Bodley Head, 1956), p. 14.

PARLIAMENTARY QUESTIONS IN THE LORDS

beginning of the day's business, but it is not of any fixed duration.[1] From 1947 to 1954 questions might be asked only on Tuesdays and Wednesdays, and not more than three questions were allowed on any one day. In 1954 a new Standing Order (No. 32) removed these limits.[2] One full day's notice must be given. The old limitation of the number of questions was only rarely found irksome; on many Tuesdays and Wednesdays less than three questions were asked. Even now, the average is about two on each day, as compared with about sixty a day actually answered in the Commons.[3] The explanation for the divergence between the two Houses in this matter is obvious. Peers have no constituents, and although only a few of the questions asked in the Commons are really constituency questions, that type of question is nevertheless an integral part of a system of questions such as has developed in the Commons. Again, the questions in the House of Commons, although many of them are not on party matters, do depend to some extent on the fact that they are asked within the context of the give-and-take of party strife.

The process of question and answer is much more leisurely in the Lords than in the Commons. A question for oral answer is put down in writing in advance in the same conditions as in the House of Commons, and when the question is reached on the order paper, the peer in whose name it has been put down stands up and intimates that he wishes to put his question. The words of his question are not read out. The question is normally addressed, not to a particular minister as in the Commons, but to Her Majesty's Government. This variant is almost inevitable, because most of the ministries are not directly represented in the Lords, and most of the questions asked relate to the activities of departments which have no representatives of their own in the upper House. As we have seen above, however, individual office-holders have the duty of answering for specific departments. In the session of 1946-7 one third of the questions asked were answered by Household officers, and a quarter by ministers or junior ministers from departments not concerned with the subject-matter of the questions.

The Government spokesman generally reads out an answer which has been supplied to him by the department concerned. It may be presumed that an outside peer, who is merely acting as the spokesman

[1] Before 1947 questions were dealt with later in the day. The old system caused inconvenience, both to the questioners and to the government spokesmen.

[2] For the changes in the Standing Orders, cf. Lords Debs., 5th February 1947, vol. 145, col. 399 and 11th May 1954, vol. 187, cols. 456 ff.

[3] As will be seen below (p. 224), the removal of the limitations did not produce any increase in the total number of questions asked. More questions were asked each year in the Commons a hundred years ago than in the Lords at present. (Cf. Howarth, op. cit., p. 106.)

of a department, will be rather more inclined to follow his brief closely than one who is actually an office-holder in the department concerned. The ministers' answers tend to be longer in the Lords than in the Commons. It is not rare to find a minister making an answer which takes three or four minutes to read. After hearing the answer the original asker of the question may ask one or more supplementary questions, and other peers may ask supplementaries also.

In the House of Commons the Speaker has to ensure that there are not too many supplementaries. He must neither seem to protect the Government from awkward questions nor allow a particular question to go on for so long that other members are prevented from putting their questions in their turn. In the Lords, however, the presiding officer has no power to bring the series of supplementaries and supplementary answers to an end. Interchanges sometimes go on for a considerable time.

During the first twelve months of the session 1955-6, eight questions occupied ten or more minutes each. Among these were Lord Elton's question, asked on the 25th October 1955, about the former Foreign Office official Maclean, and Lord Stansgate's enquiry of 17th November regarding security measures in relation to civil service entrants. On this occasion Lord Stansgate himself asked no fewer than six supplementaries. On 1st December the House spent a long time on a question asked by Lord Elibank about the Government's proposal to forbid the manufacture of heroin, and Lord Elibank reverted to the same subject a week later. Lord Silkin's question of 13th March 1956, relating to the Home Office spokesman's earlier refutation of some newspaper allegations about hanging, led to a small impromptu debate, which lasted for a quarter of an hour, and in which five peers took part. On 6th June 1956 the Lord Chancellor himself gave a fifteen-minute answer to a question asked by Lord Jowitt regarding Crown privilege for documents. His exceptionally long answer was followed by a fairly long discussion.

During the twelve months under review, 129 questions were asked by 48 peers. In another twelve-month period, the session of 1946-7, which has been analysed for the sake of comparison, the number of peers who asked questions was again 48; the number of questions asked was 134. The number of peers who ask questions almost exactly corresponds with the number of active peers of class I as defined in our study of Chapter III, when we adjust that figure by deducting from it, as we must in this context, all the office-holders. The peers who ask questions are, in fact, with few exceptions, the same persons as the peers comprising our first class of regular attenders.

PARLIAMENTARY QUESTIONS IN THE LORDS

There is little evidence of any tendency for peers on the Government side to be slower to ask questions than those of the Opposition. In our period of 1955-6, 41 questions were asked by 21 Conservative peers and 29 by 14 Labour peers. Liberal and non-party peers were relatively very active; 34 questions were asked by five Liberals and 25 by eight non-party peers. In 1946-7, with a Labour Government in power, the pattern was rather different. Only four Labour peers asked questions, and their questions numbered only ten. Three-quarters of all the questions of the session were put from the Conservative benches.

When we compare the two periods, we find evidence of a fairly high level of continuity of activity in asking questions. Of the 30 Conservative peers who asked questions in 1946-7, one third also addressed questions to their own Government nine years later, and another third held office.

It seems that there are always a few peers who are particularly inclined to make use of the right of asking questions. In 1946-7 nine peers asked between them 45 questions, or a third of the total, and in 1955-6 seven peers asked almost half of all the questions. A parallel phenomenon has been observed in the House of Commons, where it appears that half the questions are asked by a tenth of the members.[1]

It would be difficult to generalize about the content of questions in the House of Lords. Questions concerning defence and foreign and commonwealth affairs are relatively rather frequent, but far less so than forty years ago. Questions with a party slant are less common in the Lords than in the lower House; Opposition peers rarely ask questions with the intention of embarrassing or annoying the Government. Although there can be no 'constituency questions' in the Lords, it is not rare for a peer to ask a question having a local interest for his particular part of the country.

Individual peers have a tendency to specialize; those who asked several questions in 1955-6 each tended to concentrate on particular fields of interest. Lord Vansittart asked 16 questions, all related to foreign affairs; Lord Elibank asked 15, seven of them related to his demand for increased facilities for trade with China, and the rest about the ban on the manufacture of heroin, the proposed guided missile range in the Hebrides, or the working of the legal aid system. No other peer approached either of these two in the number of questions asked. Lord Barnby, a Conservative, asked nine questions, all

---

[1] Cf. R. W. McCulloch, 'Question Time in the British House of Commons', in the *American Political Science Review*, 1933, pp. 172 ff. Mr. McCulloch's survey covered the period 1924-33; similar results were found by Mr. Peter Jeffreys, in an unpublished paper on sample periods of 1950 and 1951.

of them relating to financial matters. Lord Lucas of Chilworth asked seven, all of them relating to transport. Lord Jeffreys asked four, three of them concerned with officers' pensions.

When we look in particular at the questions asked by the Opposition peers, we are at once struck by a great difference from the House of Commons. In the Commons, members of the Opposition Front Bench ask many of the private notice questions but relatively few of the others. Question time is generally regarded as above all a back-benchers' occasion. In the Lords on the other hand, during the period of 1955-6 under review, 24 of the 29 questions asked by Labour peers were asked by peers on the Front Bench. Few of these front-bench questions reflected party policy; although Lord Lucas' questions were all concerned with transport (and he had been Parliamentary Secretary to the Minister of Transport while his Party was in power), most of them were not shadow-cabinet questions. His question on the cost of the Government's vehicle testing unit at Hendon (18th April) was indeed clearly related to a matter which was then at the centre of political controversy, but some of his other questions, such as one about the Oxford ring road (26th July 1955) were of a much more restricted interest.

The explanation for the preponderance of questions asked by members of the Labour Front Bench is presumably to be found partly in the fact that by now not many Labour peers except those on the Front Bench are in close and continuous contact with the proceedings of the House.[1] A more general explanation would seem to be, however, that the conditions of the House of Lords do not produce so clear a distinction between front-bench and back-bench members of parties as do the conditions in the House of Commons. In the Commons, where it is always difficult to catch the Speaker's eye, back-benchers are somewhat jealous of their 'rights', whether formally or informally recognized. In the Lords, where a peer who wishes to make himself heard need have no fear of being unable to do so, there is no such ground for the distinction between front-bench and back-bench members. Again, while every utterance of a member of the Opposition Front Bench in the House of Commons is regarded as a statement of Opposition policy, a parallel extension of the rule of collective responsibility has not yet been consummated in the House of Lords.

Questions are often asked in order to urge the Government to act in some way or other; it would probably be fair to say that the

---

[1] When the Conservatives are in opposition the proportion of questions asked from the Opposition Front Bench is much smaller; in 1946-7 it was only a quarter of all questions asked by Conservatives. But this proportion is still incomparably greater than in the House of Commons.

Government pays neither more nor less attention to questions of this kind asked in the Lords than in the Commons. If an individual peer gets a reputation for continually riding a particular hobby-horse, the Government may take all the less notice of him for that.

The system of parliamentary questions requires a safety valve for members who are dissatisfied with the answers they receive. In the Commons a dissatisfied member can rarely get a full-scale debate, but must usually be content with his right to raise the matter again during the half-hour adjournment discussion at the end of a day—provided that he is successful in the ballot for that time. In the Lords, however, if a peer is dissatisfied he can always put down an unstarred question or a motion for some future day, when he can set out his grievances at his leisure, and a government spokesman will be bound to answer him.

2. GENERAL DEBATES IN THE HOUSE OF LORDS

Debates in the Lords on general questions are perhaps the most characteristic of the activities of the House. Various forms may be used for such debates, though the distinction between the forms is not very important. A common device is to move to call attention to some event and 'to move for papers'. A motion for papers is preceded sometimes by an extended question addressed to the Government, and sometimes by a substantive motion. Alternatively the debate may be founded on an unstarred question or on a motion without the addition of that cryptic motion for papers which, as we have seen, has no real meaning except to give the original mover of the motion the right to reply at the end of the debate.[1] The motion may take the form of an expression of regret at some action or omission of the Government. It may be pressed to a division; nearly always, however, it is withdrawn, never having been intended to be anything but a peg on which to hang the debate. It is the debate that matters, rather than the vote of the House at the end. The only divisions taken on debates of this kind in the session of 1955–6 were on the Opposition's motion 'to call attention to the Government's statement on the Egypt-Israel situation' on 1st November 1956,[2] and on a motion on 31st January 1956 calling upon the Government to take steps to ensure that no cruel methods were used in the training of performing animals. (Both motions were defeated, the latter on a free vote in a thinly-attended House.)

[1] Cf. above, p. 90 f.
[2] The debate on the Suez Canal on 12th and 13th September 1956 was based, first on a ministerial statement, and then on a Government motion to which the Opposition moved an amendment.

THE HOUSE OF LORDS AND GENERAL DEBATES

These various forms of debate may be said to combine the functions performed in the House of Commons by debates in Committee of Supply on the Estimates, by Friday debates on private members' motions, and by debates in time provided by the Government as a result of requests made to the Whips. The different conditions which apply in the Lords make it unnecessary for there to be any clear distinction between types of business in the time-table, or between private members' debates and debates arranged by the front benches. Any peer may put down a motion for any day. The only formal restriction is that on Tuesdays and Thursdays motions are taken after bills; otherwise all motions down for a particular day are taken in the order in which they have been put down. This is not to say that the front benches and the private members are really on a completely equal footing with one another; if a private member's motion is standing in the way of a motion backed by one of the front benches, the Whips can press him to let the front bench motion take precedence, and their pressure will usually be effective. They have no means of forcing him to give way, however. It should be remembered that when they do apply pressure of this kind, they are not necessarily acting only on behalf of the Party leaders; they are often acting on behalf of the generality of the peers, who may collectively want to see priority given to a subject of wider interest.

The past fifty years have seen an immense increase in the number and variety of subjects debated on motions in the Lords, and in the time devoted to such general topics. In 1909 there were nine 'general' debates; in 1912 there were twenty; in more recent times the number has increased to about fifty a year. In the session of 1947–8, when the House was under very great pressure because of the Government's exceptionally extensive legislative programme, it nevertheless found time for holding 47 debates on general questions. In the long session of 1955–6 the total number of such debates was 56, of which 47 were held during the period between the summer recess of 1955 and that of 1956—that is to say, during a period equivalent to a normal parliamentary session.

When we compare the session of 1947–8, when a Labour Government was in power, with that of 1955–6 under a Conservative Government, we find rather substantial differences in the distribution of the originators of these debates according to party membership and other factors. In 1947–8 only three of the debates were originated by back-benchers on the Government side. Twenty-five were originated by Conservatives, of whom only six were front-bench members. In the session of 1955–6 on the other hand, 28, or half of the total, were originated by Conservative back-benchers, or half the total as against less than a tenth by government supporters in the earlier period. This discrepancy is too great to be accounted for merely by the increased number of back-bench government peers during a Conservative administration as compared with their number during a Labour administration. Four-fifths of the Conservatives originating debates in 1947-8 were back-benchers; five-sixths of the debates originated by Labour members in 1955-6 on the other hand were originated by front-bench members. It would be wrong to attempt to draw from this great discrepancy any conclusions about an increasing importance of front-bench peers *vis-à-vis* back-bench peers. As we have already seen, there are not very many back-bench Labour peers who are constantly active about the affairs of the House; in any case we cannot rigidly distinguish between front-bench and back-bench debates in the House of Lords. Another change which needs to be noticed, though it is perhaps not of great importance, is the decline in the number of debates originated by independent or Liberal peers. The total fell from twenty in 1946-7 and nineteen in 1947-8 to only seven in 1955-6. This development, combined with that which we have noticed above, might apparently be taken to suggest a tendency for the House to become more and more dominated by the Parties, but it would probably be unwise to draw such a conclusion. This short-run change is mainly due to personal factors.

It is so difficult to generalize about the work of the House of Lords in holding debates on these varied topics that it seems that the best thing that we can do is to give a list of the subjects discussed during the session of 1955-6.[1] Some of them were very general, some of them very narrow. Some of them related to the highest national policy in defence or international affairs, others to large questions such as the control of the nationalized industries, or to agricultural policy or the economic situation or primary education. Some dealt with broad questions of the moment which had just come into special prominence, such as the victimization of non-strikers. There was a debate (introduced by Lord Lucas of Chilworth, the Labour Opposition's front-bench spokesman on transport) on motor racing on public roads and having particular reference to a particular scheme for motor racing on certain specified roads. Lord Hampton initiated a debate on the Government's failure to remove purchase tax from motor-cyclists' crash helmets. Lord Lucas raised the question of noise from aircraft at American aerodromes, and at one specified aerodrome in particular. Lord Vansittart initiated a debate on the desirability of conducting international relationships more through the usual and well-established methods of diplomacy, rather than through the newer methods of conferences and visits.

Several debates in 1956 arose out of unsatisfactory replies to

[1] Cf. below, pp. 233 ff.

starred questions. On 15th May, for example, Lord Ogmore introduced a debate on changes in the Board of the British Overseas Airways Corporation. The next day Lord Elibank, who had failed earlier to persuade the Government to adopt his proposal that the Post Office should issue pictorial stamps of low value, bearing illustrations to show the world some of the scenery of the British Isles, initiated a general debate on the subject. On 7th June, Lord Hankey raised the question of flour improvers, which had also been the subject of an earlier parliamentary question.

There is often a good deal of delay before it is found convenient to fit in a debate for which there is a demand. Furthermore, it is sometimes useful for notice of a forthcoming debate to be given several weeks in advance. At the very beginning of May 1956 Lord Ogmore, a Labour front-bench peer from Wales, tabled a motion relating to Welsh forestry. The motion was down on the order paper for two or three weeks without any date named. Towards the end of May a date was fixed—Tuesday, 5th June. The Labour peers had apparently expected that the reply on behalf of the Government would be given by Lord Mancroft, the Under-Secretary of State at the Home Office, because the Home Secretary had a special responsibility for Welsh affairs. The Government decided, however, that the reply was to be given by Earl St. Aldwyn, the Parliamentary Secretary to the Ministry of Agriculture. As the date fixed for the debate approached, however, Earl St. Aldwyn began to be doubtful whether he would be able to be ready by that date with the information which he considered to be necessary for him to give an adequate reply. He accordingly asked Lord Ogmore to allow the debate to be postponed. Lord Ogmore, after discussion with his own Leader, decided not to accede to this request. On the Friday four days before the debate was due to take place, Earl St. Aldwyn had become certain that he would not have the necessary information available in time, and so he once again approached Lord Ogmore, who this time agreed, somewhat unwillingly, to a postponement. (The Labour Leader, Viscount Alexander of Hillsborough, later expressed strong disapproval of the change.) The debate did not in fact take place until 18th June.

It may be a good deal harder for a general debate to be fitted in during the last two months before the summer recess, when the House is very busy with bills which have been through the House of Commons, than earlier in the session. Thus in the session of 1947–8, when the House was peculiarly hard pressed, all the general debates which took place in May, June and July were held on Wednesdays, and some of them could not start until fairly late in the day—after 5 o'clock on two occasions and after 10 o'clock on one occasion. Even during the session of 1955–6, when the House was much less hard pressed, only two general debates were held during the equivalent three months on days other than Wednesdays, and one of these began after 5 p.m.

An assessment of the effectiveness of the intervention of peers either at question time or in these general debates would be very difficult. We could indeed point to a number of instances in which pressure applied by a peer has been followed by the Government's taking the action demanded; this happened, for example, after the agitation about the Government's proposal to forbid the manufacture of heroin. But in such cases the agitation has been carried on not only in the House of Lords but by means of letters to *The Times* and other newspapers, and also in many cases by parallel agitation in the House of Commons. It would therefore not be possible to say to what extent a Government's change of plan has been directly due in any particular instance to the pressure that has been applied in the House of Lords.

In most cases what matters is what is said in the course of speeches, rather than the voting in divisions. The contribution of the House of Lords is a part of the whole complex of the political system and of the channels through which public opinion is expressed. A British Government is subject to a vast number of influences and pressures with respect to almost every decision of any moment that it has to make. There are letters in the newspapers, speeches and perhaps questions in both Houses of Parliament, informal approaches to ministers by M.P.s and peers acting alone or in groups or in party committees, and probably representations made by organizations of interested persons. None of these stand alone. The Government must balance them all against one another. The House of Lords is valuable because it is a place where opinions may be expressed, in the form of political debate, in relation to forthcoming governmental decisions, by men of varied background, experience and opinion, including great experts. On almost any subject the House will be able to hear one or two speeches, or maybe more, from men possessing a great wealth of specialized knowledge, and also other speeches from peers who, though lacking specialized knowledge in the narrow sense, may nevertheless be particularly well qualified to see the subject under discussion in its proper relationship with the rest of the national interest as a whole. Peers are less subject than members of the House of Commons to sectional pressures or party discipline; they can make speeches on these occasions without needing to consider party advantage or their own political careers. In general debates the unreformed House of Lords combines, in a fascinating way, the characteristics of a senate, an ordinary political assembly and an assembly of specialists such as might be found in an economic council.

THE HOUSE OF LORDS AND GENERAL DEBATES

It is much to the credit of the House that it has in the past generation so greatly extended its activity in the field of the discussion of general subjects. This reflection should not, however, give ground for complacency. Even in this field, rather too large a proportion of the work of the House falls upon the shoulders of the few peers who comprise the nucleus of regular attenders; this aspect of the work of the House would probably be improved still further if there were more extensive contributions from the particularly well-qualified specialists among peers of first creation.

Although lately the peers, while introducing fewer bills than in the past, have brought forward more subjects for debate, their debates on administrative questions have not, as a rule, been very much co-ordinated with those of the House of Commons. The pressure of business in the lower House is such that there are always many topics competing for time, and many which cannot be debated at all. The House of Lords clearly has great potentialities as a forum for debating questions which cannot be fitted in to the crowded time-table of the Commons; Opposition leaders in the two Houses do not appear, however, to have developed any regular practice of conferring together in order to make the fullest use of the House of Lords for their combined purposes. If there is any fault here, it is the Commons rather than the Lords who are to blame; there may in fact be more co-ordination, in a scarcely perceptible form, than is commonly supposed.

It would be agreeable to end this discussion of general debates with a reference to their educative effect on public opinion, and to suggest that, because it now holds so many debates of this kind, the House would deserve the praise of Walter Bagehot. Regrettably, however, we must express some doubt whether the educative effect is as great as it might be. If there is a fault here, we must blame, not the House of Lords, but the popular Press and its readers, who apparently do not want to be educated by reading reports of the speeches of their Lordships in the House. It would be naïve to express indignation, or even surprise, at the fact that the most widely-reported oration of recent times there was one of twelve words, containing no argument, spoken in a disorderly interruption by a famous actress; or that such fascinating topics as the manner of her escorted withdrawal from the Chamber, and her subsequent movements, were recounted (albeit with bewildering variety) more generously than the whole of any twenty sage debates put together; but the fact deserves attention. To be fair, though, we must also remember the commonplace that in our day parliamentary speeches, set down in print, cannot hope to rival in ease of access and communication the much more readily digested messages of those who speak on radio and television. If the

LIST OF SUBJECTS DISCUSSED

debates in the Lords have any educative effect on the public mind, that effect is very indirect. It may be hoped that what they lose in public éclat the debates gain in intimacy, in honest reasonableness, perhaps even, in the long run, in real constructive effect.

LIST OF SUBJECTS OF GENERAL DEBATES IN THE HOUSE OF LORDS, SESSION 1955-6

A. *Subjects introduced by Conservative Peers*

Date	Peer Introducing: Lord	
1955		
22 June	Balfour of Burleigh	Urban Congestion and the Green Belt.
5 July	Glyn	Exemptions from National Service. (Lord Glyn introduced the discussion in the first place about the exemption of stewards on merchant ships.)
7 July	Furness	The Tourist Industry and Hotels.
26 July	Howe	The Government's Road Programme.
27 Oct.	Polwarth	Guided Missile Range in the Hebrides.
2 Nov.	Raglan	The Sudan.
8 Nov.	Swinton	Defence (two days).
16 Nov.	Mansfield	Forestry Policy (second subject).
22 Nov.	Saltoun	Persecution of Railway non-strikers.
,,	Astor	Burgess and Maclean (second subject).
8 Dec.	Jessel	Encouragement of Exports (short debate).
10 Dec.	Hampton	Purchase Tax on Motor Cycle Crash Helmets.
14 Dec.	Gifford	Immigration facilities at Ports (second subject).
1956		
25 Jan.	Teynham	Officers' Pay.
26 Jan.	Monkswell	British Railways Finance and Electrification.
1 Feb.	Brabazon	Commercial Aircraft Construction.
22 Feb.	Gage	Overloading of the Building Industry.
28 Feb.	Swinton	Attendance of Peers at Lords' Debates.
20 Mar.	Glyn	Reorganization of the Colonial Service.
28 Mar.	Teviot	Manpower in the Coalmining Industry.
3 May	Rochdale	Industrial Accidents Claims and Legal Aid.
16 May	Balfour of Inchrye	Air Estimates.
29 May	Duke of Sutherland	Provision of Playing Fields.
31 May	Earl of Portsmouth	African Deforestation.

THE HOUSE OF LORDS AND GENERAL DEBATES

6 June	Saltoun	Former Officers' Pensions.
27 June	Astor	A motion welcoming the Government's intention to introduce a Bill on the control of betting.
5 July	Duke of Sutherland	Future of Historic Houses (short debate).

B. Subjects introduced by Labour Peers

1955   *Lord*

6 July	Ogmore	Colonial Policy.
12 July	Silkin	Primary Education.
13 July	Amwell	Industrial Relationships.
,,	Lucas of Chilworth	Motor Racing on Public Roads.
26 July	Lucan	High Commission Territories (second subject).
26 Oct.	Winster	The Merchant Shipping Industry.
1 Nov.	Pethick-Lawrence	The Economic Situation.
2 Nov.	Lucan	Home Defence.
3 Nov.	Lucas of Chilworth	Aircraft Noise.
9 Nov.	Listowel	Post Office Finance (second subject).
16 Nov.	Jowitt	Diplomatic Privileges.
30 Nov.	Ogmore	Commonwealth Development.
6 Dec.	Lucas of Chilworth	Noise near American Aerodromes (short debate; this could be regarded as a 'constituency' debate).
13 Dec.	Jowitt	The Ban on Heroin.
14 Dec.	Lucas of Chilworth	The British Transport Commission.
15 Dec.	Henderson	The Middle East.
21 Dec.	Henderson	The International Situation.

1956

8 Feb.	Silkin	Betting and the Report of the Royal Commission.
9 Feb.	Lawson	Report of the International Labour Conference.
15 Feb.	Alexander of Hillsborough	Agriculture.
7 Mar.	Pethick-Lawrence	Economic Situation (two-day debate).
13 Mar.	Ogmore	Plans for the future of the Imperial Institute.
15 Mar.	Attlee	The Situation in the Middle East and Cyprus.
27 Mar.	Henderson	International Situation.
11 Apr.	Alexander of Hillsborough	Agricultural Price Review.
18 Apr.	Silkin	The Development Plan for London.
2 May	Pethick-Lawrence	The Economic Situation.

LIST OF SUBJECTS DISCUSSED

15 May	Ogmore	Changes in the Board of the B.A.O.C. (began after 5 p.m. following the debate on a number of bills, including two private members' bills).
18 July	Ogmore	Forestry.
25 July	Attlee	Cyprus.
31 July	Lucas of Chilworth	A suggestion that the new electric super grid construction should be held up.
2 Aug.	Silkin	Suez.

C. *Subjects introduced by Liberal or non-Party Peers*

	Lord	
1955		
6 Dec.	Fraser of North Cape	Control of Nuclear Weapons.
1956		
31 Jan.	Strabolgi	Performing Animals (this motion was not withdrawn but pressed to a division and defeated by 12 votes to 18).
14 Mar.	Vansittart	A motion expressing preference for diplomacy through ordinary diplomatic channels, rather than by conferences and personal visits.
17 May	Elibank	An advocacy of postage stamps of pictorial design.
7 June	Hankey	Flour Improvers.
31 July	Moynihan	Prisons and Aftercare.

PART IV
THE MOVEMENT FOR REFORM

Chapter XVIII

THE QUESTION OF REFORM OF POWERS

THIS book is not a treatise on the reform of the House of Lords, but primarily a study of the working of the unreformed House. Nevertheless, as much of the public attention given to the Lords during the past fifty years has been concerned with reform, and as the House itself has spent much time and energy in considering the problem, it seems necessary now to look at the background to the Life Peers Bill which the Conservative Government introduced in December 1957.

Proposals for reform are concerned with two main topics, the powers of the House on the one hand and its composition on the other. The question of its powers can here be disposed of briefly, as it seems to have been settled already by the Parliament Acts of 1911 and 1949, surprising though it may be that this should be so. The Act of 1911 was intensely abhorrent to the Conservatives and was intended by its authors to be a temporary measure, to have effect until such time as the composition of the House might be reformed.[1] A conference under the chairmanship of Lord Bryce was set up in 1917, with the object of finding a solution to the problem of reform of both powers and composition. It made its report (Cd. 9038) in 1918. The report, which remains even today a most important document, contained not only a detailed exposition of the proper

---

[1] In the words of the preamble to the Act: 'Whereas it is intended to substitute for the House of Lords as at present constituted a second chamber constituted on a popular instead of a hereditary basis, but such substitution cannot immediately be brought into operation. . . .'

It is not intended here to review again the transactions of 1910–11, which have often been described in the past, and more recently in Mr. Roy Jenkins' book, *Mr. Balfour's Poodle*.

functions of the second Chamber, and of the position which it ought to hold in our constitutional system, but specific recommendations for reform.

The plans of the Bryce report regarding reform of the composition of the House will be dealt with below (Chapter XX). With regard to the power of the House of Lords to delay or to hold up legislation sent up from the Commons, the members of the Conference found it difficult to reach agreement, but they produced a plan which deserves to be studied, although it seems unlikely ever to be put into operation.

In their search for a solution to replace the two years' delaying power of the 1911 Parliament Act, the members of the Conference followed two main lines of approach, one, that the differences between the two Houses should be settled by some means of joint consultation between the members of the Houses themselves, and the other that a device such as a public referendum should be used.

The second proposal was perhaps in some ways the more satisfactory, and it did at least agree with the ideas of some of the statesmen on both sides who had been concerned with the dispute of 1909-11. If this had been accepted it would have given the Lords power to prevent the enactment of any substantial and controversial measure which was opposed by the majority of the people. The device of the referendum was at the height of its popularity during the early years of the present century. Eighteen American States had incorporated it into their constitutional systems between 1898 and 1918, and in an age when some sections at least of public opinion were particularly attracted by the idea of the equalization of political rights, the referendum had virtues in itself. Universal adult male suffrage had at last been generally accepted, and some opportunity for direct popular participation in the work of legislation seemed logically to be the next step.

There were perhaps two main objections to the referendum as a means of resolving differences between the two Houses of the British Parliament. On the one hand there was the question of expense and administrative difficulty and inconvenience; on the other hand there was the general doubt about the capacity of the majority of the people in a large nation-state to make a sufficiently well-informed decision about an intricate political question. Closely allied with this second difficulty was the problem of the Government's responsibility. If a Government's proposals should be rejected at a referendum, and if it considered that the execution of its policy was an indispensable prerequisite for its acceptance of responsibility for the management of public affairs, a difficult situation would arise. Such a Government

THE QUESTION OF REFORM OF POWERS

might well wish to resign office, in such circumstances that an alternative administration could hardly be found able to command a majority in the House of Commons. A new General Election, besides being inconvenient, might well not solve the problem, because the existing Government, though including a statement of its intentions with regard to the particular matter under review in its electoral programme, might obtain a majority. Many electors might dislike the particular item in its programme which was the subject of the dispute, and yet still prefer this Government to any alternative one. The referendum is a device which cannot work well under the British system of parliamentary responsible government.

This question of the Government's responsibility is also the basis of one of the main objections to a conference committee. And apart from this it is difficult to obtain acceptance of any specific principle regarding the relative strength of representation of the two Houses in whatever committee might be established for the making of the joint decision.

The Bryce Conference did eventually arrive at agreement on a device of a 'free conference', which was to meet in secret. There was to be a standing conference committee of perhaps 20 of the 'most experienced, most judicious and most trusted' members of each House, to whom perhaps ten from each House might be 'added *pro ne nata* in respect of special knowledge'. The committee was to make recommendations to the two Houses. Further detailed proposals were made with respect to bills which might still remain subjects of disagreement after being dealt with by the committee.

The conference committee proposed by the Bryce Conference had little in common with the 'free conferences' which had been used two hundred years earlier,[1] but the fact that there was a precedent for something on the same lines may have strengthened the arguments in favour of this solution. Nevertheless, it is difficult to see how a conference committee would fit in with the regular working of the party system.

The members of the Bryce Conference, although they disagreed on many matters, agreed in considering the essential principle of the 1911 Parliament Act to be unsuitable as a permanent solution to the problem of the settlement of differences between the two Houses. By now, however, that essential principle, the setting of a mathematical limit to the amount of time for which the Lords can delay legislation approved by the Commons, has come to receive general acceptance. The Act of 1949, which reduced the limit from three sessions to two sessions, or from two years to one year, was still within the framework of the same principle, and the discussions and disagreements which

---

[1] Cf. above, p. 133.

preceded the passing of the Act were concerned only with the exact extent of the reduction.¹

The Conservatives appear to have accepted even the detailed application of the 'one session' delay which they anathematized so strongly in 1948. When the Labour Government in 1948 insisted that the delay should mean twelve months from the first occasion of second reading in the Commons or nine months from the third reading, whichever was the greater, the Conservatives insisted on a different interpretation, and would have nothing to do with anything less than twelve months from the third reading; more recently they seem to have lost interest in the three months about which they previously cared so much. In 1955 Lord Salisbury stated the Conservatives' attitude as follows: 'Her Majesty's Government would certainly not wish now, any more than in 1948, to tie themselves to the proposition that in no circumstances should any House of Lords, however constituted, have any more power than your Lordships' House has today. That would be a matter for Parliament and the British people to decide, should such a proposition ever be put before them.² But . . . Her Majesty's Government consider that it is more immediately necessary to deal with the reform of the composition than with any question of the powers of the House.' ³ From this it seems that, for all the reservations about the future, the Conservatives are unlikely ever to try to increase the power of the Lords beyond that left to them in 1949. It is more likely that some future government of the Left will try to make a further reduction.⁴ It would indeed be easy enough for a Conservative government to bring in and have passed a bill to increase the power of the Lords, but it would be pointless for it to do so, as a future Labour government would be likely to take retaliatory action. Whatever their present attitude in the face of current political realities, many Conservatives still believe that ideally there ought to be a second Chamber with more power than the Lords now enjoy. They point to the weakness of the claim that any exercise of real power by the Lords is an interference with the popular will. They point out that often a government loses the support of a popular

---

[1] The Parliament Bill of 1947 became law at the end of the session of 1948-9, having been rejected by the House of Lords in three consecutive sessions, one of which was a short session held in the autumn of 1948 specially in order to ensure that the Bill could go for the Royal Assent in 1949 under the procedure of the 1911 Act. On the first occasion of second reading in the Lords, 23 Liberals, five Conservatives and 15 non-party peers voted for the Bill; afterwards, however, the Labour peers received virtually no support from the other parts of the House.

[2] It is difficult to see how Parliament and people would really make the decision.

[3] Lords Debs., 9th March 1955, vol. 191, col. 855.

[4] Mr. Anthony Wedgwood Benn, in his 1957 Fabian tract *The Privy Council as a Second Chamber*, speaks of a three months' delaying power.

majority long before it is required to face a new General Election, and that it is manifestly not true that every bill passed by the Commons really accords with the popular will. Particularly towards the end of a Parliament, they believe, there ought to be some device whereby a government's measures could be made subject to some real check. This argument has obvious merits, and the present strength of party solidarity in the Commons, which makes a government defeat there almost impossible, gives it yet more force. The main objection to it is the difficulty of reconciling it with the doctrine of governmental responsibility, as that doctrine is now preached and practised. It may be, indeed, that we have allowed this doctrine to be developed too far; perhaps it is not really true that all government bills are inextricably interwoven parts of a single monolithic policy. But the doctrine, whatever its intrinsic logical weaknesses, is in fact the very foundation of our present political system, and any departure from it would involve a revolutionary change in our political practice. Another objection to the Conservatives' argument is to be found in the domination of the unreformed House of Lords by a single political party; the 1957 Life Peers Bill makes no real attempt to deal with this problem, whose solution would demand a complete change in the character of the House.

If we could (and if we wanted to) revolutionize the doctrine of governmental responsibility for bills, and if we could devise a second Chamber in which the voting power was exercised by notables possessed of a wisdom that was, and was manifestly seen to be, quite above party allegiance, there might be a real case for giving such a second Chamber some more substantial power—power at least to force a referendum on a particular bill. But these are difficult conditions, and it is doubtful whether they could ever really be fulfilled.

Chapter XIX

PROPOSALS FOR MINOR MODIFICATIONS OF COMPOSITION

1. INTRODUCTORY SURVEY

PROPOSALS for reform of the composition of the House of Lords have a long history. In the seventeenth century the very existence of the House was called into question, and the House was in fact abolished during the Protectorate. Abolition has again been advocated, sporadically and half-heartedly for the most part, by some elements of modern radicalism, but even the Labour Party has in recent times been more concerned with keeping the House in check than with destroying it.

As the movement towards equal franchise for the House of Commons progressed during the nineteenth century, with successive reforms extending the right to vote to more and more classes of the population, so dissatisfaction with the basis of membership of the upper House increased. Along with egalitarian discontent went dissatisfaction with the way the Lords performed their functions. Inevitably, there were proposals for altering the composition of the House so as to make it conform more nearly with modern ideas. Not all the proposals for reform originated with people hostile to the House of Lords; indeed most were brought forward by people who wished to increase the prestige, and therefore the strength, of the House.

In this and the next chapter it is proposed to examine the proposals that have been put forward. For the sake of convenience they are divided into two classes, on the one hand proposals for minor modifications and on the other hand proposals for fundamental reconstruction. The two types cannot be altogether separated, because they overlap at many points, but there is an essential difference between them. Unlike the more ambitious schemes, the plans for minor modifications have generally been advocated by private members, and have nearly all begun with attempts to introduce new practices, or to revive old practices, without legislation. It has generally been argued that the House should be able to introduce the small changes by reviving or reinterpreting ancient precedents, without tampering with the essential basis of membership as it has been handed down from past centuries.

The main suggestions for partial reform, not involving fundamental reconstruction, have been:

(1) That the Crown should have power to create life peers;

(2) That peers inheriting titles should be free to avoid becoming members of the House of Lords, and to continue to be eligible to serve in the House of Commons;

(3) That peers should be excluded at least from voting, and perhaps from sitting also, unless they satisfy some test, judged usually with reference to amount of public services rendered inside or outside Parliament;

(4) That women should be eligible to sit in the House of Lords;

(5) That provision should be made for payment of peers who attend at the House.

2. LIFE PEERAGES[1]

It is perhaps most convenient to examine first the proposal to allow the creation of life peers. Some precedents for the granting of life peerages may be found from the very distant past. A few were, in effect, granted in the fourteenth and fifteenth centuries, and some life peerages were granted to women in the seventeenth and early eighteenth centuries. But these earlier instances have little relevance for contemporary discussion; the hereditary peerage, as we know it today, did not exist in the fifteenth century,[2] and the life peerages granted to women had nothing to do with sitting in the House of Lords.

The story of the modern attempts to allow the creation of life peers really begins in 1856, when a patent was issued granting to Sir James Parke the rank of baron 'for and during the term of his natural life'. Palmerston's Government, in attempting to grant a life peerage to Sir James Parke, had two objectives. It wanted to strengthen the number of specially qualified peers, so that the House might the better perform its tasks as the highest court of law in the land, but

[1] This subject has recently been dealt with by Mr. Sydney D. Bailey in *The Future of the House of Lords* (Hansard Society, 1954), pp. 109–20. The present study owes a debt to this work.   [2] Cf. above, p. 7.

it also hoped to prepare the ground for future grants of life peerages to peers for other than judicial services. Its first objective was to be fulfilled in the long run; its second had still not been fulfilled in 1957.

Sir James Parke was in 1856 a distinguished judge of 74 years old. He had no surviving sons, and it seemed unlikely that he would have any. Thus in his case it was really quite immaterial, from a practical point of view, whether the peerage was granted for life or in the ordinary way. If the grant of the life peerage had not been frustrated, however, it would have served as a useful precedent. It was for this reason that the enemies of the general introduction of a system of life peerages resisted the grant of the life peerage to him. Their resistance was for the time being successful. They argued that the precedents from the distant past, on which the Government relied, were invalid in the contemporary circumstances, and that the grant of life peerages had been out of use for so long that it was contrary to tradition and custom and had better not be revived. A practice of two hundred years' standing had become a rule; the Committee of Privileges, to which the case was referred, reported that 'neither the letters patent purporting to create him a baron for life nor the writ of summons which had been issued in pursuance thereof, entitled him to sit and vote'.[1] The House accepted the Committee's report, and the Government gave up the attempt to make Sir James Parke a life member. A few months later he was made a hereditary peer in the usual way.

With regard to their limited purpose of strengthening the judicial side of the House of Lords, the advocates of life peerages were not prepared finally to abandon their case. If the House was to be able to perform its judicial functions adequately, it must clearly include a larger number of judges than were at that time members. It would have been easy enough to solve the problem by granting ordinary peerages to a few judges, but this solution was not at that time acceptable, because judges were not considered wealthy enough to be able to found dynasties of the nobility. It was still felt that peers ought to be men of great substance, and that a man who inherited a peerage without great wealth would be in a situation embarrassing to himself and harmful to the prestige of the peerage as a whole.

The limited purpose of strengthening the House of Lords on its judicial side by the creation of judicial life peers was eventually achieved by the passing of the Appellate Jurisdiction Act of 1876, whereby life peerages might be given to a maximum number of two (later four) judges who were to take their seats in the House of Lords

[1] Cf. Sydney D. Bailey in *The Future of the House of Lords* (Hansard Society, 1954), p. 109.

as barons for life, known by the special title of Lords of Appeal in Ordinary, and receiving salaries.[1] Their number was later increased to six in 1913, to seven in 1929 and to nine in 1947.

The decision on the Wensleydale peerage case had very far-reaching effects. It established the principle that ancient precedents should not be revived from the distant past, refurbished and made to serve as pretexts for convenient alterations in current practice. The acceptance of this principle in 1856 has stood in the way of many other attempts at making changes since that date. In view of all this, it is remarkable that the Wensleydale decision might easily never have been made; it owed much to chance and to the efforts of one man, Lord Lyndhurst. The original issue of a patent of nobility without any remainder attracted little public attention at first, and if the new Lord Wensleydale had taken his seat on the first day of the session, as he was expected to do, it is possible that nothing further would have happened. But when the day came an attack of gout prevented him from taking his place, and Lord Lyndhurst had time to move that the House should resolve itself into a Committee of Privileges. Then, with 'astonishing ability and power', he insisted that 'no act or exercise of prerogative which had fallen into complete desuetude for centuries could be revived without the sanction of Parliament'.[2]

The more general purpose of strengthening the House of Lords as a legislative and deliberative body, by the grant of life peerages to distinguished men, has been often brought forward since 1856 and has won very wide sympathy in the past 100 years. One life peers bill was rejected (by 106 votes to 76) on third reading in 1869; others passed second reading, but made no further progress, in 1888 and (by 44 votes to 14) in 1935.[3] In 1953 a life peers bill was proposed by Lord Simon. After it had been debated for two days (3rd and 4th February 1953), Earl Fortescue, on behalf of the Government, proposed an adjournment, in order that discussions might be held between Party leaders, with a view to trying to arrive at a general agreement between them on wholesale reforms. The projected talks never took place, however, because the Labour Party believed that, as the discussions of 1948 'had revealed fundamental cleavages of opinion between the Parties on what is the proper part to be played by the House of Lords, there seemed to be no prospect of reaching agreement'.

[1] 39 & 40 Vict., c. 59. The Act provided for an annual salary of £6000 to each Lord of Appeal. This figure remained unchanged until 1954, when it was increased by the Judges' Remuneration Act to £9000.

[2] Cf. *Memoirs of the Duke of Argyll*, vol. ii, p. 11; quoted in W. C. Costin and J. S. Watson, *The Law and Working of the Constitution. Documents 1660-1914*, (A. & C. Black, 1952), vol. ii, pp. 403 f.

[3] Cf. Sydney D. Bailey, op. cit., pp. 116 ff.

PROPOSALS FOR MINOR MODIFICATIONS OF COMPOSITION

The adjourned debate on Lord Simon's Bill was never resumed, because the Government, like so many of its predecessors, insisted that any reform of the Lords ought to be of a wholesale character, initiated by the Government of the day, and preferably based on agreement between the Parties.

During the next two years the Government seemed to be moving towards the view that it really would have to take upon itself the task of dealing with Lords reform, and the Queen's Speech of November 1956 promised some action. In fact, however, the promise of the Speech was fulfilled only in the last days of the session, when a debate was arranged on the principle of life peerages for men and women. Shortly afterwards, in the new session, the Life Peerages Bill was introduced, providing that 'Her Majesty should have power by letters patent to confer on any person a peerage for life, and that a person receiving a life peerage should be entitled to receive writs of summons to attend the House of Lords and sit and vote therein accordingly'. The second reading debate was on 3rd and 5th December 1957, and the committee stage on 17th and 18th.

Although during the six days devoted by the House to this question in the autumn of 1957 there were many expressions of regret that the Government had not been more ambitious, there was little real opposition to the principle of life peerages. In the preliminary debate on 31st October, the Earl of Glasgow expressed general hostility and would have liked to divide the House, but could find nobody to act with him as teller. During the committee stage a Labour amendment to allow life peers to resign was defeated by 105 votes to 22. Lord Lucas, who spoke for himself alone and not for his colleagues on the Labour Front Bench, moved an amendment to provide that a person to whom a peerage was offered should be allowed to choose between a life peerage and a hereditary one. He feared that the Bill as it stood might create an unhealthy distinction between the two types of peers.

Lord Lucas withdrew his amendment, but his arguments indicate the most serious weakness in a reform which permits the grant of life peerages without any further reconstruction of the House. If the main purpose of the Life Peerages Bill is to make membership of the House of Lords more attractive, by allowing people to become members themselves without obliging their sons and descendants to be members after them, Lord Lucas' proposal is in accordance with the spirit of the Bill, though it involves obvious difficulties. If, on the other hand, the main purpose is to permit more extensive additions to the active current membership of the House, without thereby continuing to increase its future total membership, the amendment cannot be regarded as an improvement. Undoubtedly both purposes are present; it is hard to say which is uppermost.

3. EXCLUSION FOR NON-ATTENDANCE

In 1907 Lord Newton proposed that writs of summons to the House of Lord should be given, not to all persons who inherited peerages, but only to those who fulfilled certain requirements. Shortly afterwards a select committee of peers under Lord Rosebery accepted Lord Newton's idea, and proposed in addition that peers should elect their own representatives. Nothing further came of this for the time being, but the idea has been revived recently.

On 17th March 1953 the Marquess of Exeter brought forward a proposal that peers who failed to attend with reasonable regularity might be excluded from the right to vote in any division. The actual form of his motion was that no peer should vote in any division unless he had attended x times (or y times if he lived abroad)—unless he had obtained leave of absence under Standing Order No. 18. He relied, then, on a presumption that a *de facto* reform could be achieved by merely altering the existing practice without any alteration in the law. In doing this he was following a respectable precedent set by those who had tried at the end of the nineteenth century to show that new peers did not necessarily become deprived of their seats in the House of Commons, and also by those who argued that there was no reason why women should not be admitted to the Lords by a mere alteration of existing practice. The Marquess of Exeter pointed out that the existing Standing Order No. 19 provided that Lords might obtain leave of absence at the pleasure of the House upon cause shown, and Standing Order No. 17 provided that absent Lords might be called upon to serve on committees. The existence of these two standing orders seemed to presuppose some duty on the part of peers to attend at the House, and on the basis of some such presupposition it was surely no revolutionary step to impose upon peers who failed to perform this duty of attending the very mild penalty of exclusion from the right to vote in divisions. Lord Exeter was even able to quote precedents. From the seventeenth and early eighteenth centuries several instances are recorded in which the House imposed heavy fines or other penalties on peers who failed to obey instructions to attend.

Lord Exeter's scheme, by making it impossible for the so-called backwoodsmen to come down and flood the House with their votes, would have removed one of the most serious causes of popular distrust of the unreformed House. Lord Salisbury, speaking for the Government, praised the motion for its objectives and for the way in which it sought to attain them, but said that he could not accept it; nor could he accept the suggestion that the motion should be sent to the Committee of Privileges, because that Committee had not dealt with any general matter since 1750. It seemed to him that the revival of an ancient procedural device which had been in disuse for two centuries would in itself amount to a dangerous innovation. In any case he was not quite happy about the way the motion might affect individuals, because some peers might be unjustly penalized. Many who attended only rarely were valued members of the House not deserving of any kind of penalty. Some, being obliged to earn their living, were simply not able to give frequent attendance. Although Lord Salisbury turned down the Marquess of Exeter's motion in 1953 he was clearly very interested in it, and on 21st June 1955 he himself submitted a motion to the House proposing the appointment of a select committee to enquire into the powers of the House of Lords in relation to the attendance of its members. On this occasion there was some sharp criticism of the idea that the House might penalize its members for non-attendance. Lord Brabazon lightheartedly but pointedly averred that one of the reasons why he did not attend more frequently was that speeches were too long and therefore boring. He was afraid that if any sanction for non-attendance were introduced, and it had the effect of increasing the number of peers attending the debates, those making speeches would be tempted to speak at even greater length through having a bigger audience. He was also afraid that if a distinction were created between voters and non-voters, the former might become a claque.

Lord Salisbury assured the House that at this stage the motion for the Select Committee had no other objective than the establishment of facts. It had no implications for opening the door to a wide scheme of reform. The Select Committee was duly set up and made its report early in 1956.[1] The Committee observed that the words contained in the writ of summons to a peer undeniably imposed in solemn terms the duty of attendance in Parliament. The House had the power to require its members to attend, and that power, though it had not been used for over a hundred years, could be revived without offence to the constitution. It had been used on a number of occasions, sometimes ineffectively, before 1841; since then it had been in abeyance. The last attempt to use it, in 1841, had been futile. The Lord Chancellor had been instructed to inform all peers that the House expected their attendance during the trial of Lord Cardigan, but only 132 peers attended as against 318 who absented themselves; and of those who were absent only 36 furnished excuses.

[1] Report by the Select Committee on the Powers of the House in relation to the Attendance of its Members, 24th January 1956.

SHOULD PEERS SIT IN THE COMMONS?

The Committee considered that it would be neither right nor wise for the House to try to exclude absentee peers from the right of attending; quite apart from practical considerations, such a course 'would have the effect of derogating in greater or less degree from the right conferred on a peer by his writ to attend and take part in the proceedings of Parliament'. On the other hand, it did observe that the writ of summons imposed a clear duty to attend at the House, and that therefore it would be quite appropriate if peers, who did not wish to attend, were expected to apply for leave of absence. It would be possible to ask all peers, at the beginning of each Parliament, whether or not they wished to apply for leave of absence. Those who did apply, or who failed to answer within one month, could be granted leave of absence, and 'expected not to attend until their leave had been terminated by their giving such notice as might be prescribed by standing order'.

On 10th December 1957, between the second reading and the committee stage debates on the Life Peerages Bill, Lord Swinton (who had been chairman of the Select Committee) moved that a new committee should be set up to frame and propose to the House standing orders giving effect to the conclusions relating to leave of absence; the House agreed, without a division, that this should be done. During the debate Lord Stansgate suggested that this scheme for 'ticket of leave men' was 'a bucket of eyewash. . . . Here is an ancient structure; the timbers have decayed, it is riddled with dry rot, and the Government say, "Splendid! Let us paint the front door." And when you say you cannot occupy such a structure, it is against the by-laws, then along comes Lord Swinton and suggests that there should be a change in the by-laws.'

The scheme has some virtue in that it attacks the old 'scandal' of absence in defiance of the writ of summons. Also some peers may decline to apply for leave of absence and then feel bound to attend more than they would otherwise have done. Attendance may increase a little, but the practical effects will probably be slight.

4. SHOULD PEERS BE ALLOWED TO SIT IN THE HOUSE OF COMMONS?

The third piecemeal type of reform proposal has also been of a negative kind, being aimed at allowing persons who inherit peerages to avoid the status of membership of the House of Lords, in order that they may still be eligible to be elected to sit in the House of Commons. An age which worships equality of opportunity may envy peers their unearned privileges, but it also pities them for their handicaps. It has much sympathy for politicians who lose seats in the

Commons through inheriting peerages, and who are deprived thereby, it may be, of well-founded expectations of attaining the highest offices. But it is not merely the loss of the hope of becoming Prime Minister or Chancellor of the Exchequer that is harmful to such men; some may feel that, quite apart from the hopes of high political office, it is only in the House of Commons that they can fulfil their ambition of taking a proper part in the political life of the day. Even if he does not hold high office, either in the counsels of his party or in the Government when his party is in power, a member of the House of Commons can have a status and influence in political life to which, in modern conditions, no peer in a similar situation can aspire. The second Lord Hailsham, both while he was Mr. Quintin Hogg, M.P., and since he succeeded to his peerage, has frequently given utterance to his regrets about the disabilities which fate has placed upon him, and he has received much public sympathy in his misfortune.

The various proposals for general reform of the House of Lords which have been canvassed during the past fifty years would all of them make it possible for a man who had inherited a peerage to avoid acquiring the status of a member of the House of Lords, and so to be eligible to be elected to the House of Commons. But although there is almost universal agreement that such a choice should be open to peers, the attempts that have been made to achieve even this simple reform, which would touch only a very small part of the general pattern of the House, have so far (until 1957) been unsuccessful.

The first attempts to escape from the effects of what Curzon called 'the accident of death' were made in 1894 and 1895.[1] It was at first suggested that the desired reform could be achieved merely by a change in practice; a person inheriting a peerage could simply refrain from applying for a writ of summons to the House of Lords. As no peer might sit in the Lords until he had received a writ of summons, and as writs were not issued unless applied for, the solution seemed straightforward and simple.

To begin with, an oblique approach was made. In 1894 Mr. Bernard Coleridge, M.P., succeeded to a peerage. He did not try to avoid going to the House of Lords, but, in order that a by-election might be expedited, he applied for the Chiltern Hundreds, or, in other words, took steps to resign his seat in the House of Commons. Chamberlain and Balfour argued that the grant of his application for the Chiltern Hundreds would imply that he was still a member of the House of Commons, and the grant was refused on that ground.

In 1895, when the Earl of Selborne died, his son and heir, who had until that moment been a member of the House of Commons, did not

[1] Attempts by peers to prove that peers had a right to vote in parliamentary elections had failed in 1873.

immediately apply for a writ of summons to the Lords, but went into the House of Commons and sat down. Mr. Labouchère promptly asked the Speaker what right the new Lord Selborne had to be in the Commons Chamber, and a select committee was set up. In due course it decided that he had no right to sit in the Commons.[1] The failure of these two experiments showed that only by a positive reform could peers be enabled to avoid the political consequences of inheritance.

In 1936 Lord Ponsonby unsuccessfully moved that peers should be allowed to vote in House of Commons elections and to be elected for the House of Commons, but not to sit in the Lords if elected to the Commons. His proposal was met with objections based on arguments of substance and not only of tradition. The two main objections came from the Earl of Onslow, the Chairman of Committees, who referred to the impoverishment of the House of Lords that the acceptance of such a principle would produce, and from the Lord Chancellor, who complained that piecemeal changes of this kind were undesirable.[2]

In 1955 a spirited attempt was made with a personal bill which was to apply to one particular case. On 18th February, Mr. Anthony Wedgwood Benn, a young Labour member of the House of Commons and heir to the peerage of his father, Lord Stansgate, appeared before the Personal Bills Committee of the House of Lords to ask to be allowed to introduce a Wedgwood Benn Renunciation Bill, by which he would place his peerage in abeyance, and so avoid going to the House of Lords on the death of his father. (The right of succession of *his* children, in their turn, was not to be affected.). Mr. Benn supported his case with ample quotation of precedents from the fifteenth and sixteenth centuries, although in these cases the initiative in moving that a man should be prevented from succeeding to a peerage was taken by the enemies of the individual concerned. With regard to his particular motives for seeking to avoid going to the House of Lords Mr. Benn said that he was prompted not so much by ambition for office—mathematically he would stand a better chance of office if he went to the Lords[3]—but rather by the consideration that he could fulfil his political aspirations far better in the House of Commons. The Personal Bills Committee reported adversely; as one of its members, Lord Simonds, pointed out, a favourable decision would have established a principle which would have gone far beyond the Committee's competence.

Later Mr. Benn's Renunciation Bill was debated on the floor of the

---

[1] Cf. Lord Ronaldshay, *Life of Lord Curzon*, vol. I, p. 231.
[2] Lords Debs., 12th February 1936, vol. 99, cols. 536 ff., 550–72.
[3] Cf. above, p. 101.

PROPOSALS FOR MINOR MODIFICATIONS OF COMPOSITION

House, and rejected by 52 votes to 24. The Lord Chancellor, in opposing the Bill, said that the Government believed 'that the remedy must be one which was general in character. It must be arrived at not by a side wind but after full and frank and free consideration of all its implications.'

There was naturally some disappointment, when the Government brought forward its reform proposals in the autumn of 1957, that they ignored this question. At the committee stage Lord Silkin proposed a new clause, devised so that it should be relevant to the subject of life peerages, to allow a hereditary peer to convert his peerage into a life peerage; it was rejected in a vote which followed party lines.

There is clearly much to be said, on the ground of justice to individuals, for allowing heirs to peerages to renounce their seats in the House of Lords, either on succeeding or before the actual moment of their succession. The most valid argument against such a change is the danger that it would weaken the Lords as an effective instrument. The unreformed House of Lords owes a great deal to the comparatively young men who have inherited peerages and who, having political inclinations, take a large and active part in the day-to-day work of the House. Many of these men have served in the House of Commons before succeeding to their titles, and many of them would welcome the opportunity of remaining in the House of Commons, as Mr. Benn wished to do. But if they did so the House of Lords would be deprived of their services. As Lord Salisbury has pointed out, the House of Lords could scarcely manage to carry on if it were composed only of the very distinguished men whose services to the community have earned them the award of peerages.[1] Such men have generally far too many preoccupations outside Parliament to be able to attend frequently at the House, or to come down, week after week, to take part in the discussions on the committee stages of bills.

5. THE ADMISSION OF WOMEN

The exclusion of women from the House of Lords has been fairly generally regretted for a long time, and there is already a long record of attempts to admit them.[2] Here too, the story begins with an attempt to prove that the desired change could be brought about simply by an alteration in existing practice, without legislation. In 1919, after years of agitation for woman suffrage, the Sex Disqualification (Removal) Act was passed. Its main purpose was to allow women to sit in the House of Commons, but its terms were very

[1] Lords Debs., 9th March 1955, vol. 191, cols. 860–2; cf. col. 953.
[2] On this question, cf. Edward W. Iwi, 'Women and the House of Lords,' in *The Future of the House of Lords* (Hansard Society, 1954), pp. 102–8.

broad: 'A person shall not be disqualified by sex or marriage from the exercise of any public function.' It seemed reasonable to suppose that the Act entitled peeresses in their own right to receive writs of summons to sit in the House of Lords, and an attempt was made to allow Lady Rhondda, a peeress in her own right, to take her seat. The matter was referred to the Committee of Privileges, which found that, although there was no law or order of the House in existence to prevent a writ of summons from being issued to a woman, the fact that no woman had ever received a writ must be taken to have established a rule which could only be superseded by legislation or some other specific decision. The Act only removed disqualifications, and women were not disqualified from sitting in the House of Lords; they had no right to sit there. Furthermore, the Committee could not disregard the point that if the Act had intended to allow women to sit in the House of Lords, it could easily have made specific provision on the matter.

During the years that have passed since the Rhondda case, legislation to provide for the admission of women has been proposed on many occasions. Owing to the peculiarities of the constitutional position, the proposals have been of two clearly distinct types. Some have been concerned to reverse, by legislation, the effects of the Rhondda decision, so as to admit to the House those women who hold peerages in their own right; others have sought to make it possible to confer life peerages on women, carrying membership of the House of Lords.

The two classes of proposals, being clearly linked together, have often been discussed in conjunction with one another, though there are very important differences between them. It is arguable—and some people still hold—that the Rhondda decision was a bad one in law, and the idea that peeresses in their own right should be allowed to sit in the House has derived particular support from this fact. On the other hand, the Labour Party as a whole has been hostile because, as the Lord Chancellor said, in reply to a motion on the subject in 1949, 'by increasing the hereditary element we should be taking a step in the wrong direction'. Furthermore, as Lord Badeley, a former Clerk of the Parliaments, pointed out during the debate of 1949, the effects of admitting peeresses in their own right could not be exactly foreseen. Some of the women concerned hold baronies by writ (which are held to descend to heirs general, not only to heirs male), and others hold peerages which were originally created in such terms that they might be held by women. In 1949, Lord Badeley said, there were apparently eighteen women who might become eligible to take their seats; but in addition there might be fifty or more peeerages in abeyance. A peeresses bill might make a very considerable addition

PROPOSALS FOR MINOR MODIFICATIONS OF COMPOSITION

to the membership of the House. Nevertheless, the motion of 1949 was approved, in a division mainly on party lines, by 45 votes to 27. No further progress was made.

The Life Peerages Bill of 1957, which seems very likely to pass into law, provides only for the conferment of life peerages on women as well as men. It thus does not conflict with the Labour Party's desire not to extend the hereditary principle. An amendment to provide for the admission of peeresses in their own right would have been out of order, but many contributors to the debates expressed regret that nothing had been done about the peeresses. Of greater interest, however, were the House's reactions to the Government's actual proposals. A few objections were raised in the preliminary debate and at the second reading stage, and in committee the Earl of Airlie moved an amendment to exclude women from the Bill. He received some support during the debate, but, as Lord Gifford aptly suggested, the arguments brought forward against the admission of women were 'more suitable for a proposal to admit women to White's or Boodle's than to this House'. The amendment was defeated by 134 votes to 30.[1] The arguments for the admission of women are obvious and well-known; at last they have prevailed.

6. ABOLITION OF THE RIGHT OF TRIAL BY PEERS

One minor reform that has already been achieved is one which does not affect the composition of the House of Lords. The procedure under which peers charged with felony were tried by their peers in the House of Lords was abolished, at last, in 1948. The fact that even this reform was delayed for so long is an illustration of the difficulty of making changes concerning the upper House. The old procedure had become anachronistic long ago. The last trial of a peer in the upper House was in 1935, when Lord de Clifford had been involved in a motor accident and a coroner's jury had returned a verdict of manslaughter against him. Under the law as it then stood he had to be brought for trial before the House of Lords, and the trial took place with a great panoply and public show.[2] The evidence against

---

[1] Lords Debs., 17th December 1957, vol. 206, col. 1236.

[2] Ibid., 12th December 1935, vol. 99, cols. 215–18. There had been some argument in the House, a few days before the trial, over the question whether it should or should not be compulsory for peers attending the trial to have cocked hats. The memories of some venerable peers who had been present at a previous trial of a peer, in 1903, were searched, and so were the relevant newspaper files, and it was decided that cocked hats were required. All this business took place in the midst of a grievous international crisis, and many people found it all rather embarrassing.

him was very flimsy, and he was acquitted after a short trial. There was, inevitably, much talk of sledgehammers being used to crack nuts.

Soon afterwards Viscount Sankey brought in a bill for the abolition of trial by peers. He pointed out that at this trial the whole administration of justice was paralysed, fourteen judges were taken from their ordinary work, and there was a great waste of public money, let alone the cost involved for individuals. The privilege was of doubtful value, because it seemed unlikely that a peer would stand a better chance of being acquitted before the House of Lords than before an ordinary jury; furthermore, if a peer were convicted at a trial by peers he had no appeal, and was in that sense in a worse case than a person convicted at the ordinary Assizes. The second reading of Lord Sankey's Bill was passed by 62 votes to 37, and its third reading was passed without a division. It then made no further progress, however, and the final abolition of trial by peers had to wait until the Labour Government's Criminal Justice Act of 1948 (11 and 12 George VI, ch. 58, sec. 30). The reform was not included in the original text of the Bill, as the Government preferred to leave the House of Lords to take the first step if it so wished. A clause abolishing trial by peers was in due course proposed during the Committee stage in the Lords and agreed to after little discussion and without a division. The fairly substantial opposition of 1935 had withered away, and an old tradition was abandoned with little lamentation or even comment.

7. PAYMENT OF PEERS

Another piecemeal reform which has been carried through in advance of any general reform is the introduction of payment, in a very modest form, for peers who attend at the House. It is only in comparatively recent times that such payment has been mooted; until our own generation peers were in general supposed to be men of such substance that it would have seemed preposterous to ask them to fill in forms to claim the cost of their train journeys or their maintenance. It was probably during the war of 1939–45 that facts and ideas on these matters changed most rapidly, and the first instalment of a new régime came fairly quickly. On 21st May 1946, after negotiations behind the scenes, the House agreed to a resolution to the effect that peers regularly attending at the House ought to be able to be reimbursed for the cost of their railway travel, and the Government took the steps necessary to make this effective. The scheme has been operated under the supervision of a committee of the three

Chief Whips; it has been made to apply in practice only to peers who attend at least one-third of the sittings of the House.

The rather severe 'assiduity qualification' was perhaps necessary in order to forestall possible allegations of abuse, but it has excluded from the benefits of the scheme those peers to whom it could have been of most value—those who come occasionally from remote parts of the country to attend particular debates. Many of the peers who have benefited live in or near London during parliamentary sessions, and to them the payment of travelling costs is in any case a small item. It has long been recognized that these peers deserve—and in some cases need—some kind of further payment in addition. Furthermore, the lack of any further payment has probably kept away some peers who would have liked to attend, and whom the House would have been glad to see.

Members of most legislative assemblies in the world receive salaries, but salaries for all peers are out of the question. Even remuneration based on actual attendance at the House might lead to unpleasant criticism, and public indignation might be stirred up by complaints that men who happened to have inherited peerages could obtain largesse at the public expense in return to looking in at the House of Lords. On the more positive side, there are still many peers who like to feel that their House has, as it were, an amateur status.

Recognizing the need for payment on the one hand, and the difficulties in its way on the other hand, the Government in July 1957 adopted a solution which is probably the best available in the existing circumstances. It announced, simultaneously with increases in salaries of members of the House of Commons and of ministers, a provision that peers would in future be able to claim a maximum of three guineas in respect of expenses actually incurred in attending at any sitting of the House of Lords or its committees. The payment would not be subject to any minimum number of attendances. It would be additional to the travelling expenses, which would continue to be payable as before.[1]

---

[1] Lords Debs., 8th July 1957, vol. 204, cols. 768–84. Lord Home, in announcing the new arrangements on behalf of the Government, said, after some initial confusion, that the old travelling expenses would, as before, still only be payable to peers who attended one-third of the sittings. Later, however, he promised to 'have a word with the Chancellor of the Exchequer on this point'.

Although the new plan was reasonably well received in July, it was heavily attacked during the debates on the Life Peerages Bill in the autumn of 1957. On all sides it was said that the expenses allowance was quite inadequate for the regular attenders. As a positive contribution Lord Lucas suggested that the Conservative and Labour Chief Whips might nominate say twenty peers each (and the Liberal a few also), and that these should be paid a full parliamentary salary—perhaps £1500 a year. The Government held out little hope of any advance on the three guineas a day.

Chapter XX

PROPOSALS FOR WHOLESALE RECONSTRUCTION OF THE HOUSE

SO far we have been considering proposals for piecemeal reforms, which until now governments have tended to discourage, on the ground that any change in the composition of the House ought to proceed from a carefully considered plan prepared by the Government of the day, tackling the problem as one requiring a comprehensive solution. Meanwhile, there has been no lack of compendious proposals. Innumerable schemes have been advocated, by governments, conferences and individuals, in the form of books, pamphlets and motions moved in Parliament. It would hardly be possible to examine them all; it is proposed here to concentrate on the schemes that have actually been put forward in the House itself, though it will be useful to begin with a summary of the main lines which the schemes have followed.

The following are the main ideas which have been put forward:

(1) Some members should be elected on a regional basis, with so many for each section of the country. Electoral colleges might be composed of local councillors, whether of all types of local authority or only of the larger types.

(2) Some members should be elected by the House of Commons, by some sort of proportional representation and probably for long periods, e.g. for 12 years with one-quarter retiring every three years.

(3) Some members should be elected by and from among the holders of existing peerages.

(4) Some members should be appointed by the Crown, on nomination by the Government or by the Government and the Opposition.

(5) Some members should be appointed to represent specific

associations and other bodies. (Little has been heard of this project in recent years.)

In most of the schemes for reconstruction of the House's membership two or more of these particular devices have been combined. All the schemes, however they may have combined these particular features, have been aimed at making the membership of the House smaller than it has been hitherto, more rationally based, and less blatantly biased in favour of the Conservative Party.

It may be convenient to begin with Lord Rosebery's motion of 1884, that a select committee should be appointed with instructions to bring forward proposals for the extension of life peerages and for the representation of classes in the House of Lords, for the enlargement of the quorum necessary for the business of the House, and for the establishment of joint committees of the two Houses, for both public and private bills. His motion was defeated by 77 votes to 38. In 1888 Lord Rosebery again brought forward a motion for a select committee, this time with rather larger terms of reference. He suggested (a) that the existing peers should elect some representatives for fixed periods, much as was already done by the Scottish and Irish peers, (b) that some members of the House of Lords should hold their seats by election, the electors being members of local councils and perhaps also of the House of Commons; and (c) that there should be some peers for life and some peers appointed by virtue of their offices. The proportions of these different classes should be fixed in relation to one another. In addition the Agents General of the self-governing colonies, or representatives appointed by them, should be eligible to sit. He also suggested that any Lord not being a member of the House of Lords could sit in the Commons. This motion was also defeated.

The troubles of the Liberal Government in 1906-9, and the crisis of 1909-11, led to much discussion of ways of altering the composition of the House. On 14th March 1910 Lord Rosebery proposed that the House should go into committee to consider the best means of reforming its composition, and in the event of such motion being agreed to, to move the following resolution:

(1) That a strong and efficient second chamber is not merely an integral part of the British Constitution, but is necessary for the well-being of the State, and for the balance of Parliament.

(2) That such a chamber can best be obtained by the reform and reconstitution of the House of Lords, and

(3) That a necessary preliminary of such reform and reconstitution is the acceptance of the principle that the possession of a peerage should no longer of itself give the right to sit and vote in the House of Lords.

PROPOSALS FOR WHOLESALE RECONSTRUCTION OF THE HOUSE

The first of Lord Rosebery's principles was accepted after a debate of more than four days, and the second almost without debate. There was some objection to the third, but it too was finally approved, on division, by 175 votes to 17. But nothing concrete was achieved.

A little later the Earl of Wemyss proposed that 'important trading and other representative societies should each name three members of the existing peerage in the current and each succeeding Parliament, to speak and act on behalf of such societies, on all questions in which they are interested, and that the names of the peers so nominated be entered in the journals of the House'. He gave a list of twenty-two bodies, most of them commercial associations, but with the addition of some professional bodies, such as the Royal Institute of British Architects, and of others such as the Society of British Sculptors. The scheme aroused little interest, and was dropped.

It was generally supposed in 1910 that a thorough reform of the House of Lords would come before very long, and indeed the Parliament Act of 1911 was at the time commonly supposed to be a temporary expedient related to the House as it was then constituted. For various reasons no progress was made with the proposals for reform before 1914, and the war prevented any further action for a further four years.

Towards the end of the war there took place the famous Conference under the chairmanship of Lord Bryce. Its report proposed that the House should consist of two elements. In the first place there were to be 246 members elected by members of the House of Commons arranged in geographical areas and voting by proportional representation with a single transferable vote. It was hoped (rather optimistically perhaps) that the electors would not be excessively influenced by party considerations, and that they would tend to elect persons of local eminence. The second element, which was to consist of eighty peers, should be elected by a joint committee of both Houses of Parliament, on which all parties should be represented, though at the first election perhaps only peers, together with five or more bishops, might take part. At the second and subsequent elections only half of the vacancies were to be filled from among the hereditary peers, and from then on the choice was to be unrestricted, though the number of bishops and hereditary peers in the House was at no time to be allowed to fall below thirty. The election was to be for twelve years, with one-third retiring every four years.

The 32 members of the Bryce Conference included some of the most distinguished men in the land inside and outside Parliament. If all of them had agreed to the proposals embodied in the report, the proposals might have stood a good chance of being adopted. In fact, however, eight of the members (among them the Marquess of

Lansdowne) dissented from the scheme for the election of some of the members of the new upper House.

The volume of dissent in the Bryce Conference was such that no action was taken on its report. No further progress was made towards the reform of the House of Lords until July 1922, when the Coalition Government itself, shortly before its fall, introduced resolutions into the House restating, more or less, the principles regarding its composition which had been set out by the Bryce Conference, but leaving the details rather obscure. The House was to consist of approximately 350 members, and was to contain three elements. Some members were to be elected either directly or indirectly from outside, some hereditary peers were to be elected from among the existing peers, and some members were to be nominated by the Crown. All persons appointed to the House of Lords by these three devices, apart from holders of royal titles and the Law Lords, were to hold their membership of it only for restricted terms and not for life, though they were to be eligible for re-appointment. With regard to the settlement of differences between the two Houses, the new Government resolutions returned from the principles of the Bryce Conference to those of the Parliament Act of 1911. They provided that the decision as to whether a bill was a money bill or not should be taken out of the hands of the Speaker and given to a standing committee of both Houses, of which the Speaker was to be a member. Otherwise the provisions of the Parliament Act were to stand, except that no bill altering the composition or the powers of the House of Lords was to be allowed to pass without the agreement of the Lords.

The Government's proposals were debated on four days (18th to 21st July), but the debate was then adjourned, and no action was taken. During the ensuing years dissatisfaction with the actual composition and powers of the House still prevailed among all parties. Many Conservatives still believed that the existing House, with its powers restricted by the Parliament Act, was not effective enough, and they wished to increase its strength. They realized, however, that in order to increase its powers it would be necessary for them to accept a substantial measure of reform of its composition. Meanwhile, the Labour Party was more interested in abolition than in reform.

When the Conservatives returned to power at the end of 1924 the Government was pressed to bring forward concrete proposals for the reform of the House. It soon put forward a scheme, which followed rather closely the lines of the proposals of 1922. The upper House was to consist of 350 peers, together with the Law Lords and the Peers of the blood royal, who were to be members for life. Some of the 350 would be nominated by the Government, and others elected by the hereditary peers from among their own order. Both classes should receive their seats for twelve years, with one-third retiring every four years. The Government's resolutions were published, but they were not made the subject of any debate or vote in the House, although soon afterwards the House of Lords did approve, by 212 votes to 54, a motion expressing a wish for a general reform both as to composition and as to powers.

The proposals of 1927 were aimed almost entirely at strengthening the House of Lords as an instrument for resisting the danger of irresponsible, wild and unconstitutional measures, such as were at that time expected to be produced by a Socialist government if one should come into power with a sound majority in the Commons. Many Conservatives wanted to proceed in this way while there was still time. They were probably mistaken, even with reference to the achievement of their own ends; it could hardly be expected that any future Socialist government would allow its policies to be frustrated, even by a more rationally constituted upper House. In 1927 a scheme for strengthening the House of Lords had no hope of being accepted by the Labour Party against whom it was specifically directed, and in view of this fact good sense prevailed in preventing the Government from pursuing the scheme any further.

The actions of Mr. MacDonald's two Labour governments did not produce any serious crisis in the relations between the two Houses, and after the establishment of the National Government in 1931 attention was for the time being too much pre-occupied with other matters for it to seem appropriate to press forward with proposals for the reform of the Lords.

In December 1933 Lord Salisbury (the fourth Marquess), who then held no office in the Government, brought forward a new reform plan which was still essentially on the lines of the proposals of 1922. Contrary to the usual practice, Lord Salisbury's proposal, which was brought in in the form of a bill, was made the subject of a debate on the first reading, in order that the House might have an opportunity of expressing its opinion on the general principle of the desirability of reform before it went on to pronounce upon the specific principles contained in Lord Salisbury's Bill. The first reading was approved by 84 votes to 34. The official Government spokesman expressed hostility, but a free vote was allowed.

The second reading was debated on the 8th, 9th and 10th May 1934. Lord Hailsham expressed the Government's opinion on the first day of the debate. 'It seems to the Government that proposals for constitutional reform of this magnitude are best initiated by the Government of the day. In another place there is little prospect of their receiving any real consideration unless they are brought forward as a government measure.' Lord Hailsham's argument is a good illustration of the way in which the theory of governmental responsibility has been extended in recent years, in such a way that numerical majorities of either House of Parliament have come to be considered incompetent to make decisions on important questions. Lord Salisbury did indeed admit it would be preferable for the reform to be brought forward as a government measure, but as no government bill was forthcoming he asked the House to take its decision on his proposal. The Government announced that it would take no part in the division, but nevertheless the second reading was carried by 171 votes to 82. No further progress was made.

On 4th December 1935 a motion was moved by Lord Strickland, a former Governor of New South Wales, to call attention to some possible improvement in the functions of the House of Lords, in particular with reference to the overseas empire. His thesis was that, with actual abolition of the House of Lords having already been made an issue in the 1935 election, it was really becoming necessary to take positive steps towards the reform of the House with a due sense of urgency. As there seemed to be no prospect of general agreement on a fundamental reconstruction, it was better to proceed by a series of minor reforms and improvements which would help to improve the prestige and efficacy of the upper House. As a first step he thought it would be appropriate if a bill were considered authorizing the creation of life peers, some of whom might be appointed from the overseas empire. Lord Strickland's proposal did not arouse any active interest, and the only speech in reply was from Lord Halifax on behalf of the Government. He was non-committal, and the motion was withdrawn.

Meanwhile, the Labour Party was rapidly gaining strength, and it addressed itself from time to time to the problem of formulating its own attitude to the House of Lords. Its programme, *Labour and the New Social Order*, produced at the London conference in 1918, declared that no attempt by the Lords to control the people's representatives should be tolerated. It envisaged a reform which would ensure that a future Labour government possessing a majority in the Commons should not be in a minority in the upper House; no members of the upper House should hold their seats by virtue of hereditary right or *ex officio*. In 1933, at the Hastings conference, Sir Stafford Cripps advocated complete abolition of the House of Lords. In the party's draft programme of July 1934 the plan was to abolish the House of Lords only if it should interfere with the implementation of a Labour government's policy.[1] The very moderate report of

[1] G. D. H. Cole, *History of the Labour Party from 1914* (Routledge, 1948), pp. 65, 287, 293.

the Executive in 1936, which the Party conference, by a narrow majority, referred back, has already been mentioned above (p. 28).

Labour Party policies towards the House of Lords between the wars were based on the assumption that it was necessary to prevent any Labour government from seeing itself frustrated by a hostile upper House. The Governments of 1924 and 1929–31 were never in a position to take action, and by 1945 the policy had become one of 'wait and see what happens, but be prepared to act if necessary'.

The sweeping victory of the Labour Party at the General Election of 1945 did not at first produce any proposals for the reform of the Lords. The new Government, being fully occupied with its very extensive legislative programme, did not for the time being think it worth while to allow its attention to be diverted down a by-way of faded and uncertain attractiveness. It knew that it had a fair chance of remaining in office until the end of its five-year term, and on that assumption the 1911 Parliament Act would make it impossible for the House of Lords to block the bills that would be passed in the Commons during the first three sessions of the new Parliament. In any case, the Lords did not at first attempt to prevent the passing of government bills or even to insist on unacceptable amendments. By 1947, however, circumstances led the Government to begin to give the matter some consideration. The Government attached much importance to the achievement of its purpose of nationalizing the iron and steel industries within the life of the current Parliament, and knew that it would not be able to bring its bill forward to achieve this until the session of 1948–9. A bill brought forward for the first time during that session would not benefit from the protection of the Parliament Act of 1911, and if no action were taken and the Labour Party were to be defeated in the General Election, the bill could be prevented from going forward for the Royal Assent at all. Furthermore, this was the most controversial of the nationalization proposals, and the Conservatives claimed that public opinion was opposed to it. The Government calculated that the Lords would be tempted, when confronted with this measure, to depart from the policy of compliance which they had followed with such moderation during the years 1945–7.[1]

It was partly with this immediate and particular objective in view that the Labour Government brought forward its Parliament Bill, which proposed to amend the existing Act of 1911 by reducing the delaying period from two sessions to one. In order to protect the Iron and Steel Bill, the Government brought in the Parliament Bill in the session of 1947–8, and arranged for a short session during the autumn of 1948, during which the Bill was passed a second time, so that it

[1] Cf. C. R. Attlee, *As it Happened*, p. 163.

would be ready for its final passage in the session of 1948–9; its operation was to be, in a sense, retrospective. Thus if the Lords were to reject the Iron and Steel Bill at its first passage through Parliament in the session of 1948–9, assuming the Parliament Bill became law in 1949, the Iron and Steel Bill would be able to go forward for the Royal Assent on being passed by the Commons a second time during the session of 1949–50.

The Parliament Bill was duly introduced and passed through the House of Commons in the first part of the session 1947–8, and it went up to the Lords to be dealt with there. The second reading debate in the Lords began on the 27th January 1948, and continued on the 2nd, 3rd and 4th February. Lord Salisbury moved a reasoned amendment: 'that this House, while emphasizing its oft repeated readiness to consider proposals for modifying the basis of its membership, which may conduce to the more effective performance of its constitutional duties, declines to give a second reading to a bill which would effect no change in this respect, for which the nation has expressed no desire, which would go far to expose the country to the dangers of single chamber government, and which can only serve to distract the attention of the country from the economic crisis, and from the united effort towards recovery which is so vital at this time'.

During the first day's debate, Lord Samuel pleaded that the Government, instead of carrying through this particular reduction of the power of the Lords, should address itself to the problem of reform of the composition at the same time. He recognized that, however useful the House might have been as a part of the machinery of government during the preceding few years, and however moderately it had used its powers, it could at any time be swamped by the backwoodsmen, 'who are responsible to no-one but themselves, and do not always follow the advice of their leaders'. The public estimation of the House of Lords was influenced by this fact, rather than by the actual services which the House performed. 'If all the 800 members were to attend on all occasions the institution would instantly collapse. In fact, I think that this is the only institution in the world which is kept going by the persistent absenteeism of the great majority of its members.' Lord Samuel did not want to return to the proposals of 1922, or to any other Conservative proposals for reform of composition, because all of these would have strengthened the Conservative element 'by retaining in the House the very quintessence of the hereditary peerage'. Public opinion would continue to have misgivings about the House of Lords for so long as its composition gave it a permanent Conservative majority.

During the first day's debate Lord Salisbury appealed to the Government to postpone the Bill so as to enable discussions to take place between the leaders of the main parties, with a view to producing a comprehensive scheme of reform covering both composition and powers. Lord Addison replied that the Government regarded the passing of the Bill forthwith as essential, but that they would then be prepared to discuss reform after its passage.[1] On the second day, however, Lord Addison, on behalf of the Government, agreed to a temporary adjournment and a conference on the following terms:

'1. So far as discussions of the powers of the two chambers are concerned, they should be limited to ensuring reasonable time for the consideration of measures by the Lords, and for discussion of differences between the two Houses.
2. The Bill now before the House should either be passed, with or without agreed amendment, or rejected by this House before the end of the present session.
3. So far as the composition of the House of Lords is concerned, (a) there would be preliminary conversations on the possibility of there being established a basis for further discussion, (b) in the event of such a basis for discussion being provisionally agreed, the different parties should examine the same with their own members before the discussions were renewed, and (c) the preliminary discussions should be private and confined to a small number of the leading members of the parties concerned.
4. The different parties should also examine, with their own members, any suggestions emerging from the discussions relating to the Parliament Bill contemplated under para. 1.'[2]

The debate then proceeded, but at the end of the fourth day it was adjourned in order that discussions might take place.

The discussions began on the 19th February. The Labour Party was represented by the Prime Minister, Mr. Morrison, Mr. Whiteley, Lord Jowitt and Lord Addison, the official Opposition by Mr. Eden, Sir David Maxwell Fyfe, Lord Salisbury and Lord Swinton, and the Liberals by Viscount Samuel and Mr. Clement Davies. Seven meetings were held between February and April.

Beginning with a discussion of the possibility of reform of the composition of the House, the conference succeeded in agreeing on a statement of nine principles. The most important of these were perhaps the first two, namely that the second Chamber should be complementary to and not a rival to the lower House, and that the revised constitution of the House of Lords should be such as to secure as far as practicable that a permanent majority was not assured for any one political party. The acceptance of this principle by the Conservatives

---

[1] Lords Debs., 27th January 1928, vol. 153, cols. 651–66.
[2] Ibid., 2nd February 1948, vol. 153, col. 742.

may be considered an important step towards agreement with their opponents. It must be admitted, however, that in the absence of more detailed proposals, it is not easy to assess the value of the concession.

On the question of the Lords' powers, which demanded a more exact answer, the differences between the parties could not be resolved, and the conference was abandoned without having grappled with the details of the proposed new composition.

In the transactions over the Parliament Bill of 1947-9 much attention was given on both sides to considerations of immediate party advantage. The Government seemed to be making an important constitutional reform solely for the purpose of safeguarding the Iron and Steel Bill. The Conservatives on the other hand, in attacking the measure, relied over-much on the electioneering argument that it was inappropriate to introduce such a reform at a time of serious economic crisis.

During the debate Lord Cecil of Chelwood brought forward a proposal to the effect that the composition of the House should be left unchanged, but that on matters concerning legislation only 200 Lords should be allowed to vote. These 200 might be chosen in such a way as to give the parties a genuinely equal chance of fair representation. Each new House of Commons was, under his plan, to elect by proportional representation 100 peers to serve for the length of two Parliaments. The main weakness in Lord Cecil's scheme, if it was intended to produce a House of Lords which could exercise real power, was that the party majority among its 200 voting peers might sometimes be the opposite of that prevailing in the Commons. The scheme did have, however, the great merit of distinguishing between the ordinary deliberative functions of the Lords and its special function of voting, sometimes controversially, with reference to legislative proposals.

A reform along these lines would perhaps be more likely than any other to achieve a dual purpose on which the parties could agree. It would preserve intact the life of the House and the hereditary element, and at the same time would be compatible with the demands of the Left. Another hint of a movement towards a differentiation between voting and non-voting members could be discerned in the suggestion of 1953 that peers who failed to attend might be excluded from voting. Unfortunately, there seems to be no hope of finding a valid precedent for any such differentiation, but as it has apparently been decided that any revival of ancient but discarded precedents would amount to the same thing as innovation, this probably matters little.

The device of having two classes of members, voting and non-voting, has another point in its favour. The authors of the 1954

Fabian Society pamphlet suggest a return to the Bryce Conference plan of having some members chosen by the House of Commons and others nominated, but think that the total number should be little more than 100—corresponding, presumably, with the two most active groups of peers in the unreformed House. There is indeed much to be said for a very drastic restriction of the voting membership such as this, particularly for the sake of reassuring the Labour Party. But it is difficult to see what would be the advantages in restricting the right of attendance, and of participation in debate, to so small a number. So drastic a restriction would surely deprive the debates of much of their variety, without giving any compensating benefits. Again, we have already seen that 'expert' members, such as bishops, military commanders and so on, have tended in recent years to be infrequent attenders and rare voters. The total exclusion of all but a very few such members would surely bring no gain; on the other hand, the exclusion of many of them from voting would merely be the next step in a process which they have themselves, by their voluntary abstinence, already carried a long way.

However great its objective merits, a scheme on these lines is perhaps unlikely ever to be adopted. In the debate of October 1957 when Lord Pakenham made himself its advocate, Lord Kilmuir found it too ingenious and complicated, reminiscent of the Abbé Sieyès, logical yet unacceptable in practice; he was embarrassed by the prospect of benches shared by voting and non-voting peers. This Scotman's very English objections may seem rather insubstantial; but they seem likely in the long run to be decisive.

In January 1957 a completely new scheme for the reform of the upper House was produced by Mr. Anthony Wedgwood Benn.[1] Rather than engage in the well-worn discussions about quotas of peers elected by the whole body of peers, and so on, Mr. Benn suggests that the second Chamber should be composed of the members of the Privy Council who do not sit in the House of Commons. With the Privy Council composed as at the beginning of 1957, the membership of an upper House so composed would be 206, 125 peers and 81 others. Just under one half of the peers are Conservatives, one-sixth Labour and nearly a third non-party.

The scheme has a great deal to recommend it, if only because all other devices would involve such great difficulties in deciding on the composition of the House. A number of difficulties suggest themselves, however. Even if the Privy Council were much increased in size, it would presumably be composed only of distinguished men who had recommended themselves to the leaders of the political parties. As we have seen, much of the work of the House is in fact

[1] *The Privy Council as a Second Chamber*, Fabian Tract 305, op. cit.

performed by fairly young men who, at the time when they begin to be active in the existing House of Lords, have as yet had no opportunity of earning so great a personal distinction as appointment to the Privy Council. This disadvantage could be overcome, however, if the right to attend and speak in the House were left undisturbed, and the right to vote restricted to Privy Councillors.

It is a little ironic that, when so many government spokesmen have, over so many years, discouraged all proposals for piecemeal reforms, the scheme sponsored by the Government in 1957 should be, not a comprehensive reform at all, but merely a combination of three of the old piecemeal plans, pay, life peerages and the admission of women, with leave of absence added as an afterthought. The Queen's Speech of the session 1955-6 had indeed promised 'proposals for reforming the composition of the House of Lords', and it came as something of an anti-climax when the Government announced, in the debate of 30th-31st October 1957, that it would propose a Life Peerages Bill and no more. Not surprisingly the debates, both then and on the second reading of the Bill, were concerned more with the omissions from the Bill than with its contents. The debate of October ranged widely over the whole field of Lords reform. Nearly all the peers who took part in the debate, on both sides of the House, suggested that reforms ought to go further, and to deal with the problem of the excessive total membership. Lord Salisbury indicated his disappointment, and though he put forward no definite counter proposal during the debate, he wrote a letter to *The Times*, in which he suggested that a reformed House should consist of life peers together with some 200 hereditary peers chosen by a select committee at the beginning of each Parliament. On the other side several Labour peers spoke, but they made it clear that they were speaking for themselves only, as their Party had not yet had time to discuss and prepare its policy on the question. Lord Silkin, who wound up the debate from the Labour side, was on safe ground, from his Party's point of view, when he said that he disapproved of the hereditary principle altogether.

During the next few weeks it became clear that there were widely divergent opinions on Lords reform among members of the Labour Party; on 28th November, however, the Parliamentary Labour Party stated that the Government's Bill (which had been published five days earlier) was merely tinkering with the problem. The Bill, for all its modesty and lack of provocativeness, seemed to be producing on the Left the sort of opposition, the active hostility to the hereditary principle, which the Government had hoped to avoid.

Chapter XXI

CONCLUSION

THE main theme of our conclusions must be a reference to the wonderful capacity for adaptation which the House has shown in the changed circumstances of modern times. Critics on the Right may complain that the House, shorn of its powers, is slowly dying; critics on the Left may argue that an upper House must be either mischievous or superfluous; but a study of the House at work in recent years gives little support to either of these points of view. With its reduced formal powers and its recognition that it ought normally not to use even those powers, it has developed in recent years a most admirable vitality, so that it not only discusses subjects far more varied than before but very often discusses them in a more informed way.

Under governments of Left and Right, peers on both sides of the House—and Liberals and independents too—have induced governments to modify policies, attitudes and intentions, both by the force of their arguments on the floor of the House and by their persuasions outside. The superior voting strength of the Conservatives has, most of the time, had little to do with the final result. Whatever government has been in power, opponents and friends alike have come forward with innumerable suggestions for alteration of government policy. Governments, being reasonably sure of getting their own way in the long run, have listened most carefully to all these proposals. They have accepted many, with or without modification; others they have rejected, but only after giving full explanations of their reasons. On matters of broad national and social policy, and of administration in narrow fields, the House has held valuable debates from which ministers and civil servants have derived much advice of great worth. It has obliged governments to explain their policies and to reply to serious and well-informed criticisms and suggestions. All this is work such as the House of Commons also performs. But the House of Commons does not have unlimited time, and the Lords often do work which the Commons have no time to do. Again, they do not do it in quite the same way, and there are some of these functions which are better done the Lords' way than the Commons' way. A study of the record of the Lords in recent years amply confirms the argument that the upper House is a useful complement to the lower.

These considerations do not entitle us to be complacent, or to say that the House of Lords had better be left exactly as it is. In praising the House on pragmatic grounds we may also admit that it has defects on pragmatic grounds, and we must look for the remedies. There are two obvious defects in its composition—the potential (and occasionally the actual) voting strength of the backwoodsmen, and the dearth of representatives of the political left.

The backwoodsmen hardly ever—perhaps, in fact, never—really influence the course of events, but the dead weight of their potential voting strength is a harmful incubus, and when their cohorts do appear the reputation of the House is grievously damaged. Few people are favourably impressed by such a spectacle as the vast number of backwoodsmen who came down to take part in the legislative work of the nation on the Death Penalty Bill in 1956. It is true that the backwoodsmen's vote did not really affect the final result, but it brought forth an outcry against this apparent abuse of power by a body of persons whose claim to be legislators is manifestly unacceptable in a country whose underlying assumptions are those prevailing in modern Britain. Some means must be found of preventing the backwoodsmen from coming down in large numbers and depriving the voice of the House as a whole of any authority in the eyes of the public.

Many ways of excluding backwoodsmen have been proposed. Conservative politicians, both leaders and back-benchers, have been most ingenious in the extent and variety of the devices which they have brought forward. The Labour Party has looked with suspicion on all these proposals, because they would all apparently leave the Conservatives with a permanent majority in the House. The Labour Party is interested only in a reform of composition which would give the Labour Party a majority during periods of Labour rule; but such a reform, unless based on the device of restricted voting rights rather than a change in the basis of membership, would involve so complete a reconstruction that the thread of continuity in the life of the House would be broken. The Labour Party itself is not positively enthusiastic for an entirely new second Chamber. According to its sentiments and its principles, it would prefer to have no second Chamber at all;

CONCLUSION

it is only the consideration of political realities that makes it accept an institution which has no place in its ideals.

However much we may be forced to admit the desirability of dealing with the problem of the backwoodsmen's vote, the question of their membership and right to speak needs to be seen in its proper perspective. There are indeed some impressive arguments against making any change at all in the actual membership of the House. The most important of these is that, in the modern world, dominated as it is (some people might even say 'suffocated') by committees and associations and organizations, there is a positive merit in the presence in the Legislature of some persons who do not owe their seats to the favour of any association or institution or group whatever. The twelfth Duke of Bedford, who died in 1953, held some rather peculiar opinions, which he voiced from time to time in the House of Lords. It is difficult to see how a place would be awarded to such a man under any of the systems of election or appointment that have been advocated. Yet when we assess his highly individual contributions to debate against the whole of the activity of Parliament, we may well feel that something worth keeping would have been lost if he had been deprived of his seat through the operation of some rational or perfectionist plan. Furthermore, however diligently we may search for evidence of damage or obstruction to the business of the House through the presence of unworthy members, we do not find it.

Again, we must remember that in the unreformed House it is still possible for a peer suddenly to emerge from political obscurity and to make a valuable contribution. The twelfth Earl of Waldegrave succeeded to his peerage in 1936, and for twenty years did not speak in the House of Lords. He is a prominent man in the county of Somerset, and has been chairman of its Agricultural Executive Committee. On 30th January 1957 he came down to the House of Lords for a debate on agricultural policy and made a maiden speech which rightly earned for him the warmest and most admiring congratulations of every peer who spoke after him, from all parts of the House. A little before this the second Lord Westwood, heir to a Labour peer, had made a most valuable maiden speech on the Cinematograph Films Bill, about whose subject-matter he happened to have expert knowledge. Many other examples of the same kind could be cited. Time after time, in the unreformed House, a peer who has been accustomed to speak little or not at all comes down, often from a quite unexpected quarter, and gives the House the benefit of the expert knowledge which he happens to possess. It is difficult to see how any reform which restricted membership of the House to three hundred elected or appointed persons could preserve intact this advantage of the old arrangements. However important it may be to

CONCLUSION

take steps to deal with the backwoodsmen's vote, it is also important to remember the virtues of the individual's contribution to debate.

The second important defect in the existing composition of the House continues to be the under-representation of the Labour Party. If membership of the House could be more thoroughly separated from the notions of social superiority which are such anathema to the Left, then more members of the Labour Party might be prepared to accept peerages, even under Conservative governments, without seeming to betray their class or their principles or their friends. An increase in the number of Labour peers in the upper House would not merely increase the Party's voting strength; it would increase the number of back-bench Labour peers, as opposed to Party spokesmen, available to speak in debate.

Another objective at which it might be useful to aim would be to extend the representation of some of those groups of scientists and experts in particular spheres, who as we have suggested appear to have been so seriously under-represented. Most men of this type cannot be expected to attend at the House regularly, but an increase in their total number would be likely to increase the total amount of participation in debates by non-political experts. However large the new total membership should be, nothing very much would be lost if a small number such as the present sixty—perhaps indeed the very same persons—should continue to provide the House with its nucleus of members regularly attending day by day, whereas the others, as many of them do at present, attended from time to time and spoke only when subjects about which they had expert knowledge were being discussed.

The problem of the future of the House of Lords is not so much a problem of seeking to reform or greatly to alter the House because it is working badly, but rather to preserve an assembly which is at present of great value, in such a way that it should continue to perform its present function in much the same way as it is now doing, though with minor improvements such as might accrue from the addition of more Labour and more expert peers, and from the exclusion, at least from voting, of persons whom modern opinion cannot accept as worthy legislators.

Above all it is to be hoped that the House will in future preserve its character unimpaired, so that it may continue to need no timetables or rigid classification of types of business, no priorities for the Government or ballots for private members' time. The unreformed House has indeed shown itself unduly inclined to resist even minor changes which have, on rational grounds, become overdue. Its slowness in abolishing the peers' right of trial by peers, and in adopting the device of a committee for judicial sittings, are illustrations of this

CONCLUSION

point. But this conservatism is perhaps a small price to pay for the continuity of the habits of tolerant and responsible debate, which makes the House so valuable a part of the machinery of British government. Finally, even this conservatism is in the long run matched by the admirable adaptability in important matters which has enabled the House to preserve its vitality as a political instrument.

The Life Peerages Bill of 1957, together with the schemes for payment of expenses and for leave of absence, by which it is accompanied, falls short of the wishes of many people of all parties, and many people may wish to see further reforms brought in within the next few years. But the present reforms have two great merits. They are not really controversial, and they make several obvious improvements in the existing House of Lords without seeming likely to impair its true character in any way.

Appendix

THE ELECTION OF THE SCOTTISH REPRESENTATIVE PEERS

THE election of the sixteen Scottish Representative Peers takes place in Edinburgh, at a meeting convened by Royal proclamation. It may be 'at such time and place within Scotland' as the Queen thinks fit. From 1707 until 1951 the election generally took place in the Palace of Holyroodhouse, but in 1955 it was held for the first time in the Great Hall of the Parliament House. The date, 23rd May, was three days before the General Election to the House of Commons. The proceedings took an hour and a half. Fifty-five peers voted; of these, 32 attended in person, one voted by proxy and the rest by signed list. (Cf. *Glasgow Herald*, 24th May 1955.)

At these elections the peers assemble with very little ceremony and sit at the table in no order of precedence. The Lord Clerk Register presides, assisted by two Clerks of Session and the officials of his Department; the Principal Clerk of Session presides in his absence. At a bye-election, which is held only on intimation to the Lord Chancellor by two peers of Scotland, either representatives or qualified electors, that a vacancy has occurred, the same procedure is followed.

Each peer has sixteen votes (or, at a bye-election, as many votes as there are vacancies), and he may cast one of his votes for himself. A peer who holds two or more titles may vote in right of one only. There is no form of proportional representation; the sixteen candidates who receive most votes are elected. Electioneering is by canvassing letters exchanged between the peers. There was some real competition in 1910, but normally (particularly in recent times), there is very little competition, and such as there is concerns only the

APPENDIX

last two or three places. Most of the previous Representative Peers are generally re-elected; eight of the peers re-elected in 1955 had sat continuously since 1935. Three of the present sixteen are described in *Vacher* as belonging to no party; the rest are all Conservatives. Thirteen of the peers elected in 1955 received from 51 to 55 votes each, one received 41, and two (both of them non-party men) only 37 each.

The voting is not secret; each peer reads aloud his chosen list. Next the lists of those holding proxies are read out, and finally the signed lists sent in by the absent voters are read by a clerk. The final totals of the votes cast must be counted by the clerks in the presence of the meeting, and the result is then announced. It is the duty of the Lord Clerk Register, or of the clerks, to decide whether or not a peer claiming to vote is entitled to do so. No addition to the roll, which at present contains 115 titles, is made except by resolution of the House of Lords; the most recent addition is that of the Earl of Dundee.

In the proceedings of the House of Lords the Scottish Representative Peers do not confine themselves to speaking on Scottish questions. They have the same privileges, during the life of a Parliament, as other members of the House of Lords, and may therefore hold office in the Government. Of the present Representative Peers the Earl of Selkirk, for example, has held a number of offices, and in 1955 was brought into the Cabinet as Chancellor of the Duchy of Lancaster.

For a full discussion of the institution of the system, and of the difficulties attendant on it, cf. A. S. Turberville, *The House of Lords in the XVIIIth Century*, op. cit., ch. 5; and for particulars of the procedure at elections, cf. William Robertson, *Proceedings relating to the Peerage of Scotland*. For material in this Appendix the author must gratefully acknowledge his special debt to Sir James Fergusson of Kilkerran, Bt., Keeper of the Records of Scotland.

BIBLIOGRAPHICAL NOTE

Most of the material for this survey has been derived from the *Lords' Journal*, *Hansard* and reference books such as *Vacher's Parliamentary Companion*, *Who's Who* and *Whitaker's Almanac*, and from Erskine May's *Treatise on the Law, Privileges, Proceedings and Usage of Parliament* (Butterworth, 15th edition, 1950).

Much information and many useful ideas have been derived from recent publications on the House of Lords:

SYDNEY D. BAILEY (ed.), *The Future of the House of Lords* (Hansard Society, 1954).

FRANK HARDIE and R. S. POLLARD, *Lords and Commons* (Fabian Society, 1947).

LORD CHORLEY, BERNARD CRICK and DONALD CHAPMAN, *Reform of the Lords* (Fabian Research Series, no. 169, 1954).

ANTHONY WEDGWOOD BENN, M.P., *The Privy Council as a Second Chamber* (Fabian Tract 305, 1957).

L. G. PINE, *The Story of the Peerage* (Blackwood, 1956).

SYDNEY D. BAILEY's article in *The Spectator*, 20th November 1953, pp. 561 f.

W. L. GUTTSMAN, 'The Changing Social Structure of the British Political Elite', in *British Journal of Sociology*, vol. ii (1951), pp. 122–34.

——, 'Aristocracy and the Middle Class in the British Political Elite, 1886–1916,' in *British Journal of Sociology*, vol. v (1954), pp. 12–32.

H. R. G. GREAVES, 'Personal Origins and Interrelations of the Houses of Parliament (since 1832)', in *Economica*, vol. ix (1929), pp. 173–84.

The student of the history of the House of Lords must rely mainly on general historical works and on biographies and memoirs. Many of these are noted in the text.

Special mention must be made, however, of—

A. S. TURBERVILLE, *The House of Lords under William III*.

——, *The House of Lords in the Eighteenth Century* (Oxford U.P., 1927).

L. O. PIKE, *Constitutional History of the House of Lords* (London, 1894).

K. R. MACKENZIE, *The English Parliament* (Pelican, 1950).

J. A. R. MARRIOTT, *Second Chambers* (Oxford U.P., 1910).

RAMSAY MUIR, *Peers and Bureaucrats* (Constable, 1910).

Conference on the Reform of the Second Chamber. Report by Viscount Bryce (Cmd. 9038 of 1918).

Report by the Select Committee on the Powers of the House in Relation to the Attendance of its Members (H.M.S.O., 1956).

INDEX

Absentee peers, proposals for exclusion, 249
Addison, 1st Viscount, 86, 105, 207, 255, 267
Agriculture, debates on, 154, 192
  Ministry of, representation in H.L., 102
Ailesbury, Marquess of, 120
Alexander of Hillsborough, Viscount, 188, 230
Alexander of Tunis, Field Marshal Earl, 39 f., 73 f., 105
Alness, Lord, 204
Animals, welfare of, 202, 204, 207 f., 227
Appellate Committee, 85 f.
Appellate Jurisdiction Act, 1876, 18
Army, purchase of commissions in, 135
Askwith, Dr. W. M., Bishop of Blackburn, 1942–54, 66
Asquith and Oxford, first Earl of, 54
Atkin, Lord, 71, 84
Attlee, Earl, 23, 28, 29, 248, 267

Backwoodsmen, 46 ff.
Badeley, Lord, 76, 255
Baden-Powell, General Lord, 28
Bailey, Sydney, 33, 37
Baldwin, 1st Earl, 23
Balfour, A. J., 1st Earl, 252
Balfour of Burleigh, Lord, 150, 163
Balfour of Inchrye, Lord, 182
Banbury, 1st Lord, 202
Barnby, Lord, 225
Barnes, Dr. E. W., Bishop of Birmingham 1924–53, 55, 172
Baron, meaning of the word, 6, 8
Beauchamp, John of, Baron, 8
Bedford, 12th Duke of, 273
Bell, Dr. G. K. A., Bishop of Chichester, 45, 60 f.

Benn, A. Wedgwood, 31, 253, 269
Benson, Dr. E. W., Archbishop of Canterbury 1883–96, 22, 55
Beveridge, Lord, 27, 45, 77, 161
Bills in the House of Lords:
  amendments and pressure groups, 143 f.
  consolidation bills, 130
  general considerations, 142–5
  Lords' amendments in Commons, 132 f.
  Lords' bills, 186 ff.
  procedure, 127 ff.
  standing committees, not set up in Lords, 131
  supply bills, 129
Birds, protection of, 208
Birkenhead, 1st Earl of, 69
Bishops in H.L., 17 f., 52–66
  appointment of, 53
  attendance at the House, 56 f.
  voting in divisions, 64
Bledisloe, Viscount, 108
Bloomer, Dr. Thomas, Bishop of Carlisle, 63
Bonar Law, A., and Irish Home Rule, 137
Borrowing (Control and Guarantees) Bill, 1946, 172
Boyd-Orr, Lord, 45, 77
Brabazon, Lord, 73, 193, 250
Bristol, Earl of, 7
Brook, Dr. R., Bishop of St. Edmundsbury and Ipswich, 1940–54, 66
Bryce Conference, 127, 239 ff., 261 f.
Buckmaster, Lord, 68, 201, 204
Burnham, Lord, 131
Butler, R. A., 42, 172, 184 n.

Cairns, Lord, 69
Cambridge University, 22, 36
Canada, Senate of, 3

INDEX

Canterbury, Archbishop of
  always sits in H.L., 18
  membership of cabinet, 53
  grant of temporal peerage to, 28
  pre-eminence among prelates, 56
  See also under Benson, Davidson, Lang, Fisher, Temple
Capital punishment, abolition of, 46 ff., 62, 66, 70 f., 175, 216–20, 224
Cardigan, Lord, trial of, 1841, 250
Carrington, Lord, 106
Carson, Lord, 68 ff.
Cecil of Chelwood, Viscount, 60, 202, 255, 267
Cecil, Lord William, Bishop of Exeter 1916–36, 66
Chairman of Committees, 97
Chamberlain, Neville, 100
Chandos, Viscount (formerly Oliver Lyttelton), 169
Chatfield, Admiral of the Fleet Lord, 72 ff.
Cherwell, Viscount, 39 n., 40 n., 77, 105
Children, Legislation dealing with, 63, 187 f.
Chorley, Lord, 104, 119, 144, 209
Churchill, Sir Winston, 41, 105
Civil Aviation Bill, 1946, 161
Civil Servants, peerages and, 25 f., 75
Clerk of the Parliaments, 97
Coal Mining Legislation, (1926) 115; (1930) 32, 66; (1938) 117, 149; (1946) 60, 160
Cockin, Dr. F. A., Bishop of Bristol, 56, 66
Colonial affairs, 62, 119
Companies Bill (1948), 195
Conscientious objectors, 171, 209
Conservative Party organization in H.L., 112
Copyright Bill (1955–6), 193
Cork and Orrery, Admiral of the Fleet the Earl of, 73 f., 92
Corporal punishment, 148, 175
Crawford and Balcarres, Earl of, 47
Crewe, Marquess of, 101
Cripps, Sir L. Stafford, 150, 264
Crook, Lord, 214

Dalton, Hugh, 172
Danesfort, Lord, 202 f.
Darling, Lord, 201

Davidson, Randall, Archbishop of Canterbury, 1903–28, 28, 55 f., 58, 64 f., 133 n.
Davies, Clement, 248, 267
Dawson of Penn, Lord, 76, 204
Death penalty, see Capital punishment
Defence questions, 73
De Clifford, Lord, 256 f.
De Freitas, Geoffrey, 184
De la Warr, Earl, 155
De L'Isle, Viscount (formerly Lord De l'Isle and Dudley), 106
Denman, Lord, 68
Derby, 17th Earl of, 35
Desborough, Lord, 108
Devonshire, 8th Duke of, 35
Dioceses, division of, 152
Divisions, method of taking, 95
  frequency of, 114
Donoughmore, Earl of, Chairman of Committees 1911–31, 97
Douglas of Kirtleside, Air Chief Marshal Lord, 28, 73, 75
Dowding, Air Chief Marshal Lord, 73, 75
Drogheda, Earl of, Chairman of Committees, 1946–57, 19, 97
Du Parcq, Lord, 71, 191
Duke, rank and title of, 8
Durham, Bishop of, always sits in H.L., 18

Earl, rank and title of, 8
Easter, date of, 62
Ede, J. Chuter, 216
Eden, Sir R. Anthony, 23, 267
Education of peers, 21 f., 36, 41, 44
Education Bill, 1906, 56, 64, 135
Edwards, Dr. A. G., Bishop of St. Asaph, 1889–1920, 58
Egypt, 32, 61, 63, 66, 86, 123
Elibank, Viscount, 45, 203, 225, 230
Ellenborough, Lord, 35
  Lord Chief Justice, 68
Eltisley, Lord, 204
Elton, Lord, 45, 207, 224
Exeter, Marquess of, 249

Fabian Society pamphlets on H.L., 37, 159, 194
Falmouth, Lord, 47
Faringdon, Lord, 214
Finance Bill, 1909, 46, 57

Fisher, Dr. Geoffrey, Archbishop of Canterbury, 61 f., 66 f.
Foreign affairs, 32, 60 f., 63, 66, 73, 86, 123
Foreign office, representation of in H.L., 100, 102
Forestry Bill, 1951, 192
Fortescue, Earl, 87, 92, 248
Franchise bills, 65, 155
Fraser of North Cape, Admiral of the Fleet Lord, 75
Freyberg, General Lord, 29, 73.
Furse, Dr. M. B., Bishop of St. Albans, 1920–45, 66

Gainford, Lord, 153
Gambling, bills dealing with, 59, 62, 189
Garbett, Dr. Cyril, Archbishop of York, 1942–56, 59 f., 65 f., 172
Goddard, Lord Chief Justice, 71, 175
Gore, Dr. Charles, Bishop of Oxford 1911–19, 55, 57
Grantchester, Lord, 210

Hailsham, 1st Viscount, 263 f.
  2nd Viscount, 67, 121, 252
Haig, Field Marshal, 1st Earl, 25
Haigh, Dr. M. G., Bishop of Winchester 1942–52, 66, 206
Haldane, Viscount, 69
Halifax, Earl of, 77, 100, 113, 264
Hall, Viscount, 104
Halsbury, 1st Earl of, 35
  2nd Earl of, 205
Hampton, Lord, 229
Hankey, Lord, 45, 75, 230
Hastings, 21st Lord, 150, 190
Hawke, Lord, 183
Henderson, Lord, 108, 174
Home, Earl of, 41, 105
Horder, 1st Lord, 76
Hours of work, regulation of, 65, 184 n., 195 n.
Hunkin, Dr. J. W., Bishop of Truro, 1935–51, 206
Hunter, Dr. Leslie, Bishop of Sheffield, 63, 66

Iddesleigh, Earl of, 174, 204
Inchcape, 1st Earl of, 111
Independent peers, 45, 50, 111
India, constitutional reforms, 66, 113, 117

Interest groups and H.L., 143, 195
Ireland, Home Rule, 34, 57, 59, 68 f., 116, 137 f.
Irish representative peers, 19
Ismay, General Lord, 39 f.
Iwi, E. W., and the admission of women to H.L., 254 ff.

Jacob, Dr. Edgar, Bishop of St. Albans 1903–20, 58
Jeffreys, General Lord, 72 ff., 226
Jennings, Sir W. Ivor, 115
Jowitt, Earl, 74, 85, 93, 105, 108, 164, 179, 183, 191, 205 f., 214, 217, 255, 267
Judicial sittings, 84 f.

Keynes, Lord, 77, 113
Kilmuir, Viscount (formerly Sir David Maxwell Fyfe), 167, 267, 269
King-Hall, Commander Sir Stephen, 24

Labour Party and peerages, 28, 38, 43
Lamington, 2nd Lord, 147
Lang, Cosmo Gordon, Archbishop of Canterbury 1928–41, 56 f., 60
Lansdowne, 5th Marquess of, 101, 112
Lauderdale, Earl of, 155
Law Lords, 18, 52 f., 67–72, 84, 246
Layton, Lord, 45
Leathers, Lord, 39 f., 105
Libel, law of, 70, 213
Liberal Party peers, 45, 184 n., 205, 210
Licensing laws, 32, 59, 65, 139
Life peerages, 245 ff.
Listowel, Earl of, 108, 181
Llewellin, Lord, 164, 171, 191
Lloyd George, 1st Earl, 23
Lloyd, Lord, 208
London, Bishop of, always in H.L., 18
Londonderry, 7th Marquess of, 161, 202
Lord Chancellor, office of, 68, 95 ff., 104
Lords in Waiting, functions, 102 f.
Lucas of Chilworth, Lord, 108, 193, 206, 226, 229, 248, 258
Lyndhurst, Lord, 247

Manchester Guardian, The, article on H.L., 33
Mancroft, Lord, 62, 206, 230

INDEX

Mansfield, Earl of, 255
Martin, Dr. C. A., Bishop of Liverpool, 67
Matrimonial questions, 62, 70, 206, 201, 214
Maugham, Viscount, 162
MacDonald, J. Ramsay, 26
McKenna, Reginald, 524
Macmillan, Lord, 68, 100
Medical profession, members of in H.L., 25
Medland, H. M., 164
Mersey, Viscount, 204
Merthyr, Lord, 120, 209
Ministers in H.L., 41, 99 ff.
Money bills, 81, 129 f.
Montagu of Beaulieu, Lord, 192
Moran, Lord, 33, 49, 76, 162
Morrison, Herbert, 180, 267
Morrison, W. S., 145, 164
Mottistone, Lord, 203
Mountbatten, Admiral Earl, 29
Mountevans, Admiral Lord, 28 n.
Moynihan, Lord, 76, 203
Munster, Earl of, 106, 165, 179

Nathan, Lord, 105
National Health Service, 33, 60, 162
National Insurance, 60
Newall, Marshal of the R.A.F. Lord, 75
Newton, 2nd Lord, 84 f., 203, 249
Normand, Lord, 205

Oaksey, Lord, 71
Ogmore, Lord, 230
Onslow, 5th Earl of, 97, 253
Oranmore and Browne, Lord, 116
Owen, Dr. John, Bishop of St. Davids 1897–1927, 59
Oxford University, 25, 36

Pakenham, Lord, 105
Papers, motions for, 90 f., 227
Parliament Act, 1911, 57, 64, 113, 135 f.
Parliament Act, 1949, 32, 170, 239, 242, 265 ff.
Parsons, Dr. R. G., Bishop of Hereford, 1941–9, 63
Party discipline, 103, 110 ff.
Payment of peers, 94, 257 f.

Pearce, Dr., Bishop of Worcester 1919–31, 65
Peeresses, 64, 254 ff.
Pensions, old age, 154
Percival, Dr. J., Bishop of Hereford 1899–1918, 55–9, 64, 88
Percy of Newcastle, Lord, 26
Phillimore, Lord, 149
Pine, L. G., 26
Plymouth, 1st Earl of, 111
Pollock, Dr. B., Bishop of Norwich 1910–42, 65
Ponsonby of Shulbrede, 1st Lord, 253
Prayer-book measure, 1928, 32
Private Members' business, 90 ff., 196 ff.
Private bills, ix, 97, 122
Procedure, 81–93, 127 ff., 196–9

Questions, Parliamentary, in H.L., 221–7
Quorum rule, 197, 203

Rabbits Bill, 1928, 116, 139
Radnor, Earl of, 47, 148, 192
Ramsey, Dr. A. M., Archbishop of York, 63
Rawlinson, Dr. A. E. J., Bishop of Derby, 63
Rea, Lord, 120, 206
Reading, 2nd Marquess of, 44, 120, 161, 205
Referendum, as a means of settling differences with House of Commons, 240 f.
Rent control, 171, 183
Rhondda, Viscountess, 255
Ridley, Viscount, 47, 164
Road traffic bills, 122, 154, 192 f., 202, 229
Robertson, Lord, 69
Rochester, Lord, 107, 248
Rosebery, 5th Earl of, 55, 249, 260
Russell, 1st Earl, 247
Rutherford, Lord, 28

St. Aldwyn, Earl, 230
Salisbury, 3rd Marquess of, 54, 247
  4th Marquess of, 148, 152, 263
  5th Marquess of (succeeded 1947, but sat in H.L. as Baron Cecil of Essendon, being still known by courtesy title of Viscount Cranborne, from 1941 to 1947), 41, 47,

INDEX

87, 113, 141, 143, 145, 157, 161, 169, 207, 242, 249 f., 254, 266 f.
Saltoun, Lord, 145
Samuel, Viscount, 45, 120, 161, 163, 266, 269
Sandhurst, Lord, 121
Sankey, Viscount, 257
School-leaving age, 140
Scotland, Minister of State for, 105
Scottish representative peers, 18, 276
Selborne, 2nd Earl of, 252 f.
Selkirk, Earl of, 19, 41, 105, 161
Sempill, Lord, 204
Shepherd, Lord, 92
Silkin, Lord, 164, 179, 181, 184, 224
Silverman, Sydney, 216
Simon, Viscount, 119, 248
Simonds, Viscount, 191, 253
Sittings, days, times and length of, 82–8
Snowden, Viscount, 155
Speeches, length of, 82
 procedural rules on, 88, 90 f.
Stamp, Lord, 208
Stansgate, Viscount, 119, 224, 251 ff.
Steel industry, nationalization of, 161, 183
Strachie, 1st Lord, 58, 102
Strang, Lord, 101
Strauss, G. R., 167
Strickland, Lord, 264
Sumner, Lord, 68
Supply, the province of the House of Commons, 10, 81 f., 91, 129 f., 187
Swinton, Earl of, 105, 161, 171, 205, 207, 251, 267

Talbot, Dr. E. S., Bishop of Winchester, 1911–24, 55, 59
Tedder, Marshal of the R.A.F. Lord, 73, 123
Television, Independent, 32, 67, 87, 121, 180 f.
Temple, Frederick, Archbishop of Canterbury 1896–1903, 22

Temple, William, Archbishop of Canterbury 1941–5, 55
Templewood, Viscount, 61, 208
Teynham, Lord, 92, 206
Tovey, Admiral of the Fleet Lord, 73
Town and Country Planning, 163
Trade Unions, legislation concerning, 116
Transport, nationalization and de-nationalization of, 165, 206
Trenchard, Marshal of the R.A.F. Viscount, 73
Trial of peers, 9, 256 ff.
Tucker, Lord, 72
Tweedsmuir, Lord and Lady, 209

Ullswater, 1st Viscount, 76
Unemployment insurance, 149, 151 f.

Vansittart, Lord, 45, 75, 225, 229

Waldegrave, Earl of, 273
Wales, Church of, disestablishment, 55, 58
Wand, Dr. J. C. W., Bishop of London 1946–56, 206
Waverley, 1st Viscount, 45, 75
Webb-Johnson, Lord, 76
Wedgwood, 1st Lord, 53
Wemyss and March, Earl of, 261
Wensleydale, Lord, 246
Westwood, Lord, 273
Whips, duties of, 87, 90, 97, 102 ff., 111
Wilmot of Selmeston, Lord, 181
Wilson, Field-Marshal Lord, 74
Winchester, Bishop of, always in H.L., 18
Winnington-Ingram, Dr. A. F., Bishop of London 1901–39, 58
Winster, Lord, 123
Winterton, Earl, 19
Women and the right to sit in H.L., 64, 254 ff.
Wright, Lord, 204

For Product Safety Concerns and Information please contact our EU representative GPSR@taylorandfrancis.com
Taylor & Francis Verlag GmbH, Kaufingerstraße 24, 80331 München, Germany

www.ingramcontent.com/pod-product-compliance
Lightning Source LLC
Chambersburg PA
CBHW052154300426
44115CB00011B/1668